Journal of the Royal Asiatic Society China

Vol. 82   2022   No. 1

PUBLISHED EXCLUSIVELY FOR MEMBERS OF THE SOCIETY

The Journal of the Royal Asiatic Society China is published by Earnshaw Books on behalf of the Royal Asiatic Society China

Journal
OF THE
Royal Asiatic Society
China

Vol. 82 No. 1, 2022

PRODUCED BY
The RAS China Journal Team

Copyright 2022 RAS China

—∞—

CONTRIBUTIONS

The Journal Team invites submission of original unpublished scholarly articles, essays and book reviews on the religion and philosophy, art and architecture, archaeology, anthropology, environment, and current affairs of China and Greater Asia. Books sent for review will be donated to the Royal Asiatic Society China Library. Contributors will receive copies of the Journal.

LIBRARY POLICY

Copies and back issues of the Journal are available at the Royal Asiatic Society China Library. The library is available to members.

https://ras-china.org/

Journal of the Royal Asiatic Society China
Vol. 82 No. 1, 2022

978-988-8769-81-0

EB 177

© 2022 Royal Asiatic Society China

The copyright of each article rests with the author.

Front Cover Image: Doolittle Raiders crew #2, Tung-Sheng Liu (third from right) and unidentified man/with permission from the Tung-Sheng Liu Family, and Lori B. Lang (colourisation)
(copyright © National U.S. Air Force Museum)

Designed and produced for RAS China by Earnshaw Books Ltd
17/F, Siu Ying Commercial Building, 151-155 Queen's Road Central, Hong Kong

All rights reserved. No part of this book may be reproduced in material form by any means, whether graphic, electronic, mechanical or other, including photocopying or information storage, in whole or in part. May not be used to prepare other publications without written permission from the publisher.

*The Royal Asiatic Society China thanks Earnshaw Books
for its valuable contribution and support.*

DISCLAIMER

The opinions expressed in this publication are those of the authors. They do not purport to reflect the opinions or views of the Royal Asiatic Society (RAS) or its members. The designations employed in this publication and the presentation of material therein do not imply the expression of any opinion whatsoever on the part of RAS China.

CONTENTS

LETTER FROM THE RAS CHINA JOURNAL TEAM   1

RAS CHINA COUNCIL AND REPORT 2021-2022   4

SECTION 1: 'THIS IS LONDON CALLING CHINA…'—*Stories of World War Two*

Hsiao Ch'ien, Hsiung Shih-I, George Orwell and the BBC Eastern Service in World War Two
   By Paul French   13

In the Steps of Shanghai Jim
   By Duncan Hewitt   26

The Costs of Alliance: the Doolittle Raid and China
   By James Carter   56

SECTION 2: 'TODAY THEY ARE MERCHANTS, TOMORROW, FISHERMEN, AND AT EVERY OPPORTUNITY— ROBBERS'—*Stories of larger-than-life personalities*

Warrior Priest: The Mission of Claude-Marie Chevrier (1821-1870)
   By Jeremiah Jenne   69

A 'Queen Among Queens' in the Middle Kingdom
   By Graham Earnshaw   89

Our Man in Shanghai: A Russian Observer Visiting Asian Treaty Ports in 1853
   By Sven A. Serrano   98

SECTION 3: '[IN] CAME PU YI IN HIS PRINCE OF WALES SUIT WITH A PINK CARNATION IN HIS BUTTONHOLE'—*Stories of the cities*

Cutting Through the Haze: Reassessing Images of Shanghai Girls in Cigarette Advertisements 1910-1940
  By Julie Chun 117

Sweet Dreams: the Kiessling Café, China's First Cross-Provincial Confectionary Chain
  By George Godula 142

1978: A Year of Enormous Significance
  By John Darwin Van Fleet 172

Chinese Opera Meets Popular Culture: A Study of Li Yu's Family Troupe
  By Yufeng Lucas Wu 198

SECTION 4: REVIEWS

Scottish Mandarin: The Life and Times of Sir Reginald Johnston
  Reviewed by Frances Wood 217

Chiang Yee and His Circle: Chinese Artistic and Intellectual Life in Britain 1930-1950
  Reviewed by Duncan Hewitt 221

Sir Robert Hart (1835-1911): Whose Hero?
  Documentary film review by Edith Terry 229

LETTER FROM THE ROYAL ASIATIC SOCIETY CHINA JOURNAL TEAM

THE YEAR 2022 has been one of radical unpredictability, but as we approach its end, some trends are becoming clear. People still want to meet other people in person, despite adapting to the digital lives to which many of us resorted when the pandemic brought things to a standstill. And we still like to read.

The journal of the Royal Asiatic Society China is made for those who like to read. To be sure, virtual talks and streaming movies have become our companions in recent years, and their presence will not likely disappear anytime soon. Yet the hiatus of the Covid years has also reinforced our desire for a rollicking good read. And this year's journal does not disappoint. In the first section, author Paul French has once again honoured the journal's pages, this time with a piece on the BBC's Eastern Service, which employed a young journalist called Eric Blair—you may recognise him more readily by his pen name, George Orwell. Paul's essay also highlights the cross cultural friendships forming among Asian intellectuals of the day, many of whom shared Orwell's anti-imperialist sentiments.

Historian James Carter takes a fresh look at the legacy of the American aviators known as the Doolittle Raiders. He assesses the long-term impact of their aerial bombing of Japan, which took place 80 years ago this year, from a little-understood Chinese perspective. And he found a counterintuitive glimmer of hope in the grassroots remembrances of the mission, and of the era, in which the US and China were allies.

Nearly a year ago, Duncan Hewitt agreed to contribute an article on JG Ballard to the Journal. Hewitt's curiosity about Ballard was first piqued back in 1987, when he was an extra in the filming of the Hollywood movie *Empire of the Sun*, based on Ballard's book. Hewitt's enthralling and deeply researched article explains how Ballard's experiences in WWII Shanghai influenced virtually all of his writings. Today, the sometimes surreal "Ballardian" vision is embraced by new generations of readers and has renewed resonance, perhaps due to global events (One of Ballard's short stories, *The Intensive Care Unit*, depicts people meeting only via TV screens).

Hewitt's piece is especially evocative because of his intimate first-hand knowledge of Shanghai. He also interviewed people who knew Ballard and his family, including not only Ballard's niece but also Betty Barr, now 90 and living in a Shanghai retirement home. She and her family were interned during the Japanese occupation—as was Ballard's family—in what was then called the Lunghwa Civilian Assembly Centre in Shanghai. An image from her photo collection features in Hewitt's memorable piece.

Another insightful article is written by Graham Earnshaw, who recalls the 1986 China visit by Queen Elizabeth II, whose death was mourned by millions this year. Earnshaw was the Reuters China bureau chief back then. While searching through his archives, he found a photo of the visiting monarch and Chinese leader Deng Xiaoping in a meeting that only two people were allowed to photograph; he was one of them. That rare image, plus his sometimes laugh-out-loud anecdotes, count among the journal highlights.

In a totally different period and mood, historian Jeremiah Jenne documents the startling story of 'warrior priest' Claude-Marie Chevrier and his Chinese colleagues, who were 19th century Lazarist missionaries in an impoverished area north of the Great Wall, then part of the Mongolian Vicariate. While conducting his research, Jenne felt that Chevrier's adventure-filled life as both a soldier and a priest was almost cinematic in its drama, 'part *The Mission*, part *True Grit*', as he put it. The once-wild frontier area of Xiwanzi today sits not far from the Chinese sports venues used during the 2022 Winter Olympics.

Don't miss Sven Serrano's account of Ivan Alexandrovich Goncharov's travels. This gifted writer was assigned to record the log for a secret Russian mission to Imperial Japan which had set out in 1852 aboard a small flotilla, hoping to outrace a similar US fleet under the command of Commodore Matthew Perry. Goncharov's colourful personal accounts of the voyage introduced many Russians to the teeming ports of Japan, China and Southeast Asia for the first time.

The journal's stories from the cities have something for everyone. Julie Chun analyses images of Shanghai girls in cigarette advertisements during the early 1900s against the backdrop of a fast-growing cigarette industry and the changing status of women in Chinese society. Yufeng Lucas Wu expands our appreciation of Chinese opera with an illuminating portrait of a famous family-based performing troupe and how its founder appealed to popular culture to compete for audience and patronage. Meanwhile, many who knew China in the 1980s will know about the Kiessling Café. George Godula's article about China's first cross-provincial confectionary chain evokes the atmosphere of this legendary gathering place, especially the hospitality it extended to emperors, presidents, politicians, authors, actors, socialites, criminals, spies and ordinary Westerners and Chinese alike. And check out what used to happen when Pu Yi walked through the door!

A highly original perspective is featured in John Darwin Van Fleet's examination of several crucial Chinese events that took place in 1978. The economic reforms embodied by these events reveal 1978 to have been a turning point for China, and help explain China's incredible economic growth in the last four decades.

The journal concludes with several stellar reviews. Sinologist Frances Wood reviews a book on Reginald Johnston, tutor to China's last emperor Pu Yi, and reveals that Johnston's official activities were often far less interesting than what was going on behind the scenes.

Duncan Hewitt looks at a book co-edited by Paul Bevan, Anne Witchard, and Da Sheng. It focuses on Chiang Yee, Hsiao Ch'ien and Hsiung Shih-I, artistic and intellectual figures based in Britain in the middle of the last century, whose works contributed to a "China craze" in Britain now largely forgotten.

A final review analyses a documentary film about Robert Hart, once considered the most influential foreigner in China. A hero of the British Empire, he was recognised by both Britain and the Qing for his contributions to China. The fascinating film *For China and the World: Robert Hart* about "China Customs" Hart, and his rehabilitation in the eyes of many Chinese, is thoughtfully reviewed by Edith Terry.

Sincere thanks to everyone who contributed to and worked on the journal, and especially to Earnshaw Books, publisher Graham Earnshaw, and the design team.

We would like to hear from any readers—scholars, writers, biographers, people with unusual family narratives—who have a story bursting to be told. Please email the Journal Team at raschina@raschina.org. We hope this year's edition has brought enjoyment—and has fed your desire to read.

The Royal Asiatic Society China Journal Team

RAS CHINA COUNCIL 2021-2022

Honorary President
Christopher Wood—British Consul General Shanghai

Honorary Vice Presidents for Life
Carma Elliot CMG, OBE
Peter Hibbard MBE
Liu Wei
Tess Johnston

Vice President
Parul Rewal

Treasurer
Helen Yang

Membership Director
Jonathan Crowder

Secretary
Marta Lopez

Programme Director
Rachel Rapaport

Journal Editor
RAS China Journal Team

Librarian
Sven Serrano

Convenors
Julie Chun (Art Focus)
Katherine Song (Film Club)
Gabor Holch (History Club)
Robert Martin (Stories of Things)
James Miller (Philosophy Club)

NON-COUNCIL POSITIONS

Administration Manager
Irina Carpenco

Book Club Convenor
Cordelia Crockett

Library Volunteers
Kylie Bisman, Julie Chun, Paul Hopkins,
Liang Ping, Diana Long, Robert Martin,
Coquina Restrepo, Compton Tothill, Zhang Dasheng

RAS CHINA ANNUAL REPORT 2021-2022

> Without going out the door, know the world.
> Without peeping through the window, see heaven's Tao.
> The further you travel, the less you know.
> This is why the Sage knows without budging,
> Identifies without looking,
> Does without trying.
> –Laozi, Daodejing, Chapter 47

This past year Shanghai was a time of introspection for many, as the city came to a virtual standstill for the two months of April and May, in parts for even longer, as an impact of the pandemic. While numerous expatriates chose to leave during this period of uncertainty, people who were rooted to the city exhibited great courage and resilience. From a philosophical standpoint, the concept of stillness while incorporating many changes into one's way of life is testament to Daoist ideals of acceptance and action within inaction. RAS China's activities were certainly impacted, with a dwindled audience base and revised events scheduling, especially during the anti-pandemic protocols of April and May. However the society chose not to let such challenges become defining factors for the year. Instead, we are transforming and adapting to the changing conditions—investing energy in re-scheduling events, as and when possible, and in restructuring the library.

Event Highlights: RAS Salon cast a lens on the bronzes of the E state during the Zhou dynasty, and hosted a revelatory look at how Muslims brought to Yunnan as elite hostages during the Yuan dynasty helped shape court affairs.

The Film Club squeezed in a few great film screenings before in-person gatherings were impacted, including *Dying to Survive*, a 2018 box office hit that had helped prompt health-care reforms in China. An online film discussion on *Hibiscus Town* set during the Cultural Revolution, by Xie Jin, one of the most significant directors in China, offered some interaction between speaker and audience.

This year the Art Focus theme was Places & Spaces. Participants explored the pluralist facets of art museums in Shanghai with a critical approach to discovering the built-culture and the locality of

Place, further examining the artistic works and curatorial practices within the Space of the museum. When in-person events became difficult, Art Focus went online with an expanded global outlook, taking the opportunity to engage with art museums from around the world. A discussion with the curator of the Fitzwilliam Museum of the University of Cambridge in the UK and the curator of the newly instituted Hong Kong Palace Museum were part of these exciting offerings.

The History Club hosted some great online talks covering, among other topics, China-themed pulp fiction of the 1950s, the evacuation of the Forbidden City's treasures during World War II, and a digitisation project involving historical photographs of China from the 1850s to 1950. In a fascinating talk about the material and visual culture of the Cultural Revolution, we had a revelatory look at how the Mao Suit came to embody the entire popular construct of Chinese communism in the minds of various sectors.

Our focus group on Asian Philosophies and Religions featured a discussion of philosophical ideas connected to the Chan (Zen) school of Buddhism with Ben Van Overmeire, and why it remains one of the pre-eminent representations of East-Asian spirituality across the world. In a virtual adventure, James Miller led us on 'A Journey of a Thousand Miles' reflecting on what it means to journey within Daoist philosophy, exploring the relationship between travelling worldwide through the physical landscape, and the inward, or psychological, journeys that come to shape our identities as human beings.

Stories of Things swept us away to the nightlife and financial worlds of 1930's Shanghai. A nightclub club membership card owned by raconteur extraordinaire, Dr Andrew Field, evoked what it was like to go club-hopping in those heady days, and a Bank of China currency note revealed the story of politics, design and intrigue that underpinned the issuance of money in Shanghai in that dramatic decade. To help relive that era, we got to sip absinthe-laced cocktails, popular in the clubs of old Shanghai.

RAS China Journal: This year the Journal is edited by the RAS China Journal Team, which has rich China experience and literary credentials. The 2022 journal features a brilliant piece by Duncan Hewitt on how JG Ballard's experiences in Shanghai influenced his overall writing. Author Paul French looks at the BBC Eastern Service during WWII, and the role of a man better known as George Orwell.

Other topics range from a European 'warrior priest' to the history of the Kiessling Cafe in China, to a reassessment of images of Shanghai women in cigarette ads.

Membership: Owing to a large percentage of members repatriating, and lulls in activity due to the pandemic control measures, membership dropped somewhat this year. The society extended all active and new memberships in the June quarter by three months. We will continue to drive membership to recover from the membership decline in 2022.

Finances: RAS China's revenue has naturally been impacted this year owing to the reduced number of memberships and events resulting from pandemic-control protocols. However our financial position remains strong, thanks to a healthy cash reserve. The estimated year-end cash reserve is approximately RMB 200,000, a decrease of around RMB 45,000 compared to the end of 2021, since the revenue generated was insufficient to cover our standard operating expenses. Besides our major standard expenses such as the Glue-up fee (our online membership and event management platform), publication of the journal, the administrative manager's salary and the annual AGM, this year we have the additional expense of a library move. We expect to be in a stronger financial position in 2023, as we return to our normal level of programming, assuming pandemic control measures ease.

Library and Reading Room: In September this year, the five-year contract for our library space at the House of Roosevelt, which had been implemented with the help of then British Consul General and Honorary RAS President John Edwards, came to an end. We began the process of moving our collection to the RAS Reading Room at the West Bund, which will now function as our main library. All of our old and rare books and journals stored in the locked cabinets have already been brought to the Reading Room and are in the process of being inventoried and reshelved by our brilliant team of highly enthusiastic and efficient library volunteers. During the inventory we discovered several gems, including a pencil sketch of the Bund waterfront from 1848 and an original journal article by Pearl Buck before she published any of her novels. The move of the main stacks is expected to be completed by year's end and we hope to open the Reading Room to our members following that.

We thank our loyal members and potential new members for their strong support of RAS China in Shanghai, and we ask for your continued patronage as we enter what we expect to be a strong 2023.

We are ready to unfurl our sails again to full mast and move onwards.

Parul Rewal
Vice President RAS China

RAS China Membership 2021-2022
Honorary Memberships
Honorary Members	7
(FRAS) Fellow of RAS China	2
Complimentary Institutional memberships	4

Paid Memberships
Membership Type
- Individual Members	72
- Joint/Family Members	20
- Student Members	2
- Young Professional/Pensioner	6
- Overseas - Individual Members	8
- Overseas - Household	0
- Lifetime Members	3
GRAND TOTAL	**111**

RAS Donor Friends   22

RAS China Events, 1 Dec 2021 - 30 Nov 2022
- General Program (Rachel Rapaport)	3
- Art Focus (Julie Chun)	6
- History Club (Gabor Holch)	4
- Film Club (Katherine Song)	3
- Non-Fiction Book Club (Cordelia Crockett)	10
- Stories of Things (Robert Martin)	1
- Asian Philosophies and Religions (James Miller)	2
- Additional RASBJ online lectures shared with members	9
- Additional RASHK online lectures shared with members	7
- Special Events (AGM)	1
TOTAL	**46**

SECTION 1

Stories of World War Two

'This is London Calling China...'

HSIAO CH'IEN, HSIUNG SHIH-I, GEORGE ORWELL, AND THE BBC EASTERN SERVICE IN WORLD WAR TWO

By Paul French

Abstract

During World War Two the British Broadcasting Corporation (BBC) significantly increased its overseas reach with the creation of the Eastern Service as a wartime adjunct to the pre-existing BBC Empire Service. The primary target was the Indian subcontinent, considered politically unstable due to the continuing conflict between the colonial Raj administration and the growing independence movement, and therefore in special need of targeted pro-Allied propaganda. Additionally, and targeting mostly Hong Kong and Singapore, a short-lived service for Chinese speakers was launched. Several Chinese intellectuals resident in London during the war years were hired to provide talks and commentaries on the Eastern Service. This brought them into contact with a number of well-known intellectual figures in Britain, including George Orwell, E.M. Forster and William Empson, who were all also employed by the Eastern Service. These interactions and co-operations within the BBC to aid the Allied war effort against Germany and Japan helped cement the already existing links between the small group of Chinese exile artists, poets and writers in London and wider British intellectual circles. Primary among the London-based Chinese hired by the BBC were the journalist Hsiao Ch'ien (Xiao Qian) and the playwright Hsiung Shih-I (Xiong Shiyi).

The Launch of the BBC's Eastern Service

The BBC Eastern Service commenced operations in May 1940 with a short news programme in Hindustani followed by some English language programming. Given the perceived importance of India's loyalty to the British Empire during World War Two, the resources and staff of the Eastern Service, as well as its frequencies and airtime, were soon vastly increased. From 103 staff in 1938 to 1,472 in 1940, to approximately 10,000 by the end of 1941. Along with Hindustani the Service began offering programming in Tamil, Bengali, Marathi, and

Gujarati.^A

A later, and short-lived, experiment with Mandarin, Cantonese and Hokkien broadcasting was also launched, targeting Hong Kong and Singapore.^B Naturally the role of the Eastern Service was to counter Axis propaganda, particularly that inciting Indian independence, as well as to bolster morale and loyalty to the British cause globally and accentuate the 'superiority' of British, art, literature, and culture in general. Of course, the Eastern Service was subject to the government's overall wartime censorship regimen, overseen by the Ministry of Information (MoI) and, in the case of the Eastern Service, this censorship control was conducted in consultation with both the government's India Office and London's School of Oriental and African Studies (SOAS).^C

The Chinese division of the BBC Eastern Service began later. Having been first conceived of in March 1940, it did not commence broadcasts until May 1941, and ended just eight months later with the fall of Hong Kong in December 1941. Several London-based Chinese intellectuals and journalists were hired to provide content to the service. The lecturer and correspondent Hsiao Ch'ien (Xiao Qian, 1910-1999) and the playwright Hsiung Shih-I (Xiong Shiyi, 1902-1991) being the main two Chinese commentators. Hsiung, best known in England, America, and Asia for his hit 1930s stage play *Lady Precious Stream*, was hired to write and read what the BBC called the 'Kuo Yue News Commentary' (by which they meant *Guoyu*, standard Chinese, or *putonghua*) beginning transmission on May 5, 1941. Hsiung's Kuo Yue News Commentaries were fifteen minutes long and broadcast every Tuesday at 10.30am GMT to Malaya, Singapore and Hong Kong. Hsiung had left his original home in Hampstead, North London (which had been damaged at the start of the Blitz), for the relatively safer location of St. Albans in Hertfordshire, and made the journey (about 25 miles) into London on the train for the broadcasts.^D

A   For a fuller history and discussion of the origins and initial operations of the Eastern Service, see Daniel Ryan Morse, *Radio Empire: The BBC's Eastern Service and the Emergence of the Global Anglophone Novel*, New York: Columbia University Press, 2020.

B   A Cantonese service was launched on May 5, 1941; Mandarin on May 19, 1941 and; Hokkien on October 1, 1942. While the Cantonese and Mandarin services ceased broadcast in December 1941, the Hokkien service actually continued on-and-off till February 7, 1948.

C   The School of Oriental Studies (SOS) was founded in 1916 and changed its name to the School of Oriental and African Studies (SOAS) in 1938.

D   For more on Hsiung at this time see Da Zheng, *Shih-I Hsiung: A Glorious Showman*, New Jersey: Fairleigh Dickinson University Press, 2020.

Initially Hsiung's broadcasts were introduced by the Chinese Ambassador to Britain, Kuo T'ai-Ch'i (Guo Taichi, 1888-1952) with the refrain, 'This is London Calling China…' After Paris was occupied by Germany Kuo returned to China to act as the Kuomintang's foreign minister while Wellington Koo (Koo V Kuyin, 1888-1985) left Paris to take up the post of Ambassador in London. For several months he introduced Hsiung's broadcasts. After the fall of Hong Kong on Christmas Day 1941 the Chinese division ceased broadcasts.

Hsiung also recorded a programme originally entitled *Background Newsletter* which, following the cessation of the direct airmail services between Britain and South East Asia, was changed to *London Letter for Hong Kong*. This meant the discs recorded at Broadcasting House had to be despatched by ship to Hong Kong and Singapore and replayed by the local stations, respectively the Malaya Broadcasting Corporation (MBC) across the Federated States and Singapore, and the government radio broadcasting station known as "GOW" in Hong Kong.[E] This inevitably meant they were a bit out of date by the time of broadcast, despite Hsiung trying to write scripts that didn't date too badly. Feedback from Kuala Lumpur to London recorded that, 'The relay of Chinese newsletter from London means a lot to the Chinese listeners here in Malaya. They take it in the sense of political collaboration between Great Britain and China rather than mere radio entertainment.'[F]

Every Eastern Service recording suite at Broadcasting House was equipped with a censor key, and a censor was present at every transmission or recording. The censor necessarily needed to be fluent in the language or dialect being spoken to effectively hit the switch if required. In the case of the Chinese division the Eastern Service hired the Rev. Dr. Henry Raymond Williamson (1883-1966), a missionary recently returned from long service with the Baptist Missionary Society (BMS) in China. Williamson was an accomplished Chinese scholar and linguist. According to the BBC's written archives, although Williamson was appointed, attended recordings, and was paid, he never found it necessary to flick the switch.[G]

E   GOW later becoming Radio Television Hong Kong (RTHK) and MBC later, through various incarnations, morphed into MediaCorp Pte. Ltd.
F   E.R Davies, on behalf of the BBC, to Hsiung Shih-I, April 24, 1941, The BBC Written Archives Centre, Caversham Park, Reading, UK.
G   The BBC Written Archives Centre.

ENTER ORWELL AND CH'IEN

The MoI kept a watchful eye on the Eastern Service.[H] Indian loyalty was seen as a major issue, while it was generally perceived that the new Eastern Service operation at Broadcasting House in London was thoroughly "Leftist". This was largely true and certainly many of the Indian broadcasters were sympathetic to both independence and socialism. The reliable ex-MoI employee L.F. Rushbrook Williams (1890-1978), an Oxford academic who had lived and worked in Allahabad before the war, was appointed Director of the Eastern Service, but with Zulfiqar Ali ("Z.A.") Bokhari (1904-1975), who had worked in India for British-run radio stations there and who was seen as being of a leftist disposition, hired as a programme adviser for the Indian service.

In 1941 Eric Blair (aka George Orwell) was hired to assist Bokhari. Orwell was already well-known for his extensive journalism and reviewing, as well as his first-hand studies of poverty, *Down and Out in Paris and London* (1933) and *The Road to Wigan Pier* (1937), his recollections of his time as colonial policeman in *Burmese Days* (1934), and his memoir of the International Brigades in the Spanish Civil War, *Homage to Catalonia* (1938), as well as several well-

Figure 1: George Orwell at the BBC in 1943. Image courtesy of the BBC Written Archives, Caversham, UK

H   Britain's Ministry of Information (MOI), the government department responsible for all publicity and propaganda during wartime, was founded in the First World War and reformed in the Second, before being disbanded in 1946. It was famously located in Senate House (Malet Street, WC1), University of London which of course was repurposed by Orwell as the Ministry of Truth in his novel *Nineteen Eighty-Four* (1949).

received novels. Orwell was seen firmly as a "Man of the Left". Together Bokhari and Orwell put together an impressive list of Indian contributors based in London including the writer R.K. Narayan, the Tamil poet Tambimuttu, and the author Mulk Raj Anand. However, it seems Bokhari was not interested in the development of the Chinese division. The Chinese language service may have ended in 1941 with the fall of Hong Kong but the English language Eastern Service still occasionally featured content focused on the war in China. When it came to finding some Chinese contributors, Orwell took charge and looked to other sources for advice. He confessed that he had little knowledge of the country or its culture.[I] Hsiung Shih-I had been recommended to the BBC Eastern Service (prior to Orwell's appointment) by Clementine Churchill, the wife of Prime Minister Winston Churchill. The BBC was keen to oblige the PM's wife while it was also true that Hsiung was one of the best-known Chinese intellectuals in England at the time. Though Hsiung had been working hard with the United Aid to China Fund[J] since the Japanese invasion of China in the summer of 1937, he was hardly left wing—a strong supporter, and later biographer (it would be fair to say "hagiographer") of Chiang Kai-shek.[K] Hsiao Ch'ien was decidedly more left wing.

Figure 2: Shih-I Hsiung and his wife Dymia during their residence in England. Image courtesy of the BBC Written Archives, Caversham, UK

Hsiao Ch'ien (1910-1999), whose journalistic alias in China was Ruoping (若萍), was born in Beijing and had joined the Chinese Communist Youth League in 1924. After a period of study at Fu Jen

---

I   Orwell never did visit China, though he did collect traditional Chinese ginger jars he found in London antique shops.

J   Founded by Lady Isobel Cripps as a national appeal to raise money to provide relief across war-torn China. The funds were distributed by a committee headed by Sir Horace Seymour, British Ambassador in China.

K   Hsiung Shih-I, *The Life of Chiang Kai-shek*, London: Peter Davies, 1948.

Catholic University in Beijing he transferred to Yenching University to study journalism under Edgar Snow. In June 1936 he came to England to pursue postgraduate studies at Cambridge and taught briefly at University College London (UCL). After a brief sojourn in China, and a reporting trip on the vital Burma Road, he returned to England in 1939 and took up a lecturer post at SOAS while also working as the European Correspondent for the *Takungpao* (*The Impartial*) newspaper, which had London offices on Fleet Street.[L] Hsiao worked closely with the China Campaign Committee[M] and was good friends with several other well-known Chinese intellectuals in London all living in Hampstead at the time, including Hsiung Shih-I and the artist Chiang Yee (Jiang Yi, 1903-1977). Already of a left-wing disposition his opinions became pronouncedly pro-Soviet after the launch of Operation Barbarossa and the Nazi invasion of Russia in June 1941.[N]

Hsiao Ch'ien was first brought to Orwell's attention by the novelist E.M. Forster (1879-1970), not generally seen as a "Man of the Left". but one who had been close to the Bloomsbury Group and was an anti-imperialist. He had, of course, visited India and later written *A Passage to India* (1924), a novel set against the backdrop of the competing British Raj and Indian independence movement. Orwell had commissioned Forster to produce a weekly recorded book review for the Eastern Service, hoping Forster's reputation in India would attract listeners. Forster had read Hsiao Chi'en's small study of contemporary Chinese literature, *Etching of a Tormented Age*, published by the human rights organisation PEN in 1941.[O] The two had then met at a Memorial Meeting for the recently deceased Bengali poet, philosopher, and reformer Rabindranath Tagore (1861-1941)

L   *Takungpao* is the oldest active Chinese language newspaper in China. Founded in Tianjin in 1902. Between the world wars (its heyday), its slogan was "no party affiliation, no political endorsement, no self-promotion, no ignorance". It was particularly noted for its sharp political commentary and foreign coverage after the outbreaks of the Second Sino-Japanese War. Based alternatively in Shanghai, Hankow, Guilin, Chongqing, and Hong Kong, it continued to publish, staying one step ahead of the Japanese.

M   The China Campaign Committee (CCC) existed between 1937 and 1949 as a broad movement, generally to the Left of the United Aid for China group, bringing together politicians, local councillors, religious leaders, trade councils and trade unions, co-operative societies, and peace organisations to call for aid to China and a boycott of Japanese goods. Funds raised by the CCC went to Mme Sun Yat-sen's China Defence League in Hong Kong for the International Peace Hospitals in the Liberated areas.

N   Hsiao recalls his early life and education, sojourns in Britain and personal political trajectory leftwards in his autobiography, *Traveller Without a Map*, London: Hutchison, 1990.

O   Hsiao Ch'ien, *Etching of a Tormented Age: A Glimpse of Contemporary Chinese Literature*, London: George Allen & Unwin, 1941.

organised by the English PEN Club in 1941.ᴾ Forster was impressed and recommended Hsiao to Orwell.

As did another Eastern Service employee, William Empson (1906-1984). Empson was a highly regarded English literary critic who, after a scandal at Cambridge^Q, took a job teaching at the Tokyo University of Literature and Science, and then signed a three-year contract with Peking University. He arrived to find the Japanese occupying the city and the university faculty and students relocating swiftly to Kunming. He went with them and, after some time helping establish the university in "Free China", eventually arrived back in England in January 1939. In 1941 Empson was hired to work on the BBC's daily digest of foreign broadcasts, where he met Orwell.

Orwell wrote to Hsiao with the intention of hiring him to give a couple of talks for the BBC Eastern Service.

*****

13th March 1942
Dear Mr Hsiao,
I delayed writing to thank you for the copy you sent me of "*Etching of a Tormented Age*" until I should read it. It interested me very much, it also has brought home to me how complete my ignorance of modern Chinese literature is. I wonder if you would agree to do two talks for us on this subject about the end of April? We're having a series of talks on contemporary literature, and we are starting off with six talks on English literature, followed by four on Russian and two on Chinese. I am sure you would be exactly the person to undertake the latter; they are half-hour talks, i.e. not more than about 27 minutes each, and I should want the script in each case about a week before the date of the talk. Could you let me know whether you feel ready to undertake this, and if you do, I can give you further details. In the case of your not being able to broadcast on the actual days, we can easily record the talk beforehand.

P   Tagore had famously come to China twice, in 1924 and 1928. On the first trip, in 1924, he stayed several months. On his first visit he passed through Shanghai and spent most of his time in Beijing. On his second trip he remained in Shanghai.

Q   It was alleged that Empson had been caught *in flagrante delicto* with a woman in his rooms and that condoms had been found in his belongings. For this his scholarship was revoked.

                                            Yours sincerely,
                                                Eric Blair
                                             Talks Assistant
                                             Indian Section
Dictated by Eric Blair and despatched in his absence by: (not listed)
To: Hsiao Ch'ien Esq., 13, South Hill Park Gardens, N.W.3.

*****

17th March 1942

Hsiao Ch'ien, School of Oriental Studies, University of London, W.C.1.

Dear Mr. Blair,

Thank you for your kind letter. The space allotted for the booklet I did was much too small for an entirely virgin field.^R However, I feel well repaid for the time and effort I put into that "Guidebook" if I have interested an admirable writer like yourself.

No subject delights me more to broadcast on than the ones assigned me in your letter. I welcome the idea with all my heart. What I don't feel quite so sure is the date. I can in no way complain that China has suddenly become very topical, but it does take me away from a lot of work I would undertake with more love, such as a talk about modern Chinese literature. If you could put the date a bit later, say the end of May or early June, I think I can promise you with more certainty, as at present, I am working on a book. Another reason I wish it to come later is that I want to have such a talk fully illustrated with extracts, chiefly from my own translations. It was the recommendation of many friends who read the *Etching*. I can outline you this moment many ideas how they are to be done, such as having the talk on the literature of the last 2,000 years ending in the Literary Revolution and devote the second one entirely on the creative side of present-day literary China. The question is whether you could wait that long?

I suppose you have seen those Chinese stories which

R   *Etching of a Tormented Age* is just 48 pages long.

appeared in the New Writing, both in the Penguins and in the Autumn Folio.

Kindest wishes,
Yours sincerely,
Hsiao Ch'ien

*****

In his final comments Hsiao is referring to those stories concerning China, and by Chinese authors, published by the poet and editor John Lehmann (1907-1987) in his literary journals, *Penguin New Writing* and *Folios of New Writing*, which had included translations of several Chinese pieces. These included Pai Ping-Chieh (Bai Pingjie) *Along the Yunnan-Burma Road*, Yao Hsueh-Yin's (Yao Xueyin) *Half A Cartload of Straw Short*, and Zhang Tianyi's *Mr Hua Wei*, as well as an influential article entitled *Small Talk in China*, about modern Chinese literature, from Harold Acton (who had been resident in Beijing between 1932 and 1939).[S] Lehmann was a good friend of Orwell, and had been a champion of his work at the start of his career, so it can be expected that Orwell knew the publications and writings to which Hsiao referred. Indeed, Orwell's essay set in Burma, *Shooting an Elephant*, was first published by Lehmann in the literary magazine *New Writing* in Autumn 1936.[T]

The next phase of Hsiao and Orwell's correspondence becomes more friendly after Orwell (writing as George Orwell rather than Eric Blair) suggests Hsiao drop the formality and refer to him as 'George'.

*****

29th March 1942
Hsiao Ch'ien, School of Oriental Studies, University of London, W.C.1.

Dear George,

Thanks very much for your kind letter. This should be a happy day for many, especially you and me, for the thorny

---

[S] For more details on Lehmann, *Penguin New Writing* and *Folios of New Writing* see Tessa Thorniley, Phd dissertation, 'The Bridge': How *The Penguin New Writing* (1940-1950) Redrew Twentieth-Century Responses to China, University of Westminster, London, January 2020.

[T] As Lehmann needed help securing printing facilities and paper during the War, *New Writing* became *Penguin New Writing* under the sponsorship of Allen Lane (Penguin's founder). Orwell also contributed to the Christmas 1939 edition of *New Writing* with his essay *Marrakech*.

question of India is on the way to being solved. You have been a hard-working bridge builder for India with the rest of the world and China will not fail you. So, my "yes" to the two talks is spoken with genuine enthusiasm and I shall bargain no more about the date of handing in the Mss. So, you shall have the first script on the 15th and the second one on the 22nd. And many thanks for your confidence in me. I shan't mention the political side of India, but is it all right now for me to say something about the struggle of China? I would be most grateful if you could give me some idea of the prohibitive side, unofficially, so that I won't have to rewrite the whole thing again. Perhaps you know that my handling of the Indian matter in my talks to China in the past had been so indiscreet that I have forbidden myself to do any more. I am very anxious to know what the present limit is.

Yours,
Hsiao (hand signed)

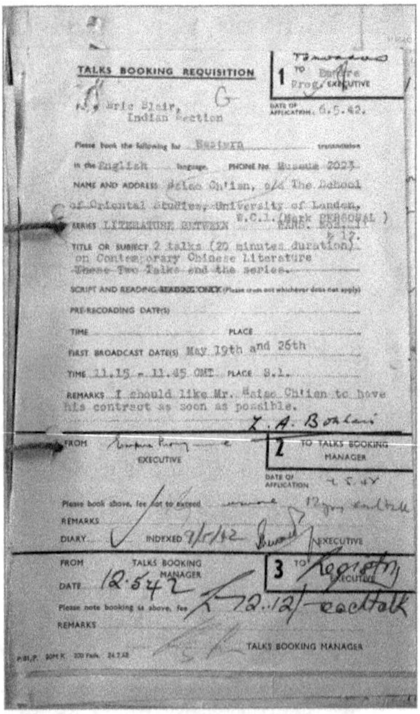

*****

And so the talks were agreed and the vital *BBC Talks Booking Requisition* form noting the broadcast dates (May 19th and May 26th, 1942), length and fee (fig 3). Just prior to Hsiao's first talk on Chinese contemporary literature, Orwell was keen to let Hsiao know that Indian listeners seemed to be appreciating the Eastern Service talks.

*****

11th May 1942

Dear Hsiao Ch'ien,

We have just received reports from India on our

Figure 3: Orwell (as Eric Blair) contracting Hsiao Ch'ien for BBC talks in 1942. Image courtesy of the BBC Written Archives, Caversham, UK

broadcasts during the first half of February. I thought you would be interested in the following, which came from Dacca[U]—

"Talk by Chinese talker on occupied China and Japan's New Order on 26th February very interesting".

We don't receive very many comments from India, so I think this is all the more encouraging! I am very much looking forward to seeing your first talk on Chinese contemporary literature.

Yours sincerely
George Orwell
Talks Producer
Indian Section
Hsiao Ch'ien Esq.,
c/o The School of Oriental Studies, Malet Street, WC1

*****

Sadly, no audio recordings or scripts of Hsiao Ch'ien's two talks remain in the BBC archives, either the sound archives or written archives. But the relationship between the BBC, Orwell and Hsiao lasted for the duration of the war, though Orwell left the BBC in March 1943. His mother died, and around the same time he started work on a new book, what would become *Animal Farm* (1945), while his health was always fragile. Orwell was apparently also depressed because he believed that not enough Indian listeners were tuning into the Eastern Service.[V]

INFLUENCE AND LEGACY

Hsiao Ch'ien remained a regular broadcaster on the Service and the wider BBC. Among his contributions was a discussion on life in China under the Japanese occupation in March 1942, and another discussion on how post-war Japan should be treated, which was aired in August 1944. This latter talk was also broadcast on the BBC service to the United States, greatly increasing Hsiao's reach and potential influence. In addition, Hsiao gave some talks on contemporary China to the BBC's "Sixth Form" service, a series of programmes aimed at

---

U Dhaka
V According to a conversation recalled by the journalist Malcolm Muggeridge and included in his introduction to *Burmese Days*, New York: Time Inc. Book Division, 1962

schoolchildren aged sixteen to eighteen that received positive feedback from the BBC commissioners.

Hsiao joined with other Eastern Service presenters on panels and discussions, notably Mulk Raj Anand (1905-2004). Anand and Hsiao had become good friends at the BBC Eastern Service and lived close to each other in North London—Anand in Primrose Hill and Hsiao in Belsize Park. The two worked together in 1942 to present a programme entitled *Letter to a Chinese Guerrilla*. Both had known the poet Wang Lixi (aka "Shelley" Wang, 1901-1939) who had lived for some years in London and then returned, with his poet wife Lu Jingqing (1907-1993), to China when the Japanese invaded. Shelley Wang died of sepsis in 1939 though news of his death took a long time to reach London. It was also said that Lu was living underground in Shanghai. Mulk Raj Anand broadcast a message to Lu, remembering Wang, and urging that the struggle to free China and defeat Japan continue. Orwell was so impressed with the contribution that he included it in a small book he compiled in 1943, shortly before leaving the BBC, of the best speeches and talks on the Eastern Service.[W] Mulk Raj Anand went on to dedicate his 1945 novel *The Big Heart* to Hsiao and 'the friendship of India and China.'[X]

Figure 4: Hsiao Ch'ien with J.M. Tambimuttu at BBC Broadcasting House in 1942. Image courtesy of the BBC Written Archives, Caversham, UK.

W   George Orwell (ed.), *Talking to India*, London: George Allen & Unwin, 1943

X   Mulk Raj Anand, *The Big Heart*, London: Hutchison International, 1945. The theme of the novel is the conflict between hereditary copper smiths and the capitalists. It is a novel about a village of artisans in Amritsar in the early 1940s whose livelihood is destroyed by the establishment of a factory producing copper utensils…The story ends with the machine emerging triumphant over humans.

The BBC Eastern Service was clearly of its time. It emphasised Empire unity and loyalty against fascism and the Japanese, while ignoring the wartime realities of famine, oppression, and anti-imperial activity ongoing in the Raj. This was despite the controlling influences of various leftist, Marxist, and anti-imperialist intellectuals such as Orwell and contributors of a similar political stripe as Anand and Hsiao Ch'ien. Apparently the combination of the oversight of the MoI and the exigencies of wartime solidarity overrode what would become prominent post-war concerns, of independence in India and Partition, as well as the end of the treaty port system in China and the eventual the communist takeover in 1949.

The Eastern Service was to be both a vehicle for Chinese intellectuals in London to attempt to communicate with, and support, the resistance at home, while collaborations between South Asian and Chinese contributors showed a unity of resistance that presaged the post-war world.

After the war, programming of the Eastern Service fell back under the rubric and control of the BBC Empire Service, which eventually morphed into the BBC World Service.

Paul French *(paul@chinarhyming.com) lived and worked in Shanghai for many years. His book* Midnight in Peking *was a New York Times Bestseller. His most recent book* City of Devils: A Shanghai Noir *has received much praise with The Economist writing, '…in Mr French the city has its champion storyteller.' Both* Midnight in Peking *and* City of Devils *are currently being developed as movies. He is currently working on a biography of the inspirational year (1924/1925) Wallis Warfield Spencer (later the Duchess of Windsor) spent in China, for publication in 2024.*

IN THE STEPS OF SHANGHAI JIM
By Duncan Hewitt

ABSTRACT:
JG Ballard is arguably the author who has done most to put wartime Shanghai on the literary map—with his novel Empire of the Sun *(later filmed by Steven Spielberg) and its sequel* The Kindness of Women. *While these books, which draw on Ballard's Shanghai childhood, were his best-selling works, many of his fans see them as separate from his true literary legacy of dystopian, science fiction-influenced novels, from* The Drowned World *to* Crash *and* High-Rise *(the latter two also made into movies). This article, however, highlights how Ballard's experience of growing up in 1930s and 40s Shanghai was a key influence on his unique worldview and literary voice throughout his career—even if this enduring literary connection is rarely acknowledged in the city of his birth itself.*

At times of crisis in contemporary urban societies, or indeed when natural disasters strike, it's become almost commonplace that someone, somewhere, will eventually liken the situation to something from the writing of JG Ballard—the Shanghai-born, British author of science fiction and disturbing, often experimental novels about contemporary society, who found global fame with *Empire of the Sun*, based on his experience of internment in a Japanese camp in Shanghai in World War II. During the early Covid-19 lockdowns in 2020, for example, the British writer Will Self drew a parallel between the isolation that many were experiencing and Ballard's 1977 short story *The Intensive Care Unit*, about a world in which people only meet via TV screens.[1] The New Statesman also published an article entitled *Why We are Living in JG Ballard's World*, arguing that 'much of our present reality now falls within the jurisdiction of Ballard's imagination.'[2]

Particularly since his death in 2009, Ballard has come to be seen by many as something of a visionary, his vivid imagination portraying the world as a fragile place, and human society as never far from disintegration. His writing covers a broad spectrum: from a London reverting to the Triassic Age after the melting of the polar ice caps in *The Drowned World* (1962), to a world of water shortages caused by pollution damage to the ecosystem in *The Drought,* and the descent of luxurious, hi-tech communities into crime, violence or terrorism in novels such as *High Rise, Cocaine Nights, Super-Cannes,* or *Millennium People.* In *The Atrocity Exhibition* (1970) Ballard predicted the use of vacuous television advertising to bring about the election of a celebrity president (in this case Ronald Reagan). His final novel *Kingdom Come* (2006), explored the thin line between consumerism, media manipulation and xenophobic populism in a suburbia draped in English flags, hinting at the forces that would propel the nation towards Brexit a decade later.

> Ballard described his fiction as being set in a kind of visionary present—recognisably the same world we live in every day, but [...] sharpened and heightened as if you were on some sort of drug. If you like, the present, five minutes ahead.[3]

His work, which included some thirty novels and more than a hundred short stories, was not to everyone's taste: the first US edition of *The Atrocity Exhibition* was pulped by its publisher after complaints about its obscenity. His 1972 novel *Crash*, focusing on the main character's erotic obsession with car accidents, was perhaps his most controversial—even two decades later, the movie version by David Cronenberg was banned by London's Westminster Council.[4]

Yet there's no doubt that Ballard's writing was highly distinctive, with its sometimes surreal, sometimes apocalyptic vision, deadpan humour and often intentionally two-dimensional characters—Ballard once said that, in his early works at least, he was 'more interested in psychological roles than in [...] novelistic characterisation'.[5] According to the novelist Martin Amis, 'nothing he ever wrote could have been written by anyone else'.[6] Indeed, the word "Ballardian" features in the Collins English Dictionary, defined as denoting 'dystopian modernity, bleak man-made landscapes and the psychological effects of technological, social or environmental developments.' And in his later years, Ballard's writing won increasingly widespread praise. The author William Boyd called him 'the most modern of writers, [whose] art engages with the artefacts and obsessions of the second half of this [20th] century in a manner and with an intensity unmatched by any other writer.'[7] Even Britain's *Mail on Sunday* newspaper, hardly a hotbed of the avant-garde, described him as 'the greatest of living English writers' in 2008, when his memoir *Miracles of Life* was published.⁸

Ballard's transition from edgy outsider to something of a national treasure by the time of his death owed much to his two biggest-selling novels, *Empire of the Sun (1984)*, and its sequel *The Kindness of Women* (1991). These were not visionary depictions of the near future, but works of semi-autobiographical fiction, drawing deeply on his childhood in Shanghai in the 1930s and 40s, in particular his experience of being interned with his family by the Japanese, between the ages of twelve and fourteen, in Lunghwa (Longhua) 'Civilian Assembly Centre' in the city's suburbs. Among some fans of Ballard's dystopian fiction, these two novels were seen as somehow tangential to his 'real' work. Yet, as Ballard himself gradually acknowledged in his later years (notably in his memoir), his experiences in Shanghai—before and during internment—influenced the style, content and imagery of his writing from his earliest works in the late 1950s onwards.

This Shanghai connection was something Ballard initially denied—not least in an attempt to integrate into life in Britain, where few seemed interested in his past when he moved there in 1946. Such denial may also have been a way of suppressing his sadness at leaving behind a city that he saw as 'unlike any other, before or since', but which soon seemed 'as remote and glamorous as ancient Rome'.⁹ Either way, he said he had

> deliberately forgotten my China background… I never mentioned it to anybody. When I married in 1955, I don't think I ever told [my wife] that I was born and brought up in Shanghai, or if I did it was only in passing.¹⁰

And when he wrote *Empire of the Sun* in the 1980s, he observed that he had 'waited forty years [...] Twenty years to forget and then twenty years to remember.'¹¹

Yet Ballard eventually recognised that 'a large part of my fiction has been an attempt to evoke [Shanghai] by means other than memory [...] The memories of Shanghai that I had tried to repress had been knocking at the floorboards under my feet, and had slipped quietly into my fiction.'¹² This article, therefore, looks at the specific ways in which Shanghai, and Ballard's childhood experiences there, shaped one of the most distinctive voices in modern English literature, influencing not only his perception of the world, and his dispassionate perspective on contemporary western societies (particularly Britain and the US), but also much of his signature imagery—from runways and crashed cars, to empty swimming pools, abandoned buildings, and chaos in elite residential compounds.

Privilege and Brutality—A Shanghai Childhood

When James Graham Ballard was born, at the General Hospital of Shanghai's International Settlement in November 1930, it was into a life of undoubted privilege. His father, also James, was a chemist who had been sent to the city the previous year as a factory manager for the Calico Printers Association, one of Britain's biggest cotton manufacturers, which in 1925 had opened a textile works in Pootung (Pudong), Shanghai (not far from today's Oriental Pearl TV tower), seeking to capitalise on East Asia's fast growing market and cheap labour. The China Printing and Finishing Company (CPF), as this new operation was known, looked after the Ballards well, housing them initially in a "Mediterranean-

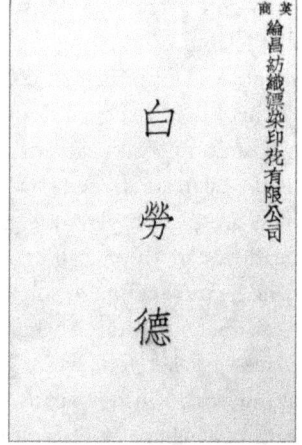

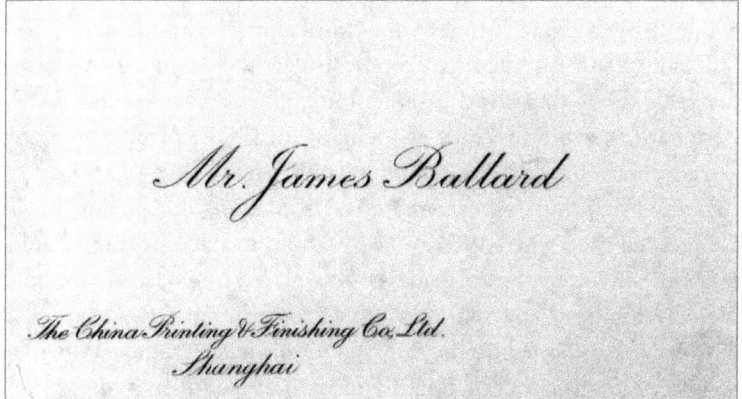

Figure 1: James Ballard senior's business card from the China Printing and Finishing Company. From the collection of Bill Salvadove.

style" villa in the prestigious new Columbia Circle development on Amherst Avenue (now Xinhua Road) in Shanghai's western suburbs, just outside the boundaries of the French concession. By the early 1940s, when they moved along the street to a larger, mock-Tudor house (after James Ballard was promoted to director of the company when his predecessor left China), the family had some ten servants, including a cook, houseboy and chauffeur, who lived in a separate building at the side of the house.

Young Jamie, as he was known, was sent to the Cathedral School, the pre-eminent British establishment in Shanghai, near the city's famous waterfront, the Bund. He travelled to school in the family's chauffeur-driven Buick, which also delivered his father to his office round the corner in Wayfoong House on Szechuen (Sichuan) Road, at the back of the imposing Hong Kong and Shanghai Bank headquarters. The school was pure British colonial: like the neighbouring Holy Trinity Cathedral, it had been designed by Sir George Gilbert Scott, architect of London's Albert Memorial and St Pancras Hotel. The mainly British boys (Asian and mixed-race students were not admitted) played plenty of sport, put on plays and revues, and studied Latin, under a British headmaster whom Ballard described as a 'brutal sadist'.[13] In his spare time he took riding lessons and swam at the Columbia Country Club near the family home, where his parents also played tennis. His father played cricket too, while his mother held frequent bridge parties, along with dinner parties at which alcohol flowed freely.[14] In the summer Ballard and his mother would spend up to two months at the northern seaside resorts of Tsingtao (Qingdao) or Weihaiwei (Weihai) with other expatriate families, sometimes joined by his father.

And yet such privilege could not insulate the young Ballard from the realities of the world around him. Illness, poverty and death were hard to avoid in 1930s Shanghai, which he remembered as 'an extraordinary brutal place,' adding, 'I think by the age of about ten I couldn't help but feel that there was something odd about this.'[15] He recalled that 'whenever I went to school in the morning I could see bodies lying by the roadside, coffins placed by the road side, put there by families who couldn't afford a proper burial.'[16] Once he saw a dead baby abandoned on the doorstep of his father's office. When he accompanied his father on the CPF ferry to the company's cotton mill at Pootung Point opposite the Bund, they would see corpses floating downstream, set adrift by families too poor to buy a coffin.[17] As a child,

Figure 2: The Ballard family moved into this house at 31 Amherst Ave, when James Ballard senior was promoted to company director. Ten servants lived in a separate building at the side of the house. Image provided with kind permission by Margaret Richardson.

he wrote, this 'unsettled me as it must have unsettled my parents.'[18]

Such unease was accentuated by the violence of Shanghai, which became more pronounced during Ballard's first decade, particularly after Japan took control of most of the city following its invasion of eastern China in 1937, and lawlessness flourished in areas under the control of its puppet government. As Ballard put it, 'There was a huge amount of crime—great gangster syndicates were operating; kidnapping and Chicago-style gangland machine gunning were commonplace.'[19] He recalled his father pointing out the car of Morris "Two Gun" Cohen, the London-raised bodyguard to Chinese warlords, on the Bund, with 'armed men standing on the running-boards, Chicago-style.'[20]

After the Japanese takeover in 1937, the Ballards initially left their home in Amherst Avenue—which was located in the so-called 'western extension roads' area, and thus technically under the control of the Japanese and their local puppets—for the relative safety of the French concession. They later returned, and British troops were stationed on Amherst Avenue in an attempt to reassure the residents. But the Ballards still had to pass through Japanese checkpoints between different zones of the city, and young Jamie soon discovered that Japanese soldiers were quite 'capable of losing their tempers and lunging with their fixed bayonets into the crowds pressing around them.'[21]

This education in violence was reinforced on weekend trips, when his parents and their friends would drive out into the Shanghai suburbs, to view recently abandoned battlefields—and take the children along. 'Today a family might go to the local garden centre or to some historic sight. We visited these battlegrounds, with bodies lying [there]', as well as dead horses beside the road, Ballard reminisced— adding, 'perhaps too little was hidden in Shanghai.'[22] He surmised that violence in the city was simply 'so pervasive that my parents and the various nannies never tried to shield me from all the brutality going on.'[23]

There was also the notorious bombing of downtown Shanghai (mainly accidentally by China's own air force) on 'Bloody Saturday' in August 1937, which left more than a thousand civilians dead. Ballard was only six at the time, but he certainly heard about these events, and described them in detail in *The Kindness of Women*.[24] (Strikingly, when I interviewed his younger sister Margaret Richardson in 2010, she was quick to show me her copy of *Four Months of War*, a book of images of the 1937 conflict, published the following year by Shanghai's North China Daily News). The Ballard family also encountered the trauma of war in autumn 1939, when they sailed from Liverpool to Canada, en route back to China after a trip home. They found themselves on a ship filled with survivors of the sinking of the SS Athenia, which had been torpedoed by the German navy a few weeks earlier with the loss of almost 100 lives. According to Margaret Richardson, this was 'very upsetting for everyone. The survivors were absolutely terrified and thought the whole thing was going to happen again, and that meant that we were terrified.'[25]

And while the Ballards never directly fell victim to violence in Shanghai themselves, it was never far away. There was at least one kidnapping in Amherst Avenue while they lived there, and the daughter of a maid working for an American family living in the same street was assaulted and killed by Japanese soldiers in a nearby shanty town.[26] The young Ballard may not have known about these incidents, but he discovered that his father kept a loaded pistol between the shirts in his wardrobe, after he was threatened during a labour dispute at the CPF mill.[27] The mill's location in Pudong also made it vulnerable in the fighting of 1937; its roof was damaged when the Japanese seized control of the area. And in 1938 a visitor from the firm's British head office reported a company delegation being fired on by the Japanese military while crossing the river back to the Bund at the end of the day and inadvertently breaking a Japanese curfew.[28]

In May 1939, the mill itself was the scene of violent clashes when workers demanding higher pay attacked British members of staff, prompting the British military of the International settlement to land a detachment of troops at the plant. After the Japanese ordered the British to withdraw, there was a skirmish in which Japanese troops fatally injured the CPF's British chief security officer, Maurice Tinkler, a former police officer in Shanghai's international settlement. The incident made headlines around the world.[29]

Later, when his family was interned in Lunghwa, Ballard had further opportunities to see Japanese troops in action. The camp's first commandant, Tomohiko Hayashi, a former London-based diplomat, was generally respectful towards the inmates, and got on well with Ballard's parents, even giving them his family tea set as a gift; after the war Ballard's father testified on Hayashi's behalf at a war crimes trial, at which he was found not guilty.[30] Ballard himself also struck up a friendship 'of a kind' with some of the young Japanese guards, who allowed him to join in their fencing practice. Yet he knew 'they could be viciously brutal, especially when acting under the orders of their NCOs'; after Hayashi was replaced as camp commandant, Ballard witnessed two guards beat a Chinese rickshaw driver to death.[31] And at the war's end, when he left the camp for a day, hoping to visit the family home, he encountered a group of Japanese soldiers who had tied a young Chinese man to a telegraph pole and were strangling him with telephone wire. After one of the soldiers demanded Ballard's American plastic belt, the 14 year-old boy felt he had no choice but to stay there, watching, until the man died and the soldiers lost interest in him; only then did he dare to walk away.[32]

The Fragility of "Civilised Society"

No wonder then, that, by the end of the war, Ballard felt that 'I had changed, and I knew that childhood had passed for good.'[33] His experiences led him, as he put it later, 'to regard the human race as potentially quite dangerous. People brought up in the comfortable suburbs of western Europe and North America tend to think that human beings are [...] thoughtful and humane above all'; he, however, was 'not convinced that human beings can be trusted beyond a certain point'.³⁴ Indeed, he described them as 'a race of partly civilised hunter killers who've adapted loosely to living in large enclaves.'³⁵

And he acknowledged that his wartime experiences had 'left me with a very sceptical eye, which I've turned onto something even as settled as English suburbia—nothing is as secure as we like to think it is.'³⁶ In fact, he added: 'A large part of my fiction tries to analyse [...] whether we are much different people from the civilised human beings we imagine ourselves to be.'³⁷ It's a question that informs much of Ballard's writing: in *High Rise*, for example, well-paid professionals—architects, accountants, doctors, television producers—quickly go "rogue", embracing violence, tribalism and a brutal reordering of society. In *Millennium People*, meanwhile, the residents of a luxurious estate in Chelsea wage a terrorist campaign against the middle-class world around them.

Of course Ballard's childhood cannot be taken in isolation; subsequent world events also reinforced his view of humanity. He regarded the 1960s as

> an era of inexplicable deaths: the murder of Kennedy; the threat of nuclear war [...] Vietnam was really getting into full swing, and nightly atrocities were shown on television. Murder and death seemed to be in the air [...] electrified by this new medium of TV.³⁸

This led, he said, to a 'deadening of the emotions'.³⁹ And Ballard was also affected by tragedy in his own life, when his wife Mary died suddenly from pneumonia on a family holiday in Spain in 1963, leaving him with three small children. He later acknowledged that the resulting trauma had influenced the direction of his subsequent work: 'I occasionally have glanced back at *Crash*, and my first reaction is, the man who wrote this is mad!' he told the BBC. 'It was a sort of piece of willed insanity.' His work at this time was, he said, an attempt to

> make sense of my wife's death. If you look at *The Atrocity Exhibition* or *Crash*, these are books that attempt to prove that black is white, that two and two do make five, [...] and therefore in a way everything is alright, the world makes sense.⁴⁰

Yet Ballard also saw these events as the continuation of 'a deep pathology that I had witnessed in Shanghai,' and his early experiences clearly lay at the root of his wariness of human nature.[41] As he put it in the early 1990s: 'Obviously we are all influenced by our childhoods. But mine was, as it happens, particularly traumatic and it has spread itself to my fiction.'[42]

Ballard's view of the fragility of "civilised society" was intensified by seeing Britain and other colonial powers initially defeated by the Japanese in Asia. Until this point he was 'intensely patriotic', having grown up reading publications like the Boy's Own Paper, which regaled readers with tales of British adventure and military success.[43] Even the street he lived on had imperial connotations: it was named after Lord Amherst, a former governor general of India, whose early 19th century trade mission to China was part of the process that led to the Opium Wars and the forced opening of China to foreign traders and settlers. There was also the influence of his parents and their circle. Ballard said he did not see them as racist, 'in the sense of feelings of innate biological superiority', and stressed that he was 'never allowed' to feel superior to Chinese children or servants. But there was, he said, a definite 'sense that we belonged to a superior commercial and industrial nation.'[44]

When the Japanese took over Shanghai's foreign concessions after the attack on Pearl Harbor in late 1941, however, he saw British power slipping away before his eyes. The diaries of Ruth Hill Barr, who was later interned in the same camp as the Ballards, describe how citizens of allied nations were banned from buying petrol, and eventually had to hand their cars over to the Japanese. They were also forced to wear ID denoting their status as enemy citizens, and were banned from cinemas and other entertainment venues.[45] The Cathedral School was closed and forced to relocate to temporary premises. (These were at least closer to Ballard's home, which was convenient as he now had to cycle to school). He recalled Japanese military police officers coming to the family house to assess its suitability for future occupation, and his father watching them walk around 'without a word… [He] had no answer to them.'[46] Seeing his parents in this situation made him realise that 'everything was changing', something that was

> […] quite a surprise to an eleven year old[…] I suddenly realised that British power had ended, and the whole great

western party, which had been running in Shanghai since something like the 1890s, was over.⁴⁷

The fall of Singapore 'without a fight' fuelled this impression. 'Even at the age of 11 or 12 I knew that no amount of patriotic newsreels would put the Union Jack jigsaw together again', he wrote. 'From then on I was slightly suspicious of all British adults.'⁴⁸

Ballard's sense that 'the British Empire had failed' only intensified when his family, along with many other British and allied citizens—including Felix Hookham, father of the ballerina Margot Fonteyn, and Cyril Goldbert, who, under the stage name Peter Wyngarde, later starred as Jason King in the 1960s' British TV spy drama *Department S*—were summoned by the Japanese to the Columbia Country Club in March 1943, and taken on buses to be interned at the Lunghwa Civilian Assembly Centre, on the grounds of the former Shanghai High School.⁴⁹

For the young Ballard, life in the camp did have some positive aspects: he appreciated spending more time with his parents, who had previously often left him with nannies and servants, and 'flourished in all this intimacy'. He also noted 'a great sense of solidarity' among many of the internees.⁵⁰ And despite the threats of sickness, cold and, in the last months of the war, food shortages, he saw the camp overall as a 'happy, friendly place. It was a huge tenement in a sense, and I was having a good time with all the other children.'⁵¹ He did have to

Figure 3: Child internees performing chores in Lunghwa Civilian Assembly Center during the war. Image supplied with kind permission by Betty Barr.

attend the camp school (except when it was closed by the Japanese to punish the adult inmates for some misdemeanour) but the general atmosphere was now far less formal, a 'relaxed and easy going world that I'd never known'. Thus for Ballard, Lunghwa was a 'prison where I found freedom.'[52]

Yet there was inevitable conflict amid such tight confinement: Ballard witnessed quarrels that 'sometimes came to blows', while Ruth Hill Barr, who took part in lectures and debates with Ballard's father, and whose son's birthday party the young Jamie attended in the camp, noted in her diaries a decline in morals among the internees as their time there dragged on.[53] For Ballard, the experience of seeing his parents and other authority figures 'humiliated and frightened, [...] stripped of all the garments of authority that protect adults generally in their dealings with children' undoubtedly added to his growing scepticism about the adult world.[54]

ECHOES OF SHANGHAI—BALLARD'S IMAGERY

The collapse of the sophisticated, "civilised" world that humans seek to create is symbolised in Ballard's fiction by a range of imagery, much of it recurring, and much of it clearly inspired by his experiences in Shanghai. Empty or abandoned swimming pools, for example, feature not just in *Empire of the Sun* but also in *High-Rise, Cocaine Nights* and other works. And while his own family, unlike the character Jim in *Empire of the Sun,* never had a swimming pool in their garden, Ballard recalled that, when they briefly moved to the French concession to avoid the fighting in 1937, they stayed in a rented house whose pool had been drained. It 'lay in the garden like a mysterious empty presence,' he said, which 'struck me as strangely significant in a way I have never fully grasped;' with hindsight, he suggested it represented the 'unknown', a concept that had previously 'played no part in my life.'[55]

Derelict buildings are another "Ballardian" trope. 'Abandoned houses and office buildings held a special magic', he wrote in *Miracles of Life*.[56] He recalled going to visit a school friend on the Avenue Foch (Yan'an Road) shortly before Pearl Harbor, only to find the boy's apartment 'abandoned to the wind, unwanted possessions scattered across the beds', the family having fled the city, fearing impending Japanese takeover.[57] After the Japanese takeover of the city, he and his father once took a short-cut through a derelict compound in an attempt to reach his school, on a day when the military checkpoints into the French concession were shut, and found themselves walking through the abandoned Del Monte Casino, once one of Shanghai's most lavish night spots, on Avenue Haig (Huashan Lu). As his father searched for the exit, Ballard found himself wandering alone among the gilded statues, overturned roulette tables, and fallen chandeliers. It was an experience that reinforced his sense of 'the surrealism of everyday life', he wrote.[58] The centre of Lunghwa Camp, meanwhile, contained the remains of ruined buildings, bombed during the fighting of 1937.[59] And at the end of the war, Ballard went to look for old family friends, the Kendall-Wards, who lived near the family home on Amherst Avenue. When he reached their house, however, all that remained was a brick shell—its contents, fittings, floorboards, even its tiles and roof beams had been stripped bare by looters.[60]

Such experiences fuelled his sense that 'reality itself was a stage set that could be dismantled at any moment, and that no matter how magnificent anything appeared, it could be swept aside into the debris of the past.'[61] This perception had a significant influence on Ballard's work: the central characters in many of his stories are, he suggested, often willing to accept the collapse of the norms of "civilised" society and 'embrace the cataclysm, because they're seeking some sort of psychological truth about themselves: '[...] in many ways the characters are finding that the so-called real world isn't convincing any more.'[62]

The war in Shanghai contributed to another recurring element of Ballard's writing—his fascination with aeroplanes, aviators and runways. Flying, he said, had played 'a very large role in my fiction. My characters are forever dreaming of runways and looking into those skies where they can transcend themselves.'[63] The fascination, he acknowledged, dated to his childhood and 'in particular the air-war over Shanghai'. He recalled his excitement at 'the first sight of the American B29s which began to bomb Shanghai in 1944', and subsequent attacks on the city by Mustang fighters. These

> flew so low over Lunghwa camp that I remember looking down at them from the second and third floor of buildings during the air raids—they were flying within ten feet of the paddy fields.[64]

Figure 4: In Steven Spielberg's film version of *Empire of the Sun*, a toy aeroplane symbolises the young Jim's fascination with planes and flight.

It's an interest shared by Jim, the Ballard-avatar in *Empire of the Sun*, who watches in awe as American fighters fly over the camp, but is equally obsessed with Japanese planes and pilots. The scene in the book where Jim chances on a crashed Chinese fighter was inspired by a childhood experience, when the young Ballard strayed onto the original Hungjao (Hongqiao) aerodrome in Shanghai's western suburbs, abandoned due to fighting, while visiting family friends nearby.[65]

Flight is also a theme in many of Ballard's other works. In *The Unlimited Dream Company*, the main character steals a Cessna aircraft from Heathrow and crash-lands it in the Thames at Shepperton, the small suburban town where Ballard lived for the last five decades of his life. Indeed Ballard—who briefly trained as an RAF pilot in Canada after dropping out of university—acknowledged that Shepperton's proximity to Heathrow Airport was part of its appeal. 'Runways have always had a special magic for me[...] This hotel close to Terminal 4 is almost my spiritual home', he said in a BBC interview which, at his request, was filmed in a hotel lobby beside the airport, adding 'I'm never happier than when inside this extraordinary atrium surrounded by resting air crew.'[66] Ballard's fascination with planes was picked up on by Steven Spielberg and screenwriter Tom Stoppard, who used the young Jim's toy aeroplane as a recurring leitmotif in the film version of *Empire of the Sun*.

Another recurring aspect of Ballard's imagery—the crashed car—may also have its earliest roots in Shanghai, with the 'Hell-Drivers', described in *the Kindness of Women* as a

> troupe of American dare-devil drivers who crashed their battered Fords and Chevrolets through wooden barricades covered with flaming gasoline. The sight of these thrillingly rehearsed accidents eclipsed the humdrum street crashes of Shanghai.[67]

Ballard's experience of war, and the constant threat of sickness in Shanghai, seems also to have contributed to his fascination with medical issues. As a child, he contracted dysentery and spent weeks in the International Settlement's General Hospital.[68] He and his friends were regularly given 'unlimited Coca Cola and ice cream' to take their minds off the ear-ache they contracted in the infected waters of the Country Club swimming pool.[69] His sister Margaret also got dysentery in Lunghwa, while the diaries of Ruth Hill Barr, the Ballards' acquaintance in the camp, highlight the danger of catching malaria there.[70] Added to his experience of seeing death and suffering in Shanghai, it's perhaps not surprising that Ballard initially studied medicine at Cambridge University (he quit after two years mainly spent dissecting cadavers), nor that many of his central characters are doctors, and his works frequently investigate the limits of the human body and mind.

Childhood memories also appear to have informed Ballard's sense of the futility of humans' attempts to impose their will on the natural world, a theme of early works such as *The Drowned World* or *The Drought*. For all Shanghai's modernity, its sewers were frequently overwhelmed in summer, when the nearby Yangtze River burst its banks. Ballard recalled downtown streets 'two or three feet deep in brown silt-laden water', while, in the surrounding countryside, 'water lay as far as the eye could see.'[71] During his time in Lunghwa, he would sometimes look out across the fields towards the city centre and see the distant apartment buildings of the French concession 'rising from these great sheets of water.'[72] Even the images of crocodiles and alligators roaming through London in *The Drowned World* could, he suggested, be traced back to childhood visits to the reptile house at the zoo in Shanghai's Jessfield (now Zhongshan) Park, with its 'enormous ancient alligator housed in a concrete pit half-filled with cigarette packets and ice-cream cartons.'[73]

'A Self-generating Fantasy'

More broadly, the sheer spectacle of pre-war Shanghai clearly left a deep mark on Ballard's imagination: the startling juxtaposition of violence, poverty and chaos with the glamour and modernity of what young Jim's father in *The Kindness of Women* called 'the most advanced city in the world' made Shanghai 'a bright but bloody kaleidoscope,' where

> unlimited venture capitalism rode in gaudy style down streets lined with beggars showing of their sores and wounds [...] Anything was possible, and everything could be bought and sold.[74]

To young Jim in the novel, the city was

> a waking dream where everything I could imagine had already been taken to its extreme. The garish billboards and nightclub neon signs, the young Chinese gangsters and violent beggars [...] were part of an over-lit realm more exhilarating than the American comics and radio serials I so adored.[75]

The result, for an imaginative child like the young Ballard, was almost limitless stimulation. In Shanghai, 'the fantastic, which for most people lies inside their heads, lay all around me', he wrote.[76] '[It was] a magical place, a self-generating fantasy that left my own little mind far behind'.[77] On trips around the city in the family car, he would routinely 'see something strange and mysterious, but treat it as normal'.[78] As he got older, and particularly after the family's car was confiscated by the Japanese, he began going for long solo bike rides around the city (often telling his parents that he was visiting friends), during which he was 'always on the lookout for something new, and rarely disappointed.'[79]

This experience of Shanghai seems to have cemented in Ballard's mind the idea of a city as a unique construct of human endeavour—which could also be the venue for, or indeed give rise to, great extremes of behaviour. His career-long interest in the implications of rampant consumerism and constant media messaging may owe much to his exposure to Shanghai's blend of mass consumption, ubiquitous advertising and latent violence. In *Kingdom Come*, for example, violence erupts in and around a huge suburban shopping mall, complete with its own 24 hour cable TV station.[80]

Ballard's sister Margaret Richardson remembered family trips to the legendary Wing On department store on Shanghai's Nanking Road, which she said was 'marvellous, [and] full of wonderful things', while Ballard himself recalled that 'bizarre advertising displays were part of the everyday reality of the city.'[81] Notably, he described attending the Shanghai premiere of the film *The Hunchback of Notre Dame*, and seeing an 'honour guard of about 50 hunchbacks whom the management had recruited from the back alleys of Shanghai, all doing their little bit to imitate Charles Laughton, as the westerners stepped from their limousines in evening dress. Even at the time', he said, 'I thought it was pretty bizarre.'[82] Margaret, meanwhile, recalled seeing *National Velvet* at the Majestic Cinema after the war—and being greeted by two horses from the nearby racecourse, complete with jockeys in livery.[83]

Such state-of-the-art cinemas, showing the latest western releases alongside the work of Shanghai's own movie industry (the city was dubbed the "Hollywood of the East"), were part of a media culture that also encompassed competing tabloid newspapers and multiple radio stations. The literary historian Leo Ou-fan Lee has described Shanghai as 'the center of cultural production for ideas about modernity', while to Ballard it was 'a media city before its time', and 'a portent of the media cities of the future.'[84]

Ballard's own fascination with cinema lasted a lifetime: he wrote of his love of American thrillers and *film noir*, as well as European directors like Cocteau and Clouzot.[85] Indeed, his sister Margaret described movies as 'the most important thing to him—terrifically important'.[86] This love of film had begun in Shanghai, where he recalled seeing his first movie, *Snow White* (which 'frightened the wits out of me') at the Grand Theatre on the Nanking (Nanjing) Road, and attending the premiere of the *Wizard of Oz* with his school.[87] Later there were private movie screenings in the house opposite his home in Amherst Avenue, courtesy of the US intelligence officers who were billeted there after the war.[88]

Yet while there was clearly much in Shanghai to fire Ballard's imagination, his desire to create stories may, ironically, also have been stimulated by the amount of time he spent alone, forced to amuse himself, as a child. His parents went out socialising most nights of the week, leaving him alone with a Russian nanny, or with the family's Chinese servants, with whom he had little communication. It was, he said, typical of middle-class expatriate British families in an era when 'children were an appendage to the parents[...] and were never seen as a significant measure of a family's health or the centre of its life.'[89] Such children, he noted,

> lived in large houses where no one shared a bedroom, they never saw their parents dressing or undressing, never saw them brush their teeth [...] The vistas of polished furniture turned a family home into a deserted museum, with a few partly colonised rooms where people slept alone, read and bathed alone.[90]

The near seven-year age gap between Ballard and his sister also meant they were hardly ideal playmates. (Ballard even recalled making a plywood screen and placing it across the family dining table so that he did not have to talk to her at breakfast time).[91] Thus they spent a lot of time reading or making their own entertainment. And when they played with their toys, it was always in their bedrooms, never downstairs with their parents. 'Children had their place', Margaret recalled. 'I was happy to play in my room, but it was an isolated thing.' Nevertheless, she added, 'I'm sure it did wonders for both our imaginations.'[92]

It may be no coincidence that many of the central characters in Ballard's fiction—most of them men—'tend to be solitary,' and relatively isolated from their families and others around them.[93] *High-Rise*'s Robert Laing, a recently divorced paediatrician who moves to the luxury compound in search of peace and quiet, and Richard Pearson, the washed-up former advertising man in *Kingdom Come*, are just two examples.

Another distinctive aspect of Ballard's writing, the rather transatlantic quality and vocabulary of his works and his obsession with the trappings of Americana (from large cars and freeways to motels and film studios), may have been influenced by his childhood in a city he called '90 per cent Chinese and 100 per cent Americanised.'[94] Even his very British parents were 'internationalised by Shanghai', and 'drove American cars and cooled their vermouth in American refrigerators.'[95] The easy-going American merchant seamen in Lunghwa camp who lent Ballard copies of *Life* magazine and *Popular Mechanics* also made an impression on him (helping to inspire the character Basie in *Empire of the Sun*), as did the 'very likeable' US intelligence officers who became his neighbours after the war, and not only showed him movies, but also took him with them to visit captured Japanese soldiers.[96] As his sister Margaret put it, '[after the war] we all felt terribly pro-American. They were the heroes for me, they liberated us, so we felt that very strongly—and we didn't feel that about the British at all.'[97] No wonder then that Ballard, despite retaining the languid, upper-middle class British accent of his childhood expatriate milieu, frequently peppered his writing with Americanisms. In *High-Rise*, for example, the inhabitants of the London residential compound drive 'automobiles' and live in 'apartments', which they access via 'elevators'.

ARCHITECTURAL VISIONS

Ballard's interest in modern architecture and its potential implications may also derive from the sophisticated, cosmopolitan surroundings of his childhood. This fascination with the urban environment is evident not just in *High-Rise*, with its "visionary" architect character (Anthony Royal), but also in works like *Super-Cannes*, which depicts the sinister underside of attempts to create a new, "ideal" world in a security-obsessed high-technology park on the Côte d'Azur . (In his foreword to *Super-Cannes*, Ballard also made a point of recommending several actual examples of modernist architecture in the region, including the Pierre Cardin Foundation—'one of the strangest buildings in Europe'[98]).

Once again, the influence of Shanghai, a city which was at the cutting edge of experiments in architecture in the 1930s, is relevant. The cinemas Ballard attended as a child were 'vast art deco theatres that loomed over Shanghai.'[99] The apartment buildings he recalled seeing on the city's skyline from Lunghwa camp included some of the world's most modern residential compounds: the upmarket Grosvenor House, the Dauphine, and other elegant art deco blocks along the Avenue Joffre (Huaihai Road), the main street of Shanghai's French concession. Even the Ballards' own first home at 100 Amherst Avenue is reported to have been designed by the renowned Hungarian-Slovak architect Laszlo Hudec, who built many of the city's best-known art deco buildings, including the Park Hotel and the Grand Theatre.¹⁰⁰

That the Ballard family had an interest in architecture during their time in Shanghai was underlined by Margaret Richardson, who recalled that their mother Edna 'was always very interested in buildings. She loved looking at them', and would often point out those she liked or disliked to her children. (Margaret herself became a curator at the Royal Institute of British Architects and the Sir John Soane's Museum in London, and president of the Twentieth Century Society, which champions modern architecture in Britain).

After his sole return trip to Shanghai, for a BBC television documentary in 1991, Ballard himself enthusiastically described the city's former French concession as 'one of the largest collections of domestic art deco architecture in the world.'¹⁰¹ Shanghai's 'faded art deco suburbs', he wrote, still seemed

> bracingly new […]The paintwork was shabby, but there were the porthole windows and marina balconies, fluted pilasters borrowed from some car factory in Detroit in the 1930s.¹⁰²

And yet, as Ballard knew well, many of Shanghai's most prestigious buildings were repurposed during the war, foreshadowing the way in which, in his fiction, the seemingly perfect world of elite residential compounds often degenerates into something far more precarious.

Figure 5: 'D Block', residential quarters at Lunghwa camp. Before the war, the site had housed the elite Shanghai High School. Image provided with kind permission by the History Club of Shanghai High School International School.

Victor Sassoon's famous Embankment Building, with its indoor swimming pool, became a shelter for Jewish refugees from Europe, while the high-rise Hamilton House became the headquarters of the feared Japanese military police, the *Kempeitai*, who also used another block, Bridge House, as a prison and torture centre for allied nationals. Other luxurious buildings (including the Ballards' own home) served as accommodation for senior Japanese officers or those with links to the puppet government, while the Columbia Country Club became a transfer centre for internees en route to the camps. Even the Lunghwa camp itself was formerly an elite high school, and featured some stylish art deco design. Such transformations—like those of the abandoned buildings Ballard encountered during the war—would have made the budding writer aware that, however idealistic the vision behind such architecture, it could also take on more sinister overtones.

'A Strange Fiction'

Ballard's experience of Shanghai and its modernity also coloured his perceptions of Britain—something which made him arguably one of the more interesting and perspicacious observers of British society (and indeed western societies in general). Having previously spent only a few months in Britain as a child, he found it a depressing place with 'grey, unhappy people' when he, his mother and sister were "repatriated" there on a British troop ship in late 1945.[103] 'I was sorry to leave Shanghai', he recalled, 'and I was even sorrier when I arrived in England.'[104] He described his shock, upon docking at Southampton, at seeing the streets lined with 'what seemed to be black perambulators, some kind of mobile coal scuttle, I assumed.'[105] These were, in fact, small pre-war British cars. 'It amazed me that anyone could design anything like that', Ballard remarked.[106]

In contrast to Shanghai and its obsession with novelty, he found an 'enormous resistance to change' in Britain—which included widespread hostility to the opening of the country's first supermarkets and motorways: 'There was a feeling that mobility wasn't a good thing, that getting from A to B as quickly as possible was somehow rather unBritish.'[107] In 1954, after dropping out of two universities, and a brief spell as an advertising copywriter, Ballard was happy to leave Britain again and head to Canada for his RAF pilot's training. 'I still hadn't found myself in England, which seemed to be a very very strange place,' he recalled.[108]

No wonder, then, that Ballard observed that he later 'treated England as if it were a strange fiction', something amply reflected in works like *Concrete Island*, where a driver becomes stranded between motorways after crashing his car off a flyover, as well as *Crash*, *High-Rise* and his later works *Millennium People* and *Kingdom Come*.[109] Significantly, he also suggested that one of his motivations for 'transforming London with a huge flood' in *The Drowned World* was 'to create a new London that in some ways reminded me of Shanghai with all its lurid freedom.'[110]

Ballard's dispassionate yet insightful observations of Britain, his sense of the hostility under the surface of society, and his interest in conflict between humans and nature have drawn comparisons with the work of Joseph Conrad, who similarly moved to Britain from abroad and found his literary voice in the country. Wilder, the film maker gone rogue in Ballard's *High-Rise*, for example, has something of the desperate, degenerate quality of Kurtz, the ivory trader turned jungle despot in Conrad's *Heart of Darkness*. Strikingly, Ballard described his own sense of being an outside observer of western societies by comparing himself to an anthropologist 'on a one man safari, [...] pushing through the jungle, my ears alert for some strange tom tom.'[111]

And while he became more comfortable in Britain after the rise of "counter-culture" in the later 1960s, Ballard observed in the early 1990s that he still felt like 'a bit of a visitor here after 46 years.'[112] It certainly took Britain's establishment many years to embrace him. Despite his plummy English accent, and insistence on wearing a jacket and tie throughout the hippy era, Ballard was seen by many as a dangerous radical; it was only after the publication of *Empire of the Sun* in 1984 that he began his journey to mainstream acceptance.

Recreating Shanghai

And though much of Ballard's writing focused on contemporary western society, it was notable that his ability to convey the atmosphere of Shanghai never faded, even after decades abroad. The vivid, detailed descriptions of the city in *Empire of the Sun*, *The Kindness of Women* and *Miracles of Life* conjure up life in Shanghai with unusual authenticity, suggesting both the deep impression the city left on him, and his enduring affection for it. In a BBC interview in the early 1990s, Ballard spoke of his regret at leaving Shanghai, adding

> I think in many ways I've never left. My imagination in large part is still moving around those streets. [...] It's probably true that a large part of my fiction is an attempt to [...] recreate Shanghai.[113]

Indeed, the main character in his first novel, *The Wind from Nowhere*, is an eccentric tycoon called 'Hardoon'—a name clearly derived from Shanghai, where the Iraqi-Jewish real estate magnate Silas Hardoon was renowned as the city's richest man.[114]

And even on his fleeting return visit to Shanghai in 1991, Ballard was still able to capture the essence of the place effortlessly. He described its modern districts as a 'skyscraper city newer than yesterday', while in the older neighbourhoods he saw

> the ceaseless activity of a planetary hive: porters steering new photocopiers into office entrances, smartly dressed young secretaries [...] Inside every doorway a small business was flourishing. A miasma of frying fat floated into the night, radio announcers gabbled [...] sparks flew from the lathes of a machine shop, [...] traffic horns blared, sweating young men in singlets smoked in doorways.[115]

Fading Memories

Yet if Ballard's fascination with Shanghai never died, the city he did so much to bring to global attention has shown little official interest in him. On Xinhua Road—the former Amherst Avenue—a sign commemorating the street's history notes that many foreigners once lived here, but doesn't name any of them. (It also cites the street's English name incorrectly as Amherst Road). The Ballard family's second home on the street, number 31 (lightly fictionalised as '13' in *Empire of the Sun*) still stands. It has gone through several incarnations since they left, serving as the library of a state-run electronics institute, several different restaurants, and most recently a private members' club. In the mid-2000s, the promotional material for one of these restaurants promised diners a chance to relive the atmosphere of old Shanghai, and 'imagine the historical stories that took place in this house.' Of its actual former residents there was, however, no mention—and staff showed limited interest when informed of its connection with a well-known British writer. In 2010, I went back there with Vicky

Figure 6: The first Ballard home at 100 Amherst Avenue, as it looked in the 1930s. The small boy sitting on the steps is probably JG Ballard. Image provided with kind permission by Margaret Richardson.

Richardson, daughter of Ballard's sister Margaret, who was visiting Shanghai. We walked up the wooden staircase (one of the few original fittings to have survived the various renovations) to the top floor, where her uncle's bedroom had once been, and mentioned to the manager that her mother had grown up in this house. 'Oh, lots of people say that', the young woman replied, with a disinterested shrug.

The Ballard's first house on the street, Number 100, meanwhile, was generally thought to have been demolished. Its number had vanished from the street, one end of which had been partially rebuilt, and Margaret Richardson was unable to find it when she revisited Shanghai in 1998. A few years ago, however, the journalist Bill Savadove kindly alerted me to a thesis by Feng Li, an architecture graduate of Shanghai's Tongji University, whose Master's research at Hong Kong University focused on the conservation of old houses in the 'Columbia Circle' development on the former Amherst Avenue. According to Feng, the Ballard's first home, Number 100, still stood, and had simply been renumbered.[116] Clutching an old photo of the house given to me by Margaret Richardson, I went to take a look.

The garden was overgrown, and partly obscured by a high wall; it also seemed to have been reduced in size by a widening of the sidewalk. Yet behind the washing hanging on poles from the windows, and the piled-up clutter belonging to the ten or so families who now shared the house, its distinctive architectural features—chimney, attic room, balcony and verandah—were identical to those in the photograph. An old map also seemed to confirm that this particular house had previously been number 100. Sadly, due to her health issues, I have not had a chance to show Margaret Richardson my most recent photographs of the house—with its original bathroom fittings and unusual "Moorish" internal arches—for confirmation. And despite Feng Li's links to Tongji University, which generally provides information for heritage signs on Shanghai's old buildings, the relatively new plaque on the wall outside makes no reference to its former inhabitants.

This lack of commemoration is perhaps hardly surprising, given official sensitivity about Shanghai's history of occupation and colonisation—though at least two of Ballard's novels, *Concrete Island* and *High-Rise*, have been translated and published in China in recent years. For Ballard himself, who once described nostalgia as 'that most detestable of all emotions', it would certainly be no cause for sadness.[117] After his return to Shanghai in 1991, when he visited both the former 31 Amherst Avenue and the room (now demolished) where his family lived in Lunghwa, he spoke of a 'great sense of release' at having confronted these childhood experiences and put them behind him.[118] His old house, he suggested, was a 'ghost', which 'had spent almost half a century eroding its memories of an English family that had occupied it but left without a trace.'[119]

Yet Ballard's own links to Shanghai never eroded, ultimately leaving an indelible mark on English literature—not just in his writings about the city itself, but in his work as a whole. For his readers, perhaps the one regret is that he did not have another chance to return to the city of his birth: in the decades since his 1991 visit, Shanghai has modernised at an unprecedented pace, building vast new residential areas, massive shopping malls, countless technology zones, and high-rises by the thousand, to create a new urban environment which, it could be argued, would have been ideal subject matter for the famous "Ballardian" literary gaze this city did so much to shape.[120]

Duncan Hewitt is *a former BBC China correspondent and Newsweek Shanghai correspondent, and an affiliate of the Lau China Institute, King's College London. He studied Chinese at Edinburgh University and at Northwest University, Xi'an, and later worked as a literary translator and editor at the Chinese University of Hong Kong. He is the author of* Getting Rich First—Life in a Changing China *(Vintage, UK, 2008) and* *of a chapter on Hongqiao Road in Tess Johnston's* Still More Shanghai Walks *(2011). His interest in Shanghai history—and JG Ballard—was first stirred by a brief spell as an extra during the filming of* Empire of the Sun *in Shanghai in 1987.*

BIBLIOGRAPHY

JG Ballard, *Empire of the Sun*, Fourth Estate, London, 2014
JG Ballard, *The Kindness of Women*, Harper Perennial, London, 2008
JG Ballard, *Miracles of Life*, Fourth Estate, London, 2008
JG Ballard, *High-Rise*, Fourth Estate, London, 2014
JG Ballard, 'Look Back at Empire', The Guardian, 4 March 2006
'Bookmark: Shanghai Jim', BBC Television, 25 September 1991
'Grand Tour: Shanghai'—interview with JG Ballard, BBC Radio 4, 17 November 1990; https://youtu.be/QtwlzWoUKrM [accessed 30 July 2022]
'Profile : JG Ballard', BBC Television, 9 November 2001 https://youtu.be/oURQJqJC520 [accessed 30 July 2022]

Author interview with Margaret Richardson, London, August 2010

REFERENCES

1 Will Self interview on *Today*, BBC Radio 4, 14 April 2020
2 Mark O'Connell, 'Why we are living in JG Ballard's World', *New Statesman*, 1 April 2020
3 Profile: JG Ballard, BBC Television, 9 November 2001
4 'The Crash Controversy', BFI ScreenOnline, http://www.screenonline.org.uk/film/id/591961/index.html
5 'Bookmark : Shanghai Jim', BBC Television, 9 November 1991
6 Martin Amis, interview with Channel 4 News, UK, 20 April 2009
7 William Boyd, quoted in JG Ballard, *The Kindness of Women*, Harper Perennial, London, 1994,
8 Cited in JG Ballard, *Miracles of Life* (hereafter '*Miracles*'), Fourth Estate, London 2008, inside cover
9 'Grand Tour: Shanghai'—JG Ballard interview, BBC Radio, 1991; JG Ballard, 'Look Back at Empire', The Guardian, 4 March 2006
10 BBC Bookmark, op. cit.
11 'Look Back at Empire', op. cit.

12 *Miracles*, pp. 7 & 251
13 *Miracles*, p. 17
14 *Miracles*, pp. 42, 38-9
15 'Grand Tour: Shanghai', op. cit.
16 'Grand Tour: Shanghai', op. cit.
17 *Miracles*, p. 15, 9
18 *Miracles*, p. 34
19 'Grand Tour: Shanghai', op. cit.
20 *Miracles*, p.9
21 *Miracles*, p.28. Ballard saw at least one man die after being bayoneted by Japanese soldiers on a Shanghai street: JG Ballard, 'The End of My War', in JG Ballard, *Empire of the Sun*, Fourth Estate, London, 2014, p. 309
22 BBC Profile, op. cit.; *Miracles* pp. 30, 34
23 *Miracles*, p. 27
24 *The Kindness of Women*, op. cit., pp. 22-26
25 Author interview with Margaret Richardson, London, August 2010
26 Businessman Thomas Sze was kidnapped from his house on Columbia Circle in July 1941; police eventually rescued him; unpublished Sze family memoir, courtesy of Bill Savadove; Patricia Luce Chapman, *Tea on the Great Wall*, Earnshaw Books, Hong Kong, 2014, p.294
27 *Miracles*, p. 10
28 Calico Printer's Association, 'Report on a Visit to the C.P. & F. Co's Works and Mills, Shanghai', March 1938; p. 17
29 Robert Bickers, *Empire Made Me*, Penguin, London, 2004, pp. 283-292
30 *Miracles*, pp. 77-8. In June 2013, Hayashi was honoured in the Canadian parliament for his "compassion" and humanitarian treatment of internees in Lunghwa. His son Sadayuki Hayashi later became ambassador to London and Japan's vice-foreign minister.
31 *Miracles*, pp. 78, 95
32 *Miracles*, pp. 106-7
33 *Miracles*, p. 113
34 'Papering over the Cracks', JG Ballard talks to Sarah O'Reilly, in JG Ballard, *Kingdom Come*, Harper Perennial, London, 2007, p. 284
35 BBC Profile, op. cit.
36 'An Investigative Spirit', JG Ballard talks to Travis Elborough, in *High-Rise*, p. 253.

37 *High-Rise*, p. 253.
38 Profile, op. cit.
39 BBC Bookmark, op. cit.
40 BBC Profile, op. cit.
41 *Miracles*, p. 145
42 'The Visitor—An interview with JG Ballard', Hardcore magazine, 1992: https://www.jgballard.ca/media/1992_hardcore_magazine.html
43 *Miracles*, p. 56
44 'Grand Tour: Shanghai', op. cit.
45 Ruth Hill Barr, *Ruth's Record: A Five Year Shanghai Diary*, 1941-45; Earnshaw Books, Hong Kong, 2017; various entries for 1942.
46 *Miracles*, p. 61
47 *Miracles*, p. 61; Grand Tour: Shanghai, op. cit.
48 *Miracles of Life*, p. 21; Ballard's resultant disdain for Britain's obsession with its imperial past (and for the monarchy) led him to reject the award of the CBE ('Commander of the British Empire') in 2003. Such medals, 'given out in the name of a non-existent empire… make us look a laughing stock', he said. See: Mattha Busby, 'Number of People Rejecting Queen's Honours Doubles in Past Decade', The Guardian, 1 December 2020
49 *Miracles*, pp. 56, 63
50 *Miracles*, p. 80 ; JG Ballard, interview with Thames Television's 'This Afternoon', 1977, https://youtu.be/fzoXzL5EP8E [accessed 5 August 2022]
51 *Miracles*, p. 80
52 *Miracles*, pp. 66, 80
53 *Miracles*, p. 249; Ruth Hill Barr, diary entry for 22 July 1944.
54 'Reality is a Stage Set—Travis Elborough talks to JG Ballard', in JG Ballard, *The Drowned World*, Harper Perennial, London, 2008, PS section, p. 2
55 *Miracles*, p. 27
56 *Miracles*, p. 59
57 Ballard, 'The End of My War', In *Empire of the Sun*, p. 310
58 *Miracles*, p. 58-9
59 Margaret Richardson interview, 2010.
60 *Miracles*, p. 108
61 *Miracles*, p. 58
62 Ballard, BBC Profile, op. cit.

63 BBC Bookmark, op. cit.
64 BBC Bookmark, op. cit.
65 *Miracles*, p.31
66 BBC Profile, op. cit.
67 *Kindness of Women*, p. 15; see also Miracles, p. 35.
68 *Miracles*, p. 10
69 *Miracles*, p. 5
70 Ruth Hill Barr, op. cit., diary entries for 4 June and 16 July 1943.
71 JG Ballard, 'Time, Memory and Inner Space' (1963), https://www.jgballard.ca/non_fiction/jgb_time_memory_innerspace.html; 'Reality is a Stage Set', op. cit, p. 3. The memoir of Patricia Luce Chapman, a childhood neighbour on Amherst Avenue, contains an evocative drawing showing cars and rickshaws ploughing through several feet of water. Chapman, op. cit., insert between pp. 164-5
72 'Reality is a Stage Set', op. cit, p. 3.
73 'Time, Memory and Inner Space', op. cit.
74 *The Kindness of Women*, p. 18; Miracles of Life, pp. 6, 5, 6
75 *The Kindness of Women*, p. 18
76 *Miracles*, pp.34-5
77 *Miracles*, p. 6;
78 *Miracles*, p. 6
79 *Miracles*, p. 34
80 JG Ballard, *Kingdom Come*, Harper Perennial, London, 2007
81 Margaret Richardson interview 2010; *Miracles*, p. 4
82 'Grand Tour: Shanghai', op. cit.
83 Margaret Richardson interview, op. cit.
84 Leo Ou-fan Lee, *Shanghai Modern: The Flowering of a New Urban Culture in China*, 1930–1945, Harvard UP, 1999, p. 45; *Miracles*, p. 4; Ballard, 'Look Back at Empire', op. cit.
85 *Miracles*, pp.148, 128-9
86 Margaret Richardson interview, op. cit.
87 *Miracles*, p. 19
88 *Miracles*, p. 113
89 *Miracles*, p.44
90 *Miracles*, p. 80
91 *Miracles*, p. 41
92 Margaret Richardson interview, op. cit.
93 Ballard, in BBC Bookmark, op. cit.
94 *Miracles*, p. 4

95 *Miracles*, p. 38
96 *Miracles*, p. 72, 113
97 Margaret Richardson interview, op. cit.
98 JG Ballard, *Super-Cannes*, Harper Perennial, London, 2006, Foreword.
99 *Miracles*, p. 19
100 Feng Li, 'Columbia Circle: Transaformation of the Social Fabric of a Garden Residence in Shanghai', University of Hong Kong, Master's Degree Thesis, August 2011, p. 37
101 *Miracles*, p. 268
102 *Miracles*, p. 268
103 Ballard, 'Look Back at Empire', op. cit.
104 'Grand Tour: Shanghai', op cit.
105 *Miracles*, p.121
106 Thames TV op cit.
107 J.G. Ballard, 'The Worst of Times', Interview by Danny Danziger, in *The Kindness of Women*, op. cit., PS section, p.9
108 BBC Bookmark op. cit.
109 *Miracles*, p. 35
110 'Grand Tour: Shanghai', op. cit.
111 BBC Profile, op. cit.
112 The Visitor—An interview with JG Ballard, op. cit.
113 'Grand Tour: Shanghai', op. cit.
114 Chris Beckett, 'The Progress of the Text: The Papers of JG Ballard at the British Library', British Library Journal, 2011, p. 11
115 *Miracles*, pp. 266-7
116 Feng Li, op. cit, pp. 36-7
117 JG Ballard, Letters to Peter Brigg, https://www.jgballard.ca/shanghai/jgb_shanghai_home.html#part%201 [accessed 8 July 2022]
118 *Miracles*, p. 270
119 *Miracles*, p. 270
120 Indeed, the front cover of the Chinese edition of *High-Rise* features the quote: 'High-Rise—precisely the world in which we find ourselves'; JG Ballard, *Motian Lou* 摩天楼 (*High-Rise*), Shanghai People's Publishing House, Shanghai, 2017

THE COSTS OF ALLIANCE: THE DOOLITTLE RAID AND CHINA

By James Carter

ABSTRACT

The Doolittle Raid in the spring of 1942 is often seen as a symbolic turning point in World War II, with important ramifications for both American and Japanese morale and planning. Yet, its impact on China and US-China relations is both significant and less well-known. This article illustrates how the raid both boosted Chinese hopes for American involvement against Japan but also defied Chinese wishes for how the war would be prosecuted. While the raid symbolised the friendship between China and the United States—and has for decades—its consequences included suffering by Chinese civilians.

SECRET PLANNING, UNLUCKY START

On 18 April 1942—it was a Saturday—more than a dozen American bombers crashed onto sites across eastern China. They had taken off a full day earlier from the aircraft carrier *Hornet* steaming across the northern Pacific. Specially modified and overloaded with fuel in preparation for an extra-long flight, they barely had enough runway on deck to get airborne, but they successfully completed their mission. After flying 800 miles, most of it just feet above the waves to avoid detection, the 16 B-25s dropped bombs on the Japanese cities of Osaka, Yokohama, Nagoya, and, above all, Tokyo.

This was the famous Doolittle Raid. Led by Lt. Col. James Doolittle, the attack had little tactical or strategic value in itself, but, as a symbol, it demonstrated the United States' ability to reach Japan. Tokyo's surprise attack on Pearl Harbor in December 1941 had pummeled American morale, exacerbated by a string of Japanese conquests in the Pacific. The assault on Pearl Harbor also had been a Japanese gamble, intended to inflict a blow that would dissuade the United States from entering the Pacific War, or destroy its ability to wage it. In response, President Franklin Roosevelt resolved to hit back at the Japanese homeland, with a mission planned in utmost secrecy. Just four months after 7 December, the Doolittle Raid was celebrated in headlines across the US. In Japan, it foreshadowed much deadlier

American bombing raids two years later. It also precipitated a fierce response from Japanese armies, who avenged the attack on the civilian population of China. It was, at once, a very small and enormously important moment.

Its physical impact was limited; 87 Japanese died in the attacks and 112 military and industrial installations were destroyed. However its indirect effects were immense for both the American and Japanese sides. The Doolittle Raid demonstrated that Japanese vulnerability, and American capability, were greater than many assumed. For the United States, reeling after the surprise attack on Pearl Harbor, the raid boosted morale. For Japan, expectations that the US would quit the war evaporated, undermining confidence. Whether that, or a re-oriented defensive strategy, was more damaging is hard to know, but both up-ended Japanese expectations for the war.

The raid's impact on the United States and Japan is obvious, and well-established, but its connection to China deserves attention as well.

The connection to China was baked into the raid's planning. Stripped down to bare essentials, carrying little but fuel, bombs, and their crew, the B-25 bombers, launched from beyond Japan's defensive perimeter, would barely barely reach the Japanese home islands. Even with their special modifications, the Americans had no hope of returning to the *Hornet;* their B-25s were too large, and lacked the proper gear, to allow carrier landings. This would be a one way-mission. US planners would have preferred to see the planes land in the Soviet Union; its Pacific port of Vladivostok was just 675 miles from Tokyo. However the Soviet-Japanese Neutrality Act signed in 1941 meant Moscow would not likely agree. So instead, it was decided that the planes would continue on past their targets and make for the Chinese coast and landing fields in "Free China", territory controlled by Chiang Kai-shek's Nationalist government. There, so the plan went, they would refuel and continue on to Chongqing, where they would continue the fight against Japan.

This was the plan as the sixteenth and final crew prepared to take off from the deck of the *Hornet*. It was after 9:00 in the morning, and the first of the planes had left nearly an hour earlier, a nerve-wracking wait when every minute counted. The morning had not gone according to plan; the task force including the *Hornet* was still 825 miles from its target when an escort vessel spotted a Japanese patrol boat. The Japanese ship was sunk, but not before it could radio a warning about the approaching Americans. Surprise was no longer possible; the decision was made to launch the bombers right away, before the fleet could be intercepted. Bad omens persisted right up to takeoff; as heavy seas pitched the deck, the B-25, piloted by Bill Farrow, lurched backwards, the spinning propeller taking the arm off a sailor.

Despite the heavy weather, the change of plans, and the accident prior to takeoff, the last plane, nicknamed 'Bat Out of Hell', rose off the *Hornet's* deck at 9:19 am, ship's time. Besides Farrow, co-pilot Bob Hite, navigator George Barr, bombardier Jacob Deshazer, and gunner Harold Spatz rounded out the crew.[1]

And after six hours of flying, crew #16 arrived at Nagoya, about 200 miles west of Tokyo. The last-minute changes to the schedule meant that the Americans would approach their targets in daylight; each passing minute heightened the odds that Japanese defences would be mobilised. The B-25 was able to elude Japanese fighters as it jumped in and out of cloud cover. The airmen eventually eventually spotted oil storage tanks and an aircraft factory. They dropped their bombs from 500 feet. The run was successful. Barr, the navigator, recalled their moments over Nagoya in an interview years later:

> ... we spotted our first target, a battery of oil storage tanks, and let go our first bomb.
> We had three more to go. To the north (on our left side) I could see smoke and fire coming from two different places. ....Up ahead I saw a nice long aircraft factory loom up to our left. [Pilot Farrow] saw it, too, and without any direction from me, changed course, lined the building up, and we made a run for it end to end, dropping out incendiaries.[2]

After successfully hitting their targets, Bill Farrow, like 15 of the 16 pilots, turned his B-25 southwest toward China's Yangtze River delta, seven hours flying time away. One plane did turn northwest and land in Vladivostok, where its crew was interned for a time before returning to the United States.

The plan was conceived with almost no margin for error, pushing the logistics to their very limits. The earlier-than-intended launch had eliminated that margin. If not for a lucky tailwind, none of the planes would have reached China.

'Bat Out of Hell', like most of the others, arrived over eastern China at dusk. Near the city of Nanchang, Jiangxi, with fuel running out, the five crew members bailed out, leaving the plane to crash into the countryside, like 13 of the 15 planes that made it to China (two others landed in the ocean, just off the coast). Barr landed safely in a rice paddy, but within a few hours was captured by Japanese soldiers and brought to a nearby town to be questioned and imprisoned. The co-pilot, Bob Hite, was captured that same night. The rest of the 'Bat's' crew was brought in the next day.

What followed for these five men, and three others who were also captured, was years of torture. They were sent by ship to Tokyo, where they were questioned about their objectives and actions during the raid. After six weeks in Japan, they were returned to China, held in Shanghai's infamous Bridge House, a hotel along Suzhou Creek in Chapei that had been used by the Japanese secret police since 1937.[3]

For more than two months, the eight Americans were held in a cell with more than a dozen Chinese prisoners. In late August 1942, they were moved to Jiangwan prison, north of Shanghai's international settlement. There, the eight were gathered into what became clear was a makeshift courtroom. Questioned by military authorities, with translation from another prisoner, the men were charged with war crimes, connected with allegations that they strafed a Japanese middle school during the raid on Nagoya. The trial lasted less than a day, after which all of the prisoners were returned to solitary confinement in Jiangwan; except for one, Dean Hallmark, who was too ill to stand and was taken by stretcher back to Bridge House.[4]

All eight men were convicted. In a sentence handed down in Tokyo on 10 October 1942, all eight were sentenced to death, but five of the sentences were commuted to life imprisonment, with the stipulation that none of those spared would be eligible for release in any prisoner exchange or other agreement.

George Barr was among those spared, but Farrow, the pilot of the 'Bat', and his gunner Harold Spatz were to face the firing squad, as was another pilot, Dean Hallmark. The three men were executed on the afternoon of 15 October, their remains interred at Jiangwan cemetery.

The five remaining raiders were each held in solitary confinement. They were informed that they had been sentenced to death, but that their sentences had been commuted; none of them were told of the fate of Spatz, Farrow, or Hallmark. In the spring, exactly one year after the raid, they were moved from Jiangwan to a prison in Nanjing. In December, Bob Meder died of heart failure related to malnutrition and disease. His body remained in the cell for two days before it was removed.[5]

The remaining four men passed day after monotonous day, the only exception being Christmas Day, 1944, when American air raids prompted fleeting hope that rescue was imminent. But for another six months after that nothing changed, until mid-June, when the four were moved to a military prison in Beijing.

The end to the men's ordeal in captivity came, oddly enough, at the Peking Hotel. American intelligence officers of the Office of Strategic Services had parachuted into the city in the days following Japan's surrender on 15 August 1945. Acting on intelligence that the Doolittle flyers were in the city, along with other Allied POWs, the Americans demanded their release. On 20 August—five days after Japan's surrender—the five were taken from their cells to the hotel, where they were given showers and shaves and met by OSS officers. Within days, all were back in the United States, except for George Barr. Barr was in desperate physical and psychological condition and remained in military hospitals in China for several months, and then spent more time recuperating in the United States. He was discharged from hospital in November, 1945.

MIRACULOUSLY, MOST OF THE AIRMEN SURVIVED

The experience of Barr and the others who were captured was not typical. Most of the men who took part in the raid bailed out in China but eluded capture by the Japanese. They managed this thanks to assistance from those on the ground, mostly residents of Anhui, Jiangxi, and Zhejiang who rescued, sheltered, and guided the Americans who had parachuted to safety or crash-landed as their planes ran out of fuel.

The Americans' arrival in China was poorly understood by Chinese forces and their advisors. Chiang Kai-shek was concerned about Japanese reprisals against the Chinese population and only reluctantly agreed to provide access to Chinese airfields so that the raiders could land, refuel, and continue on their way to the Chinese wartime capital in Chongqing. Even when that permission was given, numerous obstacles stood in the way; just days before the bombing was planned to take place, the airfields intended to accommodate the American B-25s came under Japanese attack, prompting pleas to delay the mission. Five airfields were eventually secured, and were slated to receive homing beacons to guide the raiders to safety, but even that provision was never implemented. When the B-25s were launched a day ahead of schedule because Japanese patrols had detected the task force, that message was never relayed to forces in China.[6] When the 15 planes approached the Chinese coast, no one knew they were coming, no beacons guided them, and they had no detailed explanation of where to go.

Even this, of course, was moot in the end. None of the planes had enough fuel to guarantee they would reach their destination. In fact, were it not for the unanticipated tailwind, none of the airmen would have made it to China at all. Even so, many of them made it close to Quzhou and other airfields where they were supposed to touch down. Crossing the coast after nightfall in rain and fog, a landing was impossible, especially since no airfield was alerted to their approach. Most of the men bailed out as their planes exhausted their fuel, parachuting into the darkness.

Lt Richard Joyce, one of the pilots, had an experience typical of many. After ordering his crew to jump, Joyce followed behind, leaving the aircraft flying, for just a few minutes more, stepping out of the hatch, he

> …dropped clear of the ship and pulled the ripcord and the chute opened and functioned perfectly except that the metal sheared on one of the leg strap buckles and the leg strap on my left leg parted and almost dropped me out of the chute. I slid down and the chest strap came up and smacked me in the chin with a stunning blow and at the same time jerked my pistol out of my shoulder holster and tossed it out into space. I was swinging quite badly and had some time to stop that but finally did. I estimate that I floated for about one minute. I heard the plane below me and it hit the side of a mountain and exploded and burst into flame. A few seconds later I hit the ground which was quite a surprise to me. I was not very far from the airplane but I realized that I was on a pretty steep slope and could see very little for the fog and rain.[7]

The dozens of men scattered across the countryside struggled in the rain and dark to find one another. The next morning, they tried to get their bearings and find shelter if they could. Few of them would have survived, or eluded capture, were it not for the aid and shelter they received from the local population. Much of this was done without the benefit of any common language. One exception to this was the help of Tung-sheng Liu, an English-speaking aeronautical engineer who was waiting to cross Japanese lines, in order to reach the Nationalists and help their war effort. Near Ningbo, villagers asked him to come with them. They introduced him to five dishevelled Americans, whom he immediately agreed to help guide to safety. Liu's assistance was instrumental in getting many of the Americans to an airfield in Hengyang, Hunan, from where they were flown to Chongqing.[8]

Regulations against transporting foreign nationals kept the men from bringing Liu with them to Chongqing, but he later emigrated to the United States, where he became a civilian employee for the Air Force.

Some of the downed airmen required medical treatment. A small hospital in Zhejiang province treated raiders for injuries and illness they suffered in the course of their missions, the most serious case being that of pilot Ted Lawson whose leg was amputated after wounds

Figure 1: Doolittle Raiders' crew #2 with Tung-Sheng Liu (third from right) and unidentified man in 1942. With permission from the Tung-Sheng Liu Family, and Lori B. Lang (colourisation)

inflicted by his crash landing became infected. In addition to the expertise provided by interpreters like Liu or the doctors in Zhejiang and elsewhere, it was above all the kindness, bravery, and dedication provided by ordinary Chinese, many of whom had never seen an American, that enabled the fliers to make it home safely. Remarkably, of the 72 airmen who survived the crash landings in China, all but 4, the three men who were executed at Jiangwan prison and Bob Meder, who died in the POW camp, returned to the United States, including all 64 who eluded capture upon landing.

This first American strike against Japan, even if largely symbolic, was vitally important to Chinese morale. As Chinese First Lady Soong May-ling would say in her speech to the American congress a few months later: 'Let us not forget that during the first four and a half years of total aggression China has borne Japan's sadistic fury unaided and alone.'[9] Doolittle's raid had been a start, at least, to joining that solitary fight.

The operation was bold and ambitious, but not without risk. And that risk extended far beyond danger to the crews of the 16 aircraft. In typically bureaucratic understatement, an American intelligence assessment of the operation noted somberly: 'Any encouragement, however, accruing to the Chinese must have been tempered by the fact that immediately following the raid the Japanese initiated a severe attack on those areas in China which they suspected had been used in the project.'[10] This had been a central concern of Chinese leaders all along. Chiang Kai-shek had opposed the plan from the beginning, worried that the operation would intensify Japanese attacks against his forces. Chiang and other Chinese leaders were kept out of the planning for the raid.

Historian Rana Mitter put it bluntly, 'What went down well with the American public had a hugely negative effect on the Chinese war effort.'[11] The 'severe attack', known as the Zhejiang-Jiangxi campaign, devastated eastern China. Japanese planners had worried that Japan was vulnerable to air attack, leading to the attacks against Chinese airfields in the weeks leading up to the raid, but the Doolittle Raid had confirmed it.

A Terrible Price was Paid

The campaign started just a month after the raid, involving some 180,000 Japanese troops.[12] Their goal was both strategic, to remove the threat of air raids against Japan from China, and punitive. The civilian population was to be punished for helping the American fliers. Documents from Catholic priests working in the region captured the scale of the atrocities. In the village of Yihuang, American priest Wendelin Dunker wrote that the Japanese 'shot any man, woman, child, cow, hog, or just about anything that moved. They raped any woman from the ages of 10–65, and before burning the town they thoroughly looted it.'[13]

Collective responsibility was assigned to entire cities. The town of Nancheng, with a population of 50,000 people, was all but levelled for its role in sheltering American pilots, but anyone found to have directly aided the raiders was singled out for particular cruelty. Ma Eng-lin, a resident of Yihuang who had sheltered an American pilot, was burned alive; his wife was forced to set him alight.[14]

In the words of Belgian-born priest Charles Meeus, 'Little did the Doolittle men realise that those same little gifts which they gave their rescuers in grateful acknowledgement of their hospitality—parachutes, gloves, nickels, dimes, cigarette packages—would, a few weeks later, become the telltale evidence of their presence and lead to the torture and death of their friends!'[15]

In all, approximately 250,000 Chinese were killed in the reprisal campaign in Zhejiang and Jiangxi, and some 20,000 square miles were laid waste. This embodies the central contradiction of the Doolittle Raid. It was at once a creative and ambitious tactic that influenced the course of the war in profound ways, but it also resulted in unspeakable cruelty against the populations that had helped the raiders return safely.

The Doolittle Raid was an American operation that appealed to the US but incurred unintended, though foreseeable, consequences, suffered almost entirely by the Chinese. Yet, on both sides of the relationship, the raid is remembered as an example of US-China cooperation.

The Doolittle Raid sits at an uncomfortable intersection in history, one that has become even more complex in the eight decades since the mission. Despite ongoing tensions in the Sino-US relationship, organisations in both China and the United States marked the 80th anniversary of the mission. Events included a virtual seminar organised and hosted by the Jiangxi Provincial Government and local historians. More than a dozen locations in the US commemorated the anniversary this year, often connected to the hometowns of children of participants in the raid. Also, during the spring, US public television stations began airing a new documentary by filmmaker Bill Einreinhofer titled *Unsettled History: America, China and the Doolittle Tokyo Raid*. A few years earlier, Chinese television viewers watched a series produced by the Shanghai Media Group that focused on the post-WWII war crimes tribunals, in which the treatment and execution of a number of the raiders featured significantly.

Could the legacy of the Doolittle Raid help serve as a catalyst for improved US-China relations? At this moment, it certainly seems like a stretch. After WWII, the 1949 communist victory in China's civil war meant that the Chinese government which had been allied with the United States in 1945 was no longer the government in Beijing, illustrating a complex and shifting geopolitical environment. Mentions of Tokyo's horrific retaliation after the Doolittle Raid can evoke anti-Japanese sentiment among some Chinese. At the same time however the number of local memorial halls and historical markers commemorating the Doolittle Raid suggest that communities in Zhejiang, Jiangxi and other provinces have not forgotten the stories of friendship, collaboration and grassroots assistance offered to the American airmen 80 years ago.

The raid deserves recognition in its own right as a remarkable event of the war, and maybe one with a glimmer of hope attached to it. The willingness of some to remember a moment of cooperation and friendship between Americans and Chinese can offer us the possibility that, while we live in a dark moment, there may be opportunities for understanding in the future.

James Carter *is an historian of modern China and presently the Dean of the College of Arts and Sciences at Saint Joseph's University in Philadelphia. He has published extensively on modern Chinese history and China's relations with the West, most recently in* Champions Day: The End of Old Shanghai *(WW Norton, 2020), and in a weekly column,* This Week in China's History *in the website The China Project.*

REFERENCES

(All websites accessed 29 August, 2022)

1. Children of the Doolittle Raiders website, http://www.childrenofthedoolittleraiders.com/crew-members/doolittle-raider-crews/crew-16/
2. Carroll V. Glines, Jr., interview with George Barr. McLean, Virginia, June 30 1965. Quoted in Carroll V. Glines, Jr., *The Doolittle Raid*, Orion Books, New York (1988), p.139
3. Eric Niderost, *Bridge House Hotel: Crimes of the Kempeitai in Shanghai*, Warfare History Network, website https://warfarehistorynetwork.com/article/bridge-house-hotel-crimes-of-the-kempeitai-in-shanghai/
4. Glines, p.176
5. Glines, p.184
6. Glines, p.74
7. Joyce Flight/mission report, May 5, 1942. Children of the Doolittle Raiders website http://www.childrenofthedoolittleraiders.com/doolittle-raiders-history/reports-interviews/
8. Glines, p.89
9. Soong Mei-Ling, "Addresses To The House Of Representatives And To The Senate," https://china.usc.edu/soong-mei-ling-%E2%80%9Caddresses-house-respresentatives-and-senate%E2%80%9D-february-18-1943
10. Headquarters, Army Air Forces Director Of Intelligence Service, Informational Intelligence Summary (Special) No. 20. Distribution: COMMAND CONFIDENTIAL: October 5, 1942 http://www.childrenofthedoolittleraiders.com/doolittle-raiders-history/reports-interviews/
11. Rana Mitter, *Forgotten Ally: China's World War II, 1937-1945*, Houghton Mifflin Harcourt (2013) p.261
12. R. Keith Schoppa, *In a Sea of Bitterness: Refugees During the Sino-Japanese War*, Harvard University Press (2011) p.28
13. James M. Scott, The Untold Story of the Vengeful Japanese Attack After the Doolittle Raid, *Smithsonian*. April 15, 2015
14. James M. Scott, *Target Tokyo: Jimmy Doolittle and the Raid that Avenged Pearl Harbor*, W. W. Norton & Company (2015), p.384
15. Scott, *Target Tokyo*, p.385

SECTION 2

Stories of Larger-than-life Personalities

'Today They are Merchants, Tomorrow, Fishermen, and at Every Opportunity—Robbers'

WARRIOR PRIEST: THE LIFE AND MISSION OF CLAUDE-MARIE CHEVRIER (1821-1870)

By Jeremiah Jenne

Abstract

This article looks at how missionaries in rural and urban areas interacted with the local authorities. Claude-Marie Chevrier (1821–1870) lived two lives, first serving as a marine in the French colonial forces before becoming a missionary and travelling to China in 1860. Chevrier first served in the wild and rugged country at the edge of the Mongolian steppe. His disputes with officials offer an example of the challenges both missionaries and magistrates faced in managing religious conflict in the years following the signing of the 1858 Treaty of Tianjin and the 1860 Beijing Convention.

In a desolate region just north of the Great Wall, two men in robes were riding ponies across the arid plain. One of the men was a foreigner, distinguishable by his large build and a long beard. The other was Chinese, less comfortable in the saddle but keeping up with his associate as best he could.

Claude-Marie Chevrier (1821–1870) and Vincent Ou (Wu Wensheng 1821–1870) were Lazarist priests attached to the mission station at Xiwanzi, a remote outpost that was part of the Mongolian Vicariate. Although most people living in the area were Chinese, the Lazarists called the area Mongolia due to the mission's location outside the Great Wall at the edge of the great steppe, which swept to the north and west.[1] It was wild country where Chinese villages and farms slowly faded into nomad huts and herds.[2] Today, Xiwanzi is part of Hebei Province and is close to the site of venues for the 2022 Winter Olympics, but in 1864, it was an impoverished area, sparsely populated, and a notoriously tough assignment for missionaries.[3]

Missionaries in 19th century China frequently found themselves in an awkward and uncomfortable position. Many believed they were doing God's work. It was axiomatic among missionaries, both Catholic and Protestant, that the people of China were primed to receive God's grace and so allow the Qing Empire to join the Christian

Figure 1: Claude-Marie Chevrier and Vincent Ou in undated photographs.

comity of nations. Missionaries, including Chevrier, interpreted resistance to their endeavours as a sign of diabolical interference or, at the very least, the meddling of jealous officials seeking to protect their elite status or ill-informed peasants led astray by rumours, innuendoes, and disinformation about the intentions and activities of the missionaries. They often failed to see how their activities could provoke a strong response from the areas and people the missionaries claimed to serve. Conversion could be a true act of pure faith, or it could be a way for one family or clan to enlist the perceived power and status of the foreigners in the service of feuds that might go back many years before the missionary arrived. The forceful way missionaries stood up for their converts in the face of persecution by officials might be a brave act to defend their flock against corrupt and anti-Christian local authorities, or it might interfere in the investigation of a crime or in the prosecution of a known criminal.

The ratification of the Treaty of Tianjin in 1858 and the 1860 Convention of Peking allowed missionaries relative freedom to move, preach, and establish churches and missions throughout the Qing Empire. These treaties had been signed after foreign troops occupied the imperial capital at Beijing and burned the imperial gardens belonging to the Qing emperors. A farmer or herder on the plains north of the Great Wall might be only dimly aware of these events. Unlike people living in the coastal regions or in the treaty ports with their growing number of foreign residents, most people in the countryside would have based their understanding of foreigners on exaggerated or sensational rumours, gossip, and stories. Moreover, a missionary like Chevrier might not have fully known how vulnerable he was, despite the official proclamations and treaties enforced by foreign gunboats that patrolled the coast and rivers. As a result, the years between 1860 and 1870 saw a steady increase in the number of reports forwarded to the central government by local officials describing violent attacks against foreigners, mostly missionaries, and asking for guidance in resolving these disputes.

Claude-Marie Chevrier had been assigned to the Mongolian Vicariate for over three years. Along with Vincent Ou, he spent long days, sometimes weeks, on horseback, riding between villages dodging bandits, hostile soldiers, and overzealous officials. Xiwanzi was far removed from the pleasant life of missionaries based in the treaty ports, and there were few comforts. Missionaries slept on a *kang*, a flat stone bench heated from within, ate the local food and suffered from frostbite and the maladies of the cold in winter while swarms of insects, vermin, and periodic outbreaks of cholera and dysentery plagued their summer months.[4]

Despite the remote location, Xiwanzi was not removed from the rumours and persecutions of Christians in the highly populated parts of China.[5] A missionary stationed in Xiwanzi recalled that in the 1850s, the mission:

> ... had been accused of magic, and I was appointed chief magician. We were accused of having made men and horses out of paper and donkey skin who, by enchantment, had received life and were preparing to take His Majesty the Emperor of China from the throne [...] It was said that our pews went every night, with those who sat on them, to Europe, to look for money, European rifles, sabres and pikes; that the chief magician climbed every day to the moon and the stars, to prevent rain and send out heat and dryness; that he trained Christians for combat, and that the army most to be feared was the army of women, and that our forty virgins had learned to fly to examine the terrain of combat.

Local officials had been sufficiently alarmed to order their soldiers to expel the missionaries. An attack was thwarted only after an urgent summons from Beijing redirected the troops southward to fight against the surging rebels of the Taiping Heavenly Kingdom, a nominally Christian rebellion which had burst out of southern China to occupy large swathes of the Yangtze region.[6]

A few years later, rumours again threatened the security of the mission at Xiwanzi. 'It is said that we Europeans went at night to cut the wings of the hens to do magic and [...] that a thousand red-haired Europeans were standing in the cellars of the Church, and a host of other nonsense.'[7] In a letter to his younger brother Jean-Louis, dated 30 November, 1864, the elder Chevrier wrote 'I can struggle as best I can, starboard to port, against the Gobi's devils, but I am hardly making progress.'[8]

Despite the hardships, Chevrier remained committed to the life of a foreign missionary. Only 43 years old in 1864, the French Lazarist had already lived two lives, having spent over a decade as a marine before retiring from the French military to become a priest. Chevrier's time as a soldier gave him grit that enabled him to endure the harsh life of the steppe and reinforced his natural tenacity and stubbornness. He was also handy with a rifle, a skill that was sometimes necessary when riding across the wild terrain of the Mongolian Vicariate.

Claude-Marie Chevrier's journey to China began near the city of Lyon, one of seven children born to the farming family of Jacques and Marie, née Giradet. After a limited education, much of it under the watchful eye of his maternal uncle and godfather who was a priest in a nearby parish, Claude-Marie enlisted in the Fourth Infantry Regiment based in Toulon.[9] The life of a soldier suited the impetuous young man. In 1845, now Sergeant Chevrier was sent overseas to Cayenne, in the colony of Guyana. Chevrier attended masses in Cayenne held by the Lazarist missionaries working in the settlement. Although his uncle's influence certainly informed Chevrier's understanding of the priesthood, it was likely in Guyana that the young man encountered his first overseas missionaries.[10]

In 1850, Chevrier left the service to enrol in seminary, first at Largentière and then at the major seminary in Lyon. It was not an easy transition. Chevrier was older than many of the other students, and it is easy to imagine him becoming restless in the settled life of a seminarian after his time overseas. A year later, he left France bound for Algiers where Chevrier completed his training and was finally ordained as a priest in 1854.

Chevrier was stationed in Lambaesa^A, an old Roman town that also served as a French penal colony. It was one of the most isolated and dangerous postings in North Africa. The mission was in a key strategic location, fortified by the French legion, whose control over the region was frequently contested by rebels, bandits, and tribal leaders.[11] As would be the case in Mongolia, Chevrier was responsible for long sorties across hostile terrain, including stretches of inhospitable Sahara Desert, sometimes ranging as much as 100 miles, to find and meet his converts.

In 1858, Chevrier was formally accepted into the Congregation of the Mission and returned to Paris to participate in an ecclesiastical retreat and receive his next assignment. When he arrived in Paris, Chevrier was greeted with a sartorial requirement that almost ended his association with the congregation before it began. The Lazarists had a rule that all members be clean-shaven. For Father Chevrier, his soldier's beard had been a point of pride since his days in Guyana and one that had served him well among the different groups in Algiers. His superiors in Paris insisted. According to one account, his immediate supervisor, Father Dumont, took a pair of scissors and while Chevrier was sleeping lopped off a large section of the offending facial hair. When the enraged novitiate awoke, he saw the result in the mirror and resigned himself to shaving the remainder.[12] Later descriptions of Chevrier in China suggest he grew the beard back once he was out of sight of his superiors in France.[13]

Chevrier left France in 1859 and sailed to China via London, arriving in Shanghai on 17 February 1860, during the tense months between the Dagu Repulse the previous year at the conclusion of the Second Opium War (1850-1960), and the arrival of the Anglo-French Expedition under Lord Elgin and Baron Gros. With the status of missionaries in the interior provinces still unsettled by the refusal of the court to ratify the Treaty of Tianjin, Chevrier and his fellow new arrivals prepared to make the dangerous overland journey from Shanghai to Xiwanzi disguised as Chinese travellers.

'The day after our arrival,' Chevrier wrote, 'Mr Aymeri thought of transforming us into Chinese. He brought in half a dozen tailors,

---

A   This is the modern spelling. The city was known as Lambesé (sometimes spelled Lambessé) while under French colonial rule, including during Chevrier's time at the post.

whom he kept for a whole week to make our costumes; this first work finished, a wigmaker presented himself to proceed to our toilet; the artist made three-quarters of my beard fall mercilessly, two-thirds of my hair, and one-eighth of the eyebrows; but on the other hand, he gave me a superb tail more than a metre long'.[14]

The elaborate measures to conceal Chevrier's foreign identity went unused. A few weeks after setting out from Shanghai, the situation in Central and Northern China turned violent. Taiping partisans and rebels belonging to the Nian movement were moving through the countryside pursued by soldiers loyal to the Qing government. There was also news of the imminent arrival of foreign troops on the coast. All made it too dangerous for the foreign missionaries to travel.[15] Chevrier returned to Shanghai for the remainder of the year. He and his colleagues took a short trip down the coast to visit an orphanage run by an order of nuns in Ningbo. The visit was mostly a social one. One evening, Chevrier caught up with a few former army buddies, and an excess of conviviality and camaraderie nearly caused him to miss his boat back to Shanghai.[16]

The signing of the Beijing Convention in October 1860 made it finally possible for Chevrier to journey to his posting, and he arrived in Xiwanzi in the spring of 1861. Soon after, Chevrier set out on his first long sortie into the westernmost sections of the Vicariate. Out on the steppe, the priest and a Chinese translator named Fan rode from village to village, sometimes staying in different hamlets to avoid overburdening the local Catholic households who might have felt obligated to provide precious food and accommodations for both visitors. Chevrier's appearances in the villages were a spectacle. At each stop, villagers gathered to watch the bearded foreigner parade his horse into town. Few of these communities had ever seen a priest, let alone a French missionary.[17]

Despite the enthusiasm, or at least the mild curiosity, of his intended audience, Chevrier often had a hard time keeping up his spirit. 'Our fatigue is due to two causes', wrote Chevrier in a report to his godfather in Lyon, 'The ignorance of Christians so rarely visited (these had not been visited for three years) and their scattering over vast spaces.'[18]

One reason for Chevrier's recurring frustration was the amount of official resistance to his presence and what Chevrier perceived to be undue hostility toward Christians on the part of Qing authorities.

Chevrier was not entirely wrong, although his understanding of local administration lacked nuance, and, as was often the case with foreign missionaries, his involvement tended only to make the situation worse.

On an early excursion to the western part of the Vicariate, Chevrier and Fan made plans to reconvene at a larger town to celebrate Holy Week. When Chevrier arrived, he found a messenger waiting for him instead of Mr Fan. This messenger told Chevrier that Fan and several other converts had been seized by local officials. Chevrier hastily rode out in the direction of the village where Fan and the Christians were being held. When Chevrier arrived, Fan told him the story of their capture. Fan and his converts had been taken at an inn by a group of soldiers employed by the local magistrate. Fan protested that he was a priest of the 'Master of Heaven Religion' [Catholicism] which was a permitted religion based on a decree issued by the emperor two years earlier. The soldiers were unmoved by Fan's arguments, and soon the Chinese priest realised he was the victim of a shakedown. They wanted money to release the prisoners. When Fan failed to provide sufficient funds, the soldiers began to torture Fan and the others to force them to apostatise.

After Chevrier heard Fan's account, the priest immediately set out for the magistrate's yamen. Serving in the military at colonial redoubts in Algeria and Guyana had convinced Chevrier that, priest or not, sometimes the best defence was a good offence, especially when dealing with recalcitrant local satraps. The magistrate at first refused to deal with the irate French priest but when Chevrier threatened to escalate the incident by taking his complaints to the circuit intendant, the magistrate relented. The magistrate turned out to be an elderly Manchu who complained to Chevrier about the unruliness and insubordination of the Chinese sub-officials with whom he was forced to work. He promised Chevrier that restitution would be made, and justice delivered if Chevrier returned the next day.

The following morning, Chevrier had Fan draw up an account of all the items stolen by the soldiers during Fan and the Christians' incarceration. The magistrate ordered the offenders brought before the tribunal where the miserable soldiers knelt and begged for the forgiveness of the court. The magistrate ordered that the runners receive the same number of beatings and tortures they had administered to the Christians, only to have Chevrier intercede. The French priest was interested in procuring a different pound of flesh.

He demanded a copy of the judgement against the soldiers as proof of the incident and their culpability, the return of stolen objects, and the reimbursement of expenses.

The officials resisted Chevrier's demand for a written copy of the judgement so vehemently that Chevrier was reluctantly forced to concede. The officials feared, probably correctly, that such a document would eventually find its way to higher authorities in Beijing with dire consequences for all involved. Chevrier, therefore, insisted the magistrate and his soldiers make good on his other two requests. Return of stolen goods was simple enough, but with the demand for reimbursement of expenses plus punitive damages, the old soldier-turned-priest showed that he wasn't above a little extortion of his own, imposing a price of over 400 francs on the local officials. The sum was raised after much protest, and Chevrier and Fan returned to Xiwanzi.[19]

The incident provides some insight both into Chevrier's attitude toward officials and his sense of mission, and the challenges of managing conflicts involving missionaries, native priests, and Christian members of the local community. One of the most common complaints by local officials in the 1860s involved foreign missionaries intervening on behalf of their congregants, even acting as 'Litigation Masters'[B] (讼师 *songshi*).[20]

The magistrate was charged with maintaining social order, a difficult job at best in a boisterous empire, and even more challenging out on the frontier against the backdrop of a bloody, ongoing civil war against the Taiping Kingdom. In the case of Fan and his colleagues: a group of Christians whose accents mark them as non-natives arrive in the county. Local soldiers swiftly identify the newcomers as possible threats to be neutralised, potential targets of opportunity for a little petty extortion, or both, but the intercession of a French priest in such a case complicated matters and raised the stakes for the officials involved.[22] Even beyond the Great Wall, the magistrate and his staff were aware of the humiliating defeat inflicted on the dynasty at the hands of these foreigners in the Opium War (1839-1842) and its recent sequel, the Second Opium War (1856-1860). No official wanted to be the cause of another war or occupation, but they also had to

---

B   For more on the historical role of 'Litigation Masters' and the problems of foreign missionary interference in civil and criminal cases, see Macauley, *Social Power and Legal Culture: Litigation Masters in Late Imperial China*.[21]

tread carefully lest the local populace view the officials as kowtowing to the foreigners. The foreigners had used their military superiority to force the Qing government to remove proscriptions on their faith, but boots, blood, and ink could not change the deep-seated prejudices felt by most non-Christians.

Chevrier's Lazarist colleague, Jean-Baptiste Anouilh was known for his blustering tactics on behalf of 'his' flock. Anouilh worked in the mission of Dengzhou, southwest of Tianjin. In one incident recorded in 1863, Anouilh accused the local magistrate of persecuting Christians in the district. Anouilh wrote that this magistrate had arrested a group of Christians on trumped-up charges, had them beaten, and forced them to apostatise or be executed. When Anouilh heard what had happened, he immediately rushed to intervene, escalating the case all the way to the highest levels of the Qing administration.

> At the news of these disasters, I felt my entrails torn like those of a mother from whom her children would be torn away. Following the example of the Good Shepherd, I rushed into the midst of the wolves: their fury was at first appeased; the timid herd regained courage. Not being able myself to drive this persecuting Mandarin out of the country, decrees in hand, I immediately went to the capital of the province, and I asked the viceroy, in the name of the treaty, to reparation for the insults that the religion of the Lord of Heaven had just received in my Vicariate. The great mandarins of the province's capital promised to examine the facts and do me justice. But, as thirteen years of experience have taught me to count for little the fine words of the mandarins, I went to Peking, and I drew up a report of the facts which had happened to M. le Comte. Kleckowski, then chargé d'affaires of France in the absence of His Excellency M. de Bourboulon, our very devoted Minister at Peking. Monsieur le Chargé d'affaires addressed his complaints to Prince Koung, who wrote to the Viceroy so that he might deal with my case according to justice.[23]

At the time, Prince Gong (Koung) and the Zongli Yamen were engaged in tense negotiations with Count Kleckowski, the French representative in Beijing, over anti-missionary violence in Guizhou and Sichuan.[24] The central government had little interest in opening another case with the irritable French minister and ordered the Zhili governor in Baoding to settle the matter in favour of the Christians. As a result of Anouilh's intervention, the magistrate was sacked, and the governor ordered reparations be paid to the Christians named in the lawsuit. 'The conditions of peace have also been very profitable to religion', Anouilh concluded. 'I was given all the pagodas in the village, thirteen in number, and the six hundred arpents of land belonging to the pagodas: this will suffice to build a chapel, erect a school, and for the expenses of the Mission'.[25]

Anouilh and other missionaries seemed willing to overlook how these actions would be received by the communities they intended to serve. Many missionaries made a sharp distinction between the elite, officials and gentry, and the common people. In this simplistic duality, the elite were holding China back, oppressing the non-elite, and preventing the common people from exercising their freedom to practice Christianity. The elite, so went this way of thinking, were vain, conservative, anxious, and jealous of the modernity and power of the Westerners. Trapped by outmoded ideas and discredited ideologies, ignorant of the modern world, the elite continually sought to obstruct China's entry into the comity of civilised Christian nations. The common people, in the eyes of the missionaries, were beholden to the economic, political, and social power of the elites and too often used as pawns, unwitting stooges easily duped into anti-foreignism by the propaganda of their political and social betters. As a result, Catholic missionaries in China like Anouilh and Chevrier tried to publicly shame and humiliate officials and other members of the elite by challenging their authority, aping their mannerisms, and appropriating their prerogatives. These tactics certainly had the effect of alienating the elite but also failed to elicit the gratitude of the 'oppressed' masses.

Although many non-elites in Chinese society felt marginalised, what missionaries often failed to see was that the common people often had reasons to fear and loathe the foreign presence generally and the missionaries especially. The common folk in places like Xiwanzi thought of foreign missionaries as 'White Devils' rather than white saviours. In times of crisis, the people were more likely to side with the devils they knew, even local gangsters or corrupt officials.

Qing officials were aware of the missionaries' tactics and the dangerous implications of attempts by foreign missionaries to sow division between elites and non-elites. In a memorial dated 7 February 1862, Chongshi, a Qing bannerman assigned to military affairs in the southwest briefed the Zongli Yamen, the office which at the time handled foreign affairs, on the question of why anti-Christian and anti-missionary cases were on the rise in many provinces across the empire. Chongshi had spent most of 1862 managing a series of anti-Christian and anti-missionary incidents in Guangxi and Sichuan and as much as anyone had developed a nuanced understanding of the complex forces at work in these cases.[26]

Chongshi argued that prior to the imposition of the Treaty of Tianjin and the Beijing Convention, clashes between Christians and non-Christians had been relatively rare. In his opinion, the Treaty of Tianjin, negotiated in 1858, and the Convention of Peking, signed in 1860 at the conclusion of the Second Opium War, entitled foreign missionaries to live and work in local communities. There the missionaries used the treaties as a cudgel to bully officials and non-Christians on behalf of members of 'their' congregations. Christianity already had a bad reputation, wrote Chongshi, the willingness of the missionaries to convert 'unworthy people' had resulted in boastful cells of false-Christians who took advantage of foreign protection to pick quarrels and disrupt the social order.[27]

Although Chongshi and other officials had a more nuanced view of anti-foreign, anti-missionary, and anti-Christian sentiments in local society than foreign missionaries like Anouilh, or Chevrier, these officials also failed to ask why Christianity might be appealing to marginalised groups, especially those referred to as 'unworthy' in official correspondence, and why these groups would be so willing to ally with outsiders offering their protection.[28]

Another group that was profoundly affected by the newly conceded right of foreign missionaries to travel freely in the interior provinces were Chinese Christian leaders, including Chinese priests. Although native Christian leaders were suspect in the eyes of officials, they acted as important intermediaries helping to settle disputes and negotiate spaces for the practice of Christianity in different jurisdictions while helping to localise Christianity to make it more compatible with community standards and expectations. Many native Christian leaders welcomed the provisions of the recent treaties that abrogated previous laws and statutes proscribing Christianity, but the sudden appearance of foreign missions in their towns and cities proved a mixed blessing.²⁹ Chinese priests may have wondered about their role in the church. For over a century, they had worked under the threat of arrest and execution to keep the faith alive and communities together during a time when strict laws meant there were few foreign missionaries in the interior. Now these local Christian leaders were being pushed aside from past leadership positions in favour of European priests, some with little Chinese language ability or experience of working in China.³⁰

During his time in Xiwanzi, Father Chevrier studied Chinese but still had to rely on his Chinese colleagues to communicate with congregants and officials. The French priest would struggle with the language for the duration of his time in China, writing to his superiors in Beijing, 'I am endeavouring to improve my sad pronunciation a bit and to add just a few words to my poor Chinese repertoire. I am also trying to introduce a tiny bit of English into my miserable noggin'.³¹ Chevrier persisted. Within a year of arriving in China, keeping with a long tradition for novice, non-native learners of Chinese, Chevrier was peppering his communications with Chinese phrases. In one letter, he mentions the missionary's job to fight against the Devil who, from 'time to time, still gives me some 'my-fan' [麻烦 *mafan*].³²

Chevrier often partnered with Father Vincent Ou, even though the Cantonese priest had an equally hard time communicating with Northern Chinese people in their own language. Chevrier could not have wished for a better partner. Father Ou was a stalwart supporter of the Lazarist mission and an outspoken writer on social and religious issues.

Born in 1821 in Guangdong, Ou had studied at a seminar in Macau and became a priest in 1842, just as the British were concluding the First Opium War. A year later, he undertook his first mission to Northern China. From the Lazarist base in Xiwanzi, Father Ou travelled the circuit translating and covering for the European priests working at the mission. Language issues were not the only hardship for a southerner. The winters were bitterly cold, a far cry from the heat and humidity of Guangdong. Nor was Ou entirely convinced of the faith of his converts. European priests liked to count their successes, but Father Ou lacked the optimism of his colleagues. 'What will I tell you about our dear Christians?' Ou wrote, 'They are not very proud and very fond of money like in all the rest of China'.[33]

Chevrier formed a particular bond with Father Ou, and the two were frequently paired for long sojourns in the backcountry. Father Ou finally managed to master the northern language, although his accent still marked him as a native of the south. Father Ou's experience and mastery of the principles of the Catholic faith meant he was very much in demand among the missionary outposts in Northern China. He shuttled between Beijing, Xiwanzi, and Tianjin but spent most of his time beyond the Great Wall riding with Chevrier. The two men were the same age, and although their backgrounds could not have been more different, they shared a common faith as well as a revulsion for infanticide and foot binding.[34] Father Ou was outspoken in his support for missionaries who sought to abolish foot binding among the followers. It also gives us an important clue about the origins of Father Ou. Ou's views on foot binding, his family's Christian faith, and his Guangdong origins are all indications that Ou was a Hakka.[35] This could be a dangerous association, as one of the few things that northern Chinese knew about the dreaded Taiping was that their leader, Hong Xiuquan, and many of his followers were Hakka from the southern provinces who believed Hong to be the younger brother of Jesus Christ. Father Ou was a southerner, a Hakka, and a professed Christian: three things which immediately aroused the ire and suspicion of officials in northern China.

Vincent Ou's uncle was a pharmacist and Lazarist missionary based in Tianjin, and Ou would help his uncle in Tianjin when he could, interspersed with extended stays at the Xiwanzi Mission. Many of the priests, like Chevrier, sent to Northern China following the opening of the interior to missionaries lacked even rudimentary language skills. Although some catechists and lay converts could help translate, their own understanding of Catholicism was far from robust and ordained native priests like Vincent Ou were a highly valuable, if not always adequately respected, commodity.

Working on the steppe could take a toll, even for an ex-marine. Chevrier frequently complained of his health. His back, as he suffered from sciatica, occasionally prevented him from riding, and Chevrier would regularly dose himself with quinine. His spirits were boosted by the arrival of his brother, Jean-Louis, in China in 1862. The younger Chevrier had followed Claude-Marie into the priesthood after much fraternal coaxing and cajoling. Claude-Marie's letters do not go into detail, but he expressed concern, perhaps also reflecting his personal temptations while a soldier, about his brother living a louche existence in Lyon.ᶜ

'Are you familiar with the all too famous language of the Celestial Empire? Do you get used to its inhabitants?' Claude-Marie wrote to his brother. 'Finally in the midst of the river of life, do you still row with force against the current which leads to the abyss?'³⁶

By the end of his final year in Xiwanzi, Chevrier's zeal was flagging. His health worsened and the demands on the missionary, one part priest, two parts fundraiser, frustrated Chevrier. 'The body is strong enough, but the soul is languishing. A little while longer, and if "Monsieur le Superieur" does not summon "Monsieur le Bursar" to open his cash register in my favour, all I must do is put all my little marmots to sleep until the next harvest. All I have in a rag is a trifle of fifty taels, which on the first day will [...] disappear.'³⁷

It may have been fortunate, then, that in the following year, 1866, Chevrier and his fellow Lazarists at Xiwanzi received the news that the Vicariate of Mongolia had been transferred to the pastoral care of Theophiel Verbist and the Belgian Congregation of the Immaculate Heart of Mary.³⁸ Chevrier spent his last few weeks in Mongolia accompanying a scientific expedition sponsored by the Natural History Museum of Paris and ministering to sick colleagues as the cholera epidemic that had afflicted Tianjin and the coastal cities in 1862–1863 finally reached the villages north of the Great Wall.

In September 1866, Father Chevrier and Vincent Ou left Xiwanzi for Beijing, about 80 kilometres to the south. The French priest did not linger long in the capital. Upon arrival, his superior, Bishop Joseph Mouly took Chevrier aside and gave the priest his new assignment as the head of the Lazarist mission in Tianjin.

Even in a treaty port like Tianjin, hostility and suspicion against foreigners in general, and missionaries in particular, could build over time, sometimes unnoticed or misinterpreted by the foreign consuls and naval officers in charge with securing the safety of the international community and, of course, steady profits for international firms operating in China. In times of crisis, tensions within a city could reach a breaking point. Chevrier survived his time on the steppe at

---

C   The letters between the Chevrier brothers hint at Jean-Louis' life in Lyons and suggest the younger brother had been involved in behaviour, never explicitly described, of which his older brother disapproved.

Xiwanzi, but he would not survive Tianjin.

In his new posting, Chevrier assisted a group from the Daughters of Charity with their growing orphanage and hospital and pushed plans for a towering church to be built next to the French consulate on the riverbank, outside the Tianjin city walls. With the assistance of Father Ou, Chevrier was successful in his endeavours, but at a cost. Missionary activities in Tianjin, combined with an outbreak of cholera and a rash of kidnappings in 1870, set the city on edge. On 12 June 1870, the city erupted in a day of rage that killed dozens of people, including all nine nuns affiliated with the Daughters of Charity, Father Vincent Ou, and Claude-Marie Chevrier. The Tianjin Massacre, as it became known around the world, was the deadliest outbreak of anti-foreign violence in China in the Qing era until the Boxer War of 1900. While some of the conditions that led to the deadly riots in Tianjin in 1870 were specific to that city and to the special circumstances of treaty ports on the China coast, the challenges and hostility that priests like Chevrier and Ou faced out on the steppe, and the choices they made to respond to these challenges, suggest how the presence of missionaries in local areas could destabilise the formal and informal structures of power which maintained order.

Claude-Marie Chevrier lived as a soldier and died a priest. Father Vincent Ou gave his life to spread a religion many in his own country thought to be a dangerous heterodoxy. Both men believed they were doing God's work, but it can be hard to be on the side of the angels, when the people you serve see devils.

Jeremiah Jenne is a writer and historian based in Beijing since 2002. He earned his Ph.D from the University of California, Davis, and taught Late Imperial and Modern Chinese History for over 15 years. His essays and articles on China have appeared in The Economist, South China Morning Post, The Journal of Asian Studies, Los Angeles Review of Books, and The World of Chinese. His writings can also be found in China in 2008: A Year of Great Significance, The Insider's Guide to Beijing, and the 2015 collection While We're Here: China Stories from a Writer's Colony. *Jeremiah is currently a Council Member for the RASBJ.*

References

1. Zhang Qin 张欣, "Wan qing Zhangjiakou diqu chuanjiao yanjiu 晚清张家口地区教案研究 [Research into Missionaries in the Zhangjiakou Region during the Late Qing]" (河北师范大学 Hebei Shifan Daxue, 2015). Luo Wei 罗薇 and 吕海平 Lü Haiping, «Saibei Tianzhujiao shengdi Xiwanzi zhujiaozuotang jiantang shimo 塞北天主教圣地西湾子主教座堂建堂始末 [The Complete Story of the Construction of the Xiwanzi Cathedral] "[The construction of the Xiwanzi Cathedral.] 南方建筑 Nanfang Jianzhu 4 (2019)
2. Xiaohong Zhang, Tao Sun, and Jianping Xu, "The relationship between the spread of the Catholic Church and the shifting agro-pastoral line in the Chahar Region of northern China," CATENA 134 (2015/11/01/ 2015). Patrick Taveirne, *Han-Mongol Encounters and Missionary Endeavors: A History of Scheut in Ordos (Hetao) 1874-1911* (Coronet Books, 2004), p. 200
3. Tiedeman Rolf G Tiedemann, "Catholic Mission Stations in Northern China: Centers of Stability and Protection in Troubled Times," in *The Church as Safe Haven: Christian Governance in China*, ed. Lars Peter Laamann (Leiden: Brill, 2019)
4. Sweeten, *China's Old Churches: The History, Architecture, and Legacy of Catholic Sacred Structures in Beijing, Tianjin, and Hebei Province*. See especially Chapter Six, "Old Churches in Hebei's Small Cities, Towns, and Villages," pp. 226–287
5. Even today, the presence of the Catholic Church and the legacy of evangelism in the region continue to make Xiwanzi a focus of state surveillance and occasional religious persecution. See United States Department of State, United States Congress House Committee on International Relations, and United States Congress Senate Committee on Foreign Relations, *Annual Report, International Religious Freedom: Report Submitted to the Committee on International Relations, U.S. House of Representatives and the Committee on Foreign Relations, United States Senate by the Department of State, in Accordance with Section 102 of the International Religious Freedom Act of 1998* (U.S. Government Printing Office, 2008), p. 143
6. Jean-Baptiste Göttlicher, July 21, 1861, in *Annales de la Congrégation de la Mission (Lazaristes) et de la Compagnie des Filles de la Charité*. Volume 28, 1863, p. 334
7. Jean-Baptiste Göttlicher, July 21, 1861, in *Annales de la Congrégation*

de la Mission (Lazaristes) et de la Compagnie des Filles de la Charité. Volume 28, 1863, p. 543

8. C.M. Chevrier to J. L. Chevrier, November 26, 1864. Sackebant, *Notices et documents sur les Prêtres de la Mission et les Filles de la Charité de S. Vincent de Paul: massacrés, le 21 Juin 1870, a Tien-tsin (Pé-tche-ly) Chine en haine de la religion catholique et de ses saintes oeuvres ; ou, les premiers martyrs de l'Oeuvre de la Sainte-Enfance.* p. 149

9. See the entry in J. Van Den Brandt, *Les Lazaristes en Chine, 1697-1935, notes biographiques recueillies et mises à jour par J. Van den Brandt* (Impr. des Lazaristes, 1936)

10. Sackebant, *Notices et documents sur les Prêtres de la Mission et les Filles de la Charité de S. Vincent de Paul: massacrés, le 21 Juin 1870, a Tien-tsin (Pé-tche-ly) Chine en haine de la religion catholique et de ses saintes oeuvres ; ou, les premiers martyrs de l'Oeuvre de la Sainte-Enfance.* p. 84

11. For a history of the mission, see J.B. Piolet and E. Lamy, *Les missions catholiques françaises au XIXe siècle* (A. Colin, 1901)., p. 81. For an overview of the Lazarist mission in Algeria and the area around Lambaesa, see Michael Greenhalgh, *The Military and Colonial Destruction of the Roman Landscape of North Africa, 1830-1900* (Leiden: Brill, 2014)

12. Sackebant, *Notices et documents sur les Prêtres de la Mission et les Filles de la Charité de S. Vincent de Paul: massacrés, le 21 Juin 1870, a Tien-tsin (Pé-tche-ly) Chine en haine de la religion catholique et de ses saintes oeuvres ; ou, les premiers martyrs de l'Oeuvre de la Sainte-Enfance,* p. 91

13. Mouly to Superior General Paris, October 27, 1868. Annales CM 1869, *Annales de la Congrégation de la Mission (Lazaristes) et de la Compagnie des Filles de la Charité.* p. 78

14. Chevrier to Procurer General Lazarists in Paris, May 14, 1860, Sackebant, *Notices et documents sur les Prêtres de la Mission et les Filles de la Charité de S. Vincent de Paul: massacrés, le 21 Juin 1870, a Tien-tsin (Pé-tche-ly) Chine en haine de la religion catholique et de ses saintes oeuvres ; ou, les premiers martyrs de l'Oeuvre de la Sainte-Enfance,* p. 95.

15. C. M Chevrier to J. L. Chevrier, May 28, 1860. Chevrier to Procurer General Lazarists in Paris, May 14, 1860, Sackebant, *Notices et documents sur les Prêtres de la Mission et les Filles de la Charité de S.*

Vincent de Paul: massacrés, le 21 Juin 1870, a Tien-tsin (Pé-tche-ly) Chine en haine de la religion catholique et de ses saintes oeuvres ; ou, les premiers martyrs de l'Oeuvre de la Sainte-Enfance, p. 98.

16. C.M. Chevrier to J.L. Chevrier, November 9, 1860, et documents sur les Prêtres de la Mission et les Filles de la Charité de S. Vincent de Paul: massacrés, le 21 Juin 1870, a Tien-tsin (Pé-tche-ly) Chine en haine de la religion catholique et de ses saintes oeuvres; ou, les premiers martyrs de l'Oeuvre de la Sainte-Enfance.109.

17. See Taveirne, *Han-Mongol Encounters and Missionary Endeavors: A History of Scheut in Ordos (Hetao) 1874-1911*; Zhang, Sun, and Xu, "The relationship between the spread of the Catholic Church and the shifting agro-pastoral line in the Chahar Region of northern China."

18. C.M. Chevrier to Abbé Giradet, October 6, 1862. et documents sur les Prêtres de la Mission et les Filles de la Charité de S. Vincent de Paul: massacrés, le 21 Juin 1870, a Tien-tsin (Pé-tche-ly) Chine en haine de la religion catholique et de ses saintes oeuvres; ou, les premiers martyrs de l'Oeuvre de la Sainte-Enfance, p. 131

19. C.M. Chevrier to Abbé Giradet, October 6, 1862. Sackebant, *Notices et documents sur les Prêtres de la Mission et les Filles de la Charité de S. Vincent de Paul: massacrés, le 21 Juin 1870, a Tien-tsin (Pé-tche-ly) Chine en haine de la religion catholique et de ses saintes oeuvres; ou, les premiers martyrs de l'Oeuvre de la Sainte-Enfance.*, p. 131

20. Lee, *The Bible and the Gun: Christianity in South China, 1860-1900*, p. 104.

21. Melissa Ann Macauley, *Social Power and Legal Culture: Litigation Masters in Late Imperial China*. Law, Society, and Culture in China, (Stanford: Stanford University Press, 1998).

22. For a similar case in Xiwanzi, see Patrick Taveirne, "The Religious Case of Fengzhen District. Reclamation and Missionary Activities in Caqar in the Late Qing Dynasty," in *The History of the Relations Between the Low Countries and China in the Qing Era (1644-1911)*, ed. W.F. Vande Walle and Noël Golvers (Leuven University Press, 2003)., p. 389

23. J.B. Anouilh, January 20, 1863, *Annales de la Congrégation de la Mission (Lazaristes) et de la Compagnie des Filles de la Charité.* Volume 31, 1866, p. 34.

24. *Qingmo jiiao'an* 清末教案 *[Anti-Missionary Cases of the Late Qing], Volume 1.*, Document Nos. 209–211

25. J.B. Anouilh, January 20, 1863, *Annales de la Congrégation de la Mission (Lazaristes) et de la Compagnie des Filles de la Charité.* Volume 31 1866, p. 34
26. Chongshi memorial dated February 7, 1862 in *Qingmo jiiao'an* 清末教案 *[Anti-Missionary Cases of the Late Qing], Volume 1.*, Document No. 222
27. Mark W. Driscoll, "The Whites Are Enemies of Heaven," in *2. Ecclesiastical Superpredators* (Duke University Press, 2020), p. 86.
28. There have been many studies of this phenomenon. For example, see Nicholas Tapp, "The Impact of Missionary Christianity upon Marginalized Ethnic Minorities: The case of the Hmong," *Journal of Southeast Asian Studies* 20, no. 1 (1989), pp. 70–95. See also Guo Wenjing, "Rethinking History of Subalterns in China from Late Qing to Nanjing Decade: Postcolonial Approach on Studying the Power Asymmetry between Chinese Subalterns and Western Missionaries within Christian Educational Institutions" (Masters Thesis University of Oslo, 2019).
29. Sweeten, "Catholic Converts in Jiangxi Province: Conflict and Accommodation, 1860-1900"; Ambrose Mong, "Catholic Missions in China: Failure to Form Native Clergy," *International Journal for the Study of the Christian Church* 19, no. 1 (2019)
30. Ambrose Mong, "Catholic missions in China: failure to form native clergy," *International Journal for the Study of the Christian Church* 19, no. 1 (2019/01/02 2019)
31. C.M. Chevrier to Monsignor Guierry, December 1866. Sackebant, *Notices et documents sur les Prêtres de la Mission et les Filles de la Charité de S. Vincent de Paul: massacrés, le 21 Juin 1870, a Tien-tsin (Pé-tche-ly) Chine en haine de la religion catholique et de ses saintes oeuvres ; ou, les premiers martyrs de l'Oeuvre de la Sainte-Enfance.*, p. 255.
32. C.M. Chevrier to J.L. Chevrier, December, 23, 1863. Sackebant, *Notices et documents sur les Prêtres de la Mission et les Filles de la Charité de S. Vincent de Paul: massacrés, le 21 Juin 1870, a Tien-tsin (Pé-tche-ly) Chine en haine de la religion catholique et de ses saintes oeuvres ; ou, les premiers martyrs de l'Oeuvre de la Sainte-Enfance.*, p. 146.
33. Vincent Ou to Joseph Mouly, December 1852. Sackebant, *Notices et documents sur les Prêtres de la Mission et les Filles de la Charité de S. Vincent de Paul: massacrés, le 21 Juin 1870, a Tien-tsin (Pé-tche-ly)*

Chine en haine de la religion catholique et de ses saintes oeuvres ; ou, les premiers martyrs de l'Oeuvre de la Sainte-Enfance. p. 66

34. Vincent Ou to J.B. Etienne, August 4, 1843. Sackebant, *Notices et documents sur les Prêtres de la Mission et les Filles de la Charité de S. Vincent de Paul: massacrés, le 21 Juin 1870, a Tien-tsin (Pé-tche-ly) Chine en haine de la religion catholique et de ses saintes oeuvres ; ou, les premiers martyrs de l'Oeuvre de la Sainte-Enfance.*, p. 60; and Vincent Ou to the Holy Childhood Association, September 4, 1865. Ibid, p. 73

35. Nicole Constable, "Christianity and Hakka Identity," in *Christianity in China: From the Eighteenth Century to the Present*, ed. D.H. Bays (Stanford: Stanford University Press, 1996)

36. C.M. Chevrier to J.L. Chevrier, December 1862, Sackebant, *Notices et documents sur les Prêtres de la Mission et les Filles de la Charité de S. Vincent de Paul: massacrés, le 21 Juin 1870, a Tien-tsin (Pé-tche-ly) Chine en haine de la religion catholique et de ses saintes oeuvres ; ou, les premiers martyrs de l'Oeuvre de la Sainte-Enfance.*, p 140.

37. C.M. Chevrier to J. L. Chevrier, November 26, 1864. Sackebant, *Notices et documents sur les Prêtres de la Mission et les Filles de la Charité de S. Vincent de Paul: massacrés, le 21 Juin 1870, a Tien-tsin (Pé-tche-ly) Chine en haine de la religion catholique et de ses saintes oeuvres ; ou, les premiers martyrs de l'Oeuvre de la Sainte-Enfance,* p. 149

38. Taveirne, *Han-Mongol Encounters and Missionary Endeavors: A History of Scheut in Ordos (Hetao) 1874-1911*, p. 212.

A 'QUEEN AMONG QUEENS' IN THE MIDDLE KINGDOM

By Graham Earnshaw

Long ago and far away, and it seems like another age, the Queen of England came to China. It was 1986, and the China she came to visit was in so many ways still struggling to make it into the modern world, after having been locked in a time warp for over three decades. But it was also a China that was desperately interested—economically, socially, culturally, technologically, every which way—in looking outside, in reconnecting to a past when it was integrated into the world. When it had been able to build relationships beyond its borders, and harmonise with the international community as it existed at that time. The enormous irony of an invitation from the communist leaders of China to an aristocrat, the hereditary monarch of Great Britain and of the British Commonwealth, successor to the British Empire, was not lost on anyone. I had the honour of being able to watch this collision of worlds at close quarters—at the time, I was the Reuters bureau chief for China and I followed her every step as she made her way along a carefully planned path through five Chinese cities.

But first, let us pause for a moment to consider her death in September, 2022, fully 36 years after her visit to China. It was a global news event, the end of an era and a moment for many people to think back over the decades, to consider the present in terms of the past. For so many whose lives she directly touched, however fleetingly, it was a time to remember that moment, but it sparked memories for almost everyone sparked memories. She had reigned as monarch for the entire life of most people on the planet. A remarkable number of people measured their lives in terms of what the Queen did during her life, or what happened to her, and her passing was marked even in China, where she symbolised the traditional 'Western' world, attracting admiration for the skill with which she performed her role. A very senior Chinese official delivered two large funeral wreaths to the British Embassy. When her funeral was televised, a modest gathering viewed it, livestreamed onto a large screen, in a private courtyard mansion in Beijing. Many attendees, both expats and Chinese, were visibly moved by the occasion. It was a rare and precious example of ordinary people, regardless of background, coming together to pay their collective respects, in a manner that reflected not only the dignity of the occasion but also an unusual sense of intimacy.

Also dignified was the way she was greeted on that historic visit in October of 1986. She was accorded a level of welcome and ceremony which was almost unprecedented in Communist China, and was never repeated. What stands out now is both the pomp and ceremony accorded her by China's communist officials, and the evident enthusiasm and warmth of the welcome displayed by ordinary Chinese people, especially in Shanghai, a city with a history closely intertwined with the British Empire.

It was, of course, a top story globally and I was filing at least two articles every day to feed the needs of subscribers and readers. I even had the opportunity to speak with her—a brief exchange of no consequence. There was an incredible sense of disconnect between the Mao-suited officials and Her Majesty and her dapper consort. The contrast in the superficials of dress that existed then don't exist now. she had no political power, so she didn't represent the British government, but she definitely represented something, in an all-encompassing and non-controversial way. And that was not so much the United Kingdom, but another world entirely, the outside world of the West and beyond as it had developed while China had been exploring ever more deeply the concept of socialism with Maoist characteristics. The long separation, with China behind the Bamboo Curtain, created the stark contrast that was the Monarch in the Middle Kingdom in 1986.

To the Chinese leadership at that time and to the Chinese people, in a conscious or unconscious way, I suppose she could also have represented continuity, respect for the past, respect for the exquisite, and the higher ideals of humanity. The image of an aristocrat one might find in fairy tales as opposed to the sometimes messy aristocratic arrogance and entitlement in reality. Not only was she above the cutthroat messiness of politics, she was also a woman. How would it have played out if the monarch of the British Isles at that moment had been a man? Differently for sure.

She was feted by all the top Chinese leaders, including Deng Xiaoping, who held no post in the government's main hierarchy, but still held all the cards (he was, after all, the Honorary President of the All-China Bridge Association). They all seemed a little over-awed in spite of the power they wielded.

But there was one political agenda to her visit, related to Hong Kong, a city which well fitted the description 'borrowed place on borrowed time', just as Shanghai had been a number of decades earlier. An agreement on the future of the cramped enclave on the south China coast had been reached two years previously, with Deng rejecting in harsh terms Mrs Thatcher's suggestion of just extending the arrangement which was clearly working so well, but offering in its place the pledge of '50 years no change.'

'Investors in Hong Kong can set their mind at ease,' Deng said one day as he stood right next to me in the Great Hall of the People, and basically they did.

It's difficult to rewind back to the days when media in China was basically one newspaper and one television channel, and nothing else. There were no other sources of information at all, apart from the rumour mill. Zero. And so the Queen being in China was something that every single Chinese person with access to the media was aware of. It was big news on the state newscasts, because they had obviously decided the visit reflected well upon them.

There was such a huge historical paradox about this man, Deng Xiaoping, who had worked so hard to overthrow the Old China and help to chase away the British imperialists, meeting the British Queen. But with hindsight, it was also significant for what it implied in terms of how China's leadership at that time wanted to mould the country's relationship with the rest of the world, not just with the UK but with the West in general. Wanting to be friends, wanting to show respect, wanting to be integrated, wanting to be a part of it. There was something special about the way he took the meeting, smiling and shaking hands, being together in the same room as her.

First, a review of the visit. Her Majesty and Prince Philip arrived on an RAF plane on October 12 and were lodged in the Diaoyutai State Guest House in Beijing. In six days, they saw Peking, Xi'an, Kunming, Shanghai and Canton (Guangzhou). She and her entourage flew in the RAF plane on the trip around China, which was a rare occasion in which the Chinese government had allowed foreign dignitaries to use their own plane in Chinese airspace.

On October 13, she visited the British Embassy, ransacked by Red Guards two decades previously during the Cultural Revolution, but October 14 was the big day. The Queen, wearing a lilac twin-set with matching hat, met first with the General-Secretary of the Chinese

Communist Party, Hu Yaobang, in Zhongnanhai, the section of the Forbidden City which has been the party's headquarters since the 1950s. Hu was a Deng protégé and a highly convivial individual. Then came lunch in another pavilion in the huge compound with Deng Xiaoping. To quote my own article from that day:

> Looking healthy and beaming broadly, Deng, 82, walked out of a pavilion into the autumn sunshine to greet the Queen as she arrived for lunch at the Spring of Contentment Hall, a pavilion favoured by Ming dynasty emperors in the 15th and 16th centuries. 'Thank you for coming to see an old man such as me,' Deng said.

He ushered her into the pavilion and they sat down on individual armchairs; a pack of cigarettes and a box of matches sat on the low table between them (he was a smoker). This was the time for a brief photo opportunity, and only two journalists out of the 200 or so who were accredited to the tour were allowed in. One was Chinese, a guy from Xinhua News Agency, and the other was me. I had been handed a camera by the *Sun* newspaper's photographer and he showed me how to press the shutter, saying, 'DO NOT touch anything else, I've made all the settings right, do not touch it, just take the damn picture, and

Figure 1: In Beijing, Deng Xiaoping greeted Her Majesty by saying, 'Thank you for coming to see an old man such as me'. Photograph taken by Graham Earnshaw.

take lots of them just in case.' 'Okay, okay', I said. And so we went into the modest room, I took the photograph, which turned out all right. It was definitely the photograph of the day, and probably the second-most important photograph of the whole visit, after the Queen on the Great Wall of China.

We were later informed that Deng started the lunch conversation with a comment on Hong Kong, directly linking the warmth of his welcome to the agreement reached two years previously for the return of Hong Kong to China in 1997.

'With the successful solution of the Hong Kong question, our duty now is to develop the friendly relations between our two countries,' he said. 'It is in this context that I wish you the warmest of welcomes.'

But they then moved on, and quite rightly too, to a discussion of the weather. Again, to quote my dispatch of the day:

> After observing that Peking is a lot drier than London, Deng said he lived in Paris as a young man. 'I was told that from the top of the Eiffel Tower it was possible to see England. I went up the tower twice, but on both occasions the weather was very bad so I could not see it,' he said.
>
> The Queen replied: 'The Eiffel Tower is a long way from England. I don't think you would see it.'

Which was a rather weak response, but then very few people in her life probably threw jokes at her in such formal exchanges.

After the lunch, described as being cordial and relaxed, it was off to the Great Wall. She and Philip walked about 500 metres along the wall, posed for photos, and then it was a mad race back to the Diaoyutai Guest House for a meeting with Deng's other 1980s protégé, Zhao Ziyang, then the number two in the party hierarchy behind Hu.

The leaders all seemed star-struck, even though Queen Margrethe of Denmark and King Juan Carlos of Spain had been through Peking not long before. I quoted a Chinese official as saying: 'We consider the Queen of England to be a queen among queens and she will be treated as such.'

That evening, there was a banquet at the Great Hall of the People, for which the richest woman in the world dressed wonderfully, dripping in ruby-encrusted jewellery. And the next morning, on to Shanghai.

Figure 2: Wu Xueqian, then China's Foreign Minister, with Her Majesty at China's state banquet in Beijing. https://www.chinadaily.com.cn/world/2015-03/02/content_19691778_11.htm [accessed 6 November 2022]

The crowds in Shanghai were the most extraordinary part of the whole trip. There were, in that year, still many people in the city old enough to remember when the city's central areas were run primarily by the British, as they were from the 1840s to the 1940s. Either out of curiosity or nostalgia, a huge number came out to mark the moment.

'For once it really is possible to talk of millions of people lining the streets,' the Queen's press secretary said. 'They were lined up 10 to 20 deep for most of the way from the guest house to the old city.' Which was about 10 kilometres.

Having trounced the Qing military in the first Opium War, the British decided in 1842 to set up a settlement next to the original walled town of Shanghai on the banks of the Huangpu River and make it the base of British military and commercial activities in China. Hong Kong was important because it was British territory, and so that is where companies like the Honkers and then Shankers (now known less poetically as HSBC) and Jardines were registered, while the Legation in Peking retained a shadow of significance. But Shanghai had the real power. The city was the financial heart of the British Empire in East Asia, handling trade and investments from India to Japan. From tea trading in Sichuan to rubber plantations in what was then Malaya, it all revolved around the solid granite buildings on the Bund.

There was something decidedly British about Shanghai and the way that it grew. The British had a deep impact on the culture of the city—the brand of English that is spoken in Shanghai has much more of an English flavour than that of other parts of China, thanks largely to the former St. John's University. English culture, English education and afternoon tea, no matter how idealised the impressions of them are, still seem to captivate Shanghai more than other places in China. And in many Shanghai attitudes, I sometimes espy a tinge of Englishness, including, could it be, maybe possibly, the arrogance of the Anglo-Saxon colonialists?

The power of the British was symbolised by both the domed Bank building on the Bund, and also the imposing British Consulate. It was the largest of the foreign consulates in old Shanghai, situated on the banks of the Huangpu River at the confluence of the Suzhou Creek, just opposite the place where the Queen's boat, the Royal Yacht *Britannia*, was docked in 1986. She definitely passed by the old Consulate, at that point a trade office and now a part of the Peninsula Hotel. It had been occupied by British diplomats up to 1966, only 20 years before the Queen's visit, when they were turfed out by Red Guards. Mao's number two, Zhou Enlai, thoughtfully had the army secure the consulate's records, and a few years later they were shipped off to London.

In the first part of the 20th century, the writ of British law held sway throughout the International Settlement, spearheaded by the British Supreme Court for China and Japan, the courtrooms and judges' chambers of which were right next to the Consulate. But Shanghai, that borrowed place on borrowed time, fell to the Japanese and the British government renounced any concessionary rights to central Shanghai in 1943. There was an echo of all that in the Hong Kong subtext to the Queen's visit 43 years later.

After a busy Shanghai day, The Queen hosted a return banquet on the *Britannia* for the then-President Li Xiannian. The following day, we flew off to Xi'an to see the Terracotta Army.

Security was quite lax by today's

Figure 3: Among the ancient terra-cotta warriors in Xi'an. https://global.chinadaily. com.cn/a/202209/09/ WS631a2875a310fd2b29e76bb8_7. html

standards and there was a rope around a section just outside the exhibition hall entrance where some English students waited to see the Queen. Prince Philip wandered up to them for a chat, and one of the students told reporters later that he had commented lightheartedly that they would end up with "slitty eyes" if they spent too long in China.

The diplomats cringed and the lizards of Fleet Street leapt on the gaffe. The Daily Mirror had it as their front page lead the next day with the spectacular headline "The Great Wally of China." This was, of course, just one of many goofs that Prince Philip made over his life, which the Queen bore stoically, at least in public.

Asked about the duke's "slitty eyes" comment at a briefing, the Queen's Press Secretary said: 'I think it is a well-known physiological fact that people's eyes in different parts of the world are different, but so what? I have sort of roundish eyes.' Which if anything compounded the Duke's appalling comment.

We then went to the city of Kunming, where the following day the Royal couple went for a cruise on a lake while we journalists watched from the shore. It was quite clear she and her husband weren't talking together at all; Her Majesty was giving him the frosty treatment.

Once back on shore after the Kunming cruise, the Duke ushered the Queen into position so that journalists could snap both of them with some dancers. 'Thank you, sir!' shouted one of the photographers. 'Well, I have got to do something right sometime,' replied the Duke.

Then the entourage flew on to Canton, where the couple boarded the *Britannia* again, and sailed off southward, bound for Hong Kong. And that was it.

With the benefit of perspective, what was the significance and value and meaning of the visit? Did it help the British position in any way? The Hong Kong decision had already been made, and that story rolled on over the next 11 years, with Elizabeth's son being the key British representative at the handover ceremony there on July 1 1997. The Queen's visit to China was probably useful in establishing the right vibe, and to some extent probably helped to stabilise Hong Kong in terms of investment sentiment (at least until other issues intervened and made things far more fraught during the run-up to the key moment).

I had seen such as those which greeted the Queen in Shanghai once before, in 1979, with the US Vice-President Walter Mondale, on his visit to Xi'an, I was absolutely blown away by the number of people, many tens of thousands at least, lining the road from the airport into the city. Unthinkable now. We went to a temple and, again, security was sensible to the point where a couple of pigtailed girls in standard Cultural Revolution winter garb, padded jackets and padded pants, came up to Mondale and said, 'Hello.' They talked to him in basic English saying, 'We listen to VOA shortwave radio all the time!' Again, there was a sense of connection at a basic level of goodwill and warmth, human beings to human beings.

As it had been with the Queen in China every day. Allusions to this symbolism welled up during quiet conversations among Chinese who signed the British Embassy's condolence book after her death and watched televised coverage of the Queen's funeral. Even laden with priceless diamonds and rubies, Her Majesty somehow came across as very human—putting on her reading glasses to peer at her menu at the state banquet, for example.

The goodwill generated by her Majesty's visit on the Chinese side was not just directed at the UK, it was about China's relationship with the rest of the world. What Deng was signalling and what the Chinese people who were able to have some access were responding to was the idea of China being a part of the world.

It is a memory to cherish which contains hope for the future.

Graham Earnshaw *is a businessman and editor with several decades of experience in the China world. He is Publisher of Earnshaw Books and was previously Reuters Editor-in-Chief for Asia, Editor-in-Chief of Xinhua Finance, and Reuters China bureau chief in the mid-1980s. He has written a number of books, including* The Great Walk of China *(2011) and* The Genius of Chinese Characters *(2021). He speaks Mandarin and Cantonese and his English is said to be acceptable.*

OUR MAN IN SHANGHAI–A RUSSIAN OBSERVER VISITING ASIAN TREATY PORTS IN 1853
By Sven A Serrano

Abstract

While Ivan Alexandrovich Goncharov (1812-1891) is remembered today mostly for his novel about the lethargic, would-be noble reformer Oblomov, he also served as a government translator at the Russian Finance Ministry. Goncharov's literary skills led to his employment in an official role charged with creating a record of a secret diplomatic mission to Imperial Japan. His lively account of the voyage secured fame and fortune for him, and was widely read in Russia over the following decades. In addition to providing a picturesque travelogue, Goncharov's account inspired and emboldened Russian industrialists and traders, who would join thousands of western entrepreneurs hoping to exploit the riches of the orient.

A Secret Diplomatic Mission

In the autumn of 1852, a small flotilla of Imperial Russian Navy sailing ships set off on an urgent diplomatic mission. On board the flagship, the frigate *Pallada*, was Admiral Yevfimiy Vasilyevich Putyatin, who had been told to sail to Japan, then ruled by the Tokugawa Shogunate, and through direct diplomacy to open that long-closed country to trade and formal relations.[1] His aim had been to complete this task before the Americans arrived, with a similar fleet of sailing and steam ships, under the command of Commodore Matthew Perry.

Also on board was the secretary to the admiral, Ivan Alexandrovich Goncharov (1812-1891), a writer of short stories and translator at the Russian Finance Ministry's Foreign commerce department. Chosen as a "literary" man who could both serve the Admiral as well as produce a record of the still-secret mission, he wrote the official log of the voyage. However, it was his personal account, written first in letters and articles before being compiled into a travelogue, *The Frigate Pallada*, that gained lasting fame for the writer.

Goncharov is today best known for his novel *Oblomov*, a complex story of a lethargic Russian noble, full of half-baked plans for

Figure 1: The Frigate Pallada painted in 1847 by Alexei Bogolyubov.[2]

progress and reform, who is inevitably unable to get out of his bed to act on them.

By contrast, his first-person account of the entrepôts of Asia, run by Europeans but powered by Asian labour, is a portrait of the modern trading world at its genesis. His descriptions of the Shanghai treaty port in November of 1853 particularly fascinated his readers in Russia. At that time, Shanghai was under the sway of aggressive British and Western merchants, salesmen, and missionaries, bustling about in their efforts to squeeze profits and save souls from Qing Dynasty China, as China was shedding its dynastic regime and becoming a modern nation.

The Frigate Pallada enjoyed great popularity in Russia and no less than ten editions[3] were published between 1858 and 1900. For Russians, it was an eye-opener, as Goncharov described Singapore, Hong Kong, Manila, and Nagasaki to readers who mostly knew Asia from accounts of Russian land and caravan expeditions. Like many books of the era by western travel writers such as Alexis de Tocqueville, Mark Twain, and Robert Louis Stevenson, it promoted imperial and colonial goals of bringing Western law, faith, medicine and civilisation to Asians.

Russian interest in China had been sparked in the 1820s and 1830s by the publication of writings by Father Yakinf, a priest who had lived in Beijing for fourteen years as a member of the Orthodox Mission.[4] This gifted polyglot, who added Mandarin, Mongolian, and Manchurian to his Greek, Latin, and French, compiled Chinese dictionaries, grammar books and translated Confucian classics into Russian. He became a celebrity at the salons in St. Petersburg where he hobnobbed with the likes of Pushkin, Glinka, Lermontov, and Krylov, telling entertaining stories and anecdotes of Chinese Imperial Court life. While Father Yakinf's residence in Beijing had given Russia knowledge equal to that of western Europeans, he was criticised for idealising the Chinese Empire at a time when it was obvious that the Qing dynasty was failing to resist the commercial and military incursions of the Western powers.[5] Goncharov's book would provide a second course on all things Chinese for Russian readers.

The official logbook of the expedition, compiled by Goncharov, has been lost to history. The official report of the expedition was written by Admiral Putyatin and published by the Russian Ministry of the Navy.[6]

Goncharov's account began with collected notes from his diary which were sent back to Russia as letters to his friends. Some of these were published unchanged in St Petersburg. In a letter dated 26 March 1854 from the Philippines, he wrote to E.P. and N.A Maikov:

> I started my [literary] studies, and to my amazement experienced such a drive that now my suitcase is stuffed with travellers' notes as a result. [Many of these notes] are in good enough order to be sent to print straight away.[7]

The other literary source of the expedition is a collection of similar letters from Voin Alexandrovich Rimsky-Korsakov, a relative of the famous composer and commander of the steam-powered schooner Vostok. He gave an initial account of meeting Goncharov, saying in it that he wished Goncharov would billet on his ship, as he would be pleasant company. Rimsky-Korsakov then changed his mind and provided a biting critique of Goncharov's character, revealing him to be, again, very close in personality to his literary character, Oblomov.

> [He] is simply the laziest of epicures, grown fat from full meals and long naps afterward, a pleasant enough person to converse with, but often hard to bear in company because of his weak-nerved, womanish temperament, which torments him with various fears, causing him to groan and everyone [else] to grieve.[8]

Rimsky-Korsakov played a sly joke on Goncharov by giving him a book on shipwrecks 'to ease his fears' which most likely had the opposite effect![9]

From October 1852 to April 1853 the Russian flotilla made stops in Portsmouth, Madeira, and South Africa. Our writer encountered the Chinese on the approach into East Asia in June 1853: first in Java, where he saw a village of Chinese settlers, then in Singapore and Hong Kong in great numbers, working on the docks, selling fruit, tea, dry goods, and opium in city shops, and, in the opulent home of a Chinese merchant,

> [w]here against the walls were pieces of furniture of delicate carvings, gilded lampshades, long covered galleries with all the appurtenances of refined luxury: bronzes, porcelain, on the walls statuettes, arabesques. European comfort and eastern luxury here went hand in hand.[10]

In Hong Kong, Goncharov noted with admiration the transformation of a sparsely uninhabited coastal island into a vibrant trading port and gave kudos to British industry and ingenuity.

> It did of course not occur to the Chinese that the useless heap of stones that they ceded to the English in 1842 [...] would one day be turned into such a city. Even less did they imagine that they, the Chinese themselves, would cut the stones, erect the walls, the fortifications, on which guns would be placed[...] All this has been done.[11]

He noted that once the colony of Hong Kong was established, it immediately attracted the attention of the native residents of Portuguese Macao. Almost 30,000 of them, lured by the wages the British offered, moved to Hong Kong to work and construct the port and commercial areas of the island.[12] The migrant workers then took up permanent residence in

> [...] this welter of noise, smells, crowding, between birdcages and all objects under the sun, the Chinese seemed somehow happier and freer: they had constructed here their little China. Here they were happy.[13]

It was if, he mused, like aquarium fish, they had been transplanted from a muddy pool 'and put into a marble basin filled with transparent water'.[14]

Upon arriving in Japanese waters, the Russian ships spent three fruitless months in Nagasaki waiting for the shogun to respond. Having failed to get permission to begin negotiations with the Tokugawa Shogunate, the Russian flotilla sailed into the mouth of the Yangtze River and anchored off of Woosung at the end of November 1853, to replenish their supplies.[15]

During the months spent at anchor in Nagasaki Bay, Admiral Putyatin was only once allowed to go ashore with his officers to meet the Kyushu governor. The rest of the time Goncharov and the ship's crew were confined to their vessels and could only survey the curtained-off streets of the city through telescopes. 'Time meanwhile dragged on[...] We waited for the answer from Yeddo, occupied ourselves and were bored, or did nothing - and also were bored.'[16] The diplomatic procedures, even for small requests, remained the same. The Japanese even refused payment for provisions, saying this would mean they were doing direct business with the Russians, something only permitted to the Dutch.

When Admiral Putyatin announced to the Japanese they were leaving, the Japanese suddenly delivered a message that had, at last, come from Edo: Four plenipotentiaries, "*groote Herren*" were coming to meet the admiral to negotiate. The message had been written by the president of the council to the governors. It said that plenipotentiaries would come, but no further details of the plenipotentiaries were given, nor was a date specified. The Russians deduced that the Japanese wanted to continue stalling them out of fear that their flotilla would sail for Tokyo Bay and attempt, as Commodore Perry had done the previous year, to demand negotiations at the seat of power. Instead of waiting any longer, the Russians took their leave with a promise to return, and the flotilla set sail for China.

Figure 2: Admiral Putiatin in Nagasaki, 1853 by an anonymous Japanese painter[17]

Respite In Shanghai

After a few days of dithering in the roadstead at the mouth of the Yangtze, Goncharov joined several of the ship's officers and men and boarded a sloop to journey up the Huangpu to the foreign concessions and the Chinese city.[18] He described the fishing boats he saw on the way, noting that often enough, they turn to piracy in the absence of any authority. 'The Chinese government is too weak, and without a fleet of [armed] boats you can't do anything about them.'[19] It is impossible, he writes, to know who they are. 'Today they are merchants, tomorrow, fishermen, and at every opportunity - robbers.'[20]

He continued with a sweeping, universal observation:

> The population of China skips out like a pea from an overfilled basket, and settles in every direction, on all nearby and far islands, as far as Java on one side, to California in the other. Chinese are always present in large numbers; they are tradesmen, excellent craftsmen, and labourers.[21]

Approaching the Bund, Goncharov was initially resigned to the possibility that the British Concession in Shanghai may be a replica of what he saw in Hong Kong, with the same sights and with similar foreign shops and restaurants. However, his descriptions of Shanghai are evocative, suggesting that his first glimpse of the city intrigued him greatly.

> [There were]ships and junks, magnificent European buildings, gilded floors, temples, Protestant churches, gardens, all this was crowded together in a hazy mass, without any perspective, just as if the church stood in the water, the ship on a street [...][22]

He had already heard that there was turmoil and disorder in the Chinese town. Three years earlier, the quasi-Christian rebel Hong Xiuquan had begun a Hakka and Han Chinese rebellion against the Manchu dynasty, capturing large swaths of central China, including the city of Nanjing, which he made the capital of his Taiping "Heavenly Kingdom." In January of 1853, the war came to Shanghai when a criminal band, the Small Swords Society [Xiǎo dāo huì 小刀会], who were loosely affiliated with the Taiping rebels, infiltrated the Chinese walled city adjacent to the foreign concessions and captured it. As his sloop pulled up to the Shanghai Bund, Goncharov could see and hear the physical sights and sounds of this battle between the local rebels and the Qing Army.

> Korsakov [with a telescope] showed me the foreign ships, French and English, [one] bought by the Chinese and commanded by an English skipper who just managed the sails and did not take part in the battles with the insurgents; a cannonade issued from them, a Chinese admiral commanded. Here I heard that in yesterday's battle two junks had been blown up.[23]

With that martial introduction, Goncharov began his tour of Shanghai. Curiously, he made no mention of their companion vessel in the flotilla, the former Russian-American Company ship, *Kniaz Menshikov*, which had visited Shanghai in 1848 on a fur trading expedition.[24] At any rate, no veteran of that earlier voyage was with the ten men ashore on this expedition. Several of them checked into Commercial (Astor) House, the crowded foreigner's hotel on Suzhou Creek which targeted the seafaring clientele of the day. Goncharov, using his rank, took up residence with Admiral Putyatin at the lavish home of Russian consular agent (and the French and American vice-consul) Edward Cunningham, co-partner of Russell & Company, the largest American trading firm on the China coast. Goncharov penned a humorous account of his initial meeting with Cunningham where the two confer while sitting in two 'elevated anti-hemorrhoidal chairs' before the Russian, after having difficulty sitting in the chair as the cushion kept rotating underneath him, took his leave.[25]

With a Baron Kreitner as his guide, Goncharov began the first of several colourful excursions in Shanghai, enchanting readers with swirling descriptions of street life in the treaty port.

> In this labyrinth, an enormous crowd of people moves about. In one shop things are so crowded one cannot get out of the store. And there is a constant coming and going of people. Here bearers push through the crowd with amazing skill, carrying the most enormous loads, with

bales and bolts of silk cloth, big as a haystack. And over there they carry two bodies, not on their shoulders but on their arms; a coolie runs with a letter and a basket of eggs is pulled along. And they all run and shout and sing to make you step aside. This man beats with a drumstick on a board, indicating that linen is sold here. That man has wild ducks in hand and dead pheasants hanging over his shoulder - or is it the other way around? Peddlers shout just as they do at home. Just as you dodge one, another puts his hand gently on your shoulder, you move back, and a third one cries out to you. You jump back because in one hand he holds some intestines, and in the other a long fish that slithers on the ground, 'Where can we go? Two cows are coming,' said Baron Kreitner, and we jumped into a little shop while the cows went past.[26]

Goncharov was obsessed with the sights, sounds, smells, and flavours of the food he saw on offer, noting that he used to think that travellers were prone to exaggeration, but that here in Shanghai he saw for himself that this was not necessary. He observed sauces

being warmed, heated, cooked, roasted, and the crackle can be heard in the hot smelly sauce and in the steam that pervades everything[...] Particularly two smells assail you: the offensive vegetable oil, sesame oil, I think, and garlic.[27]

He complained about the quality of Chinese tea, moaning in the manner of Oblomov 'Why, oh why is it impossible to get good tea in China? Every kind of tea grows in this country; the problem here is with the word "good"'.[28] Goncharov pined for a cup of orange pekoe.

More revealing of the new order in the treaty ports is his account of the relations between the Westerners and the Chinese on the Promenade, the path allotted to the new European residents for horse-riding and walking. This wide street, he noted, separated Shanghai from the outskirts, where an imperial army camped, conducting the campaign to capture the walled city from the Small Swords. Here the Chinese came to watch with curiosity the sight of English men and women on horseback cantering down the path. The locals heckled and laughed at each passing rider.

From this vantage point, our writer described the Chinese Imperial Army's siege of the bandit-occupied walled city. Unable to dislodge the Small Swords after several poorly executed attempts, the Manchu forces decided to

> seize anyone who does something out of order, declare him an insurgent[...] tie something red around his head as a sign of rebellion, then chop off his head and stick it on a pole.²⁹

The insurgents were unperturbed and continue to re-supply their fighters through a fence, buying provisions from townspeople who were only too happy to sell them what they needed. At night the Manchu Bannermen

> shot off rifles from this camp, but only blank cartridges [...] to demonstrate that they were on alert, as English officers informed us. So the attack and fire we saw at night[...] was no more than the caricature of a battle.³⁰

After spending several pages praising the business operations and methods employed by the British in Hong Kong, Singapore, and in Shanghai, Goncharov levelled criticism over their open peddling of opium and their treatment of the Chinese.

> The way the English treat the Chinese and others too, all the people subjugated by them, is not really cruel, but like victors over the vanquished, [it is] cold, rough, and disdainful, so much so, that it hurts to see it. They do not accept these people as humans, but as some sort of labouring animal that they do not beat or even tend carefully and pay generously, but do not hide their contempt for.³¹

He visited an opium shop, and was offered a sample, but refused. Like the missionaries and moralists of the Victorian era, he noted that for opium

> the Chinese gave away their tea, silk, metals, medicated herbs, sweat, blood, energy, brains—their whole life. The

English and the Americans take all this in cold blood and change it into money.'³²

The Russians could only look on with bewilderment, wishing they had something equally lucrative to sell to the Chinese in the treaty ports. Russian imperial ambitions, apart from opening trade ties with Japan, had included expanding Russian seaborne trade in coastal and inland South Asia. Furs from Siberia and Alaska were the first step. Goncharov declared that Shanghai would be the obvious starting place for trade with China, noting its favourable geographic situation on the Yangtze, near the upriver manufacturing towns like Suzhou, which served as storage and sales centres for the best silk and tea.³³ He observed that the Taiping Rebellion had disrupted normal trade routes and commercial relations but did not make a prediction about who would prevail, only that the war was not going to end soon.

After a gala dinner at the home of Mr. Cunningham, the one-month idyll in Shanghai ended abruptly on December 15 when the latest mail and newspapers arrived from Europe. These included news of an imminent break with Britain and France over Russia's ultimatum to the Ottoman Turks, which heralded the beginning of the Crimean War. Tensions mounted for the Russians as '[h]our by hour we waited for a second ship bringing the mail from East India: if it should bring news of the war, then the English warships might seize our schooner.'³⁴ Goncharov quickly prepared his luggage and papers and hurried out to catch a water taxi to the *Pallada*.

Once out of China, Admiral Putyatin's fleet split up, with Putyatin returning to Japan where the Russian delegation continued negotiations with the Japanese. Eventually, they received a promise from the Shogun that Russia would receive the same treatment as the Americans (who would eventually force through an agreement in 1854). The *Pallada* with Goncharov, left the flotilla and made its way to Russia's ramshackle eastern port of Ayan on the Sea of Okhotsk in Siberia, successfully eluding French and English warships.³⁵ The Crimean War had reached the Far East.

The rest of the delegation, still in Japan continuing negotiations, was witness to the Ansei-Tokai earthquake and tsunami on December 23, 1854, in the port of Nagasaki. The tsunami damaged the replacement Russian flagship *Diana* beyond repair and forced the Russian crew, with the assistance of their Japanese hosts, to build a

Figure 3: Ivan Goncharov and Vice-Admiral Yevfimiy Putyatin (seated 5th and 6th from the left in the first row) among officers of the frigate Pallada.³⁷

new, replacement schooner, the *Heda*, in which to return home.³⁶

From Ayan, Goncharov made his way overland through Siberia for six months, continuing to write descriptions of the Siberian peoples that the Russians had absorbed in their empire, ending his epic travel account in Irkutsk. He arrived back in St. Petersburg on Feb 25, 1855, after an absence of almost three years, to continue his literary career.

CRITICAL RESPONSE AND ENDURING RELEVANCE

Reviews almost universally praised *The Frigate Pallada* as a masterful depiction of the exotic lands and cities visited by Goncharov, full of life, human activity, and intricate detail. The liberal author and critic Stepan Dudyshkin called it 'a gallery of masterfully painted etudes which strike one by their freshness, completeness, and originality.'³⁸ A few critics noted the lack of hard historical or scientific or formal accounts of the diplomatic meetings carried out by Admiral Putiatin's delegation, but most reviews concentrated on the romance of the tale.³⁹ The book was eagerly read by all of Russia's literary classes and, thanks to its moderate descriptions of the Asian fleshpots visited, became acceptable reading for school children in the Tsarist *lycees*.

During the reigns of the final three Tsars, Russian foreign policy toward the Qing Dynasty was both aggressive and competitive, like that of the other Western powers. Goncharov's book was read in official circles, published first in serial form in the influential journal *Morskii Sbornik* (Naval Collection), a publication of the Imperial Ministry of the Navy and a mouthpiece for reforms in the Russian military.

The Treaty of Ghuljia, formalising overland trade between Russia and China, signed just before Putyatin's visit in 1851 was followed by the crowning achievement of Admiral Putyatin's expedition, the Treaty of Shimoda.[40] This document, signed on February 7, 1855, opened the ports of Nagasaki, Shimoda, and Hakodate to Russian vessels, established the position of Russian consuls in Japan, and defined the borders between Japan and Russia. Two more treaties were enacted in the shadow of the Second Opium War: the 1858 Treaty of Aigun and the 1860 Convention of Beijing, where the Qing ceded to Russia all of the Amur coast, some 600,000 sq. km of territory, and the site of the future port of Vladivostok.

References to *The Frigate Pallada* began to appear in English language literary scholarship in the 1950s, making use of a slightly censored 1949 Soviet edition of the work. The respected East Asia scholar George Lensen, writing in the 1950s, noted that besides being a piece of personal travel literature, that it had historical significance, for creating 'a stereotype of the Japanese which contributed to the reckless "we shall sink their warships" attitude prevalent in Russia at the turn of the century.'[41] Milton Ehre, in his 1973 book, *The Life and Art of Ivan Goncharov*, said the work reflected the author's disappointment when he encountered in Singapore, Hong Kong, and Shanghai

> an Orient under the rule of the several colonial powers [which] had begun to achieve a pedestrian sameness, an East not of mystery and allure, but of squalid ports, shabby European hotels, and sullen natives.[42]

Finally, in 1987, a full version in English, translated by Klaus Goetze, was published by St. Martin's Press.[43]

In a 1988 article *Oblomov's Travels,* John Bayley notes that it was in Shanghai that

> the Russians gloomily observed the sensational results of the British opium trade, the boom in business it had engendered, the demoralization of the Chinese and the lapse of the Celestial Empire into anarchy and civil war.[44]

William McOmie, in a 1995 piece on the Russian diplomatic mission to Nagasaki, said that Goncharov's account was only partially useful to historians as 'the interpretation of [the events] is literary and constantly infused with the humor and irony, sarcasm, and mockery of its cranky and gifted author.'[45]

Following the bicentenary of Goncharov's birth in 2012, renewed interest in our author saw two important studies appear in print. In Susanna Sojung Lim's book *China and Japan in the Russian Imagination 1685-1922*, an entire chapter is devoted to the importance of *The Frigate Pallada*, praising it as 'a vivid literary testament and paean to the Russian presence in the East,' and noting that in his descriptions of Hong Kong and Shanghai he maintains the then almost universal Romantic belief in a stagnant, decaying, China. However, according to Lim, Goncharov pushed back against this view, observing that Chinese labour and money had emerged as 'indispensable elements of progress, as engines assisting the West.' It was in China, Lim observes, that economic realities would ensure 'that the front lines of the battle between Russia and the West were to be drawn.'[46]

Yale Professor Edyta Bojanowska's breakthrough 2018 book *A World of Empires—the Russian Voyage of the Frigate Pallada* finally gave Goncharov's *The Frigate Pallada* the place it deserves. She points out that it is the modern globalism of 'trade, tariffs, flows of global capital, and skyrocketing profits'[47] that captured Goncharov's attention, as he visited the trading enclaves and European run-ports of Asia.

Shanghai, along with Manila, Singapore, and Hong Kong were depicted then as they are today:

> vibrant trading hubs whose networks encircle the globe, as testaments to the emerging world economy, the globalizing forces Euro-American imperialism, and Asia's incredible economic potential.'[48]

Goncharov provided a guidebook for the officials, bankers, merchants, and railroad builders of the Russian empire to participate in this new world. This rush to join oriental profiteering would later put Russian Empire on a collision course with Imperial Japan - which had been so assiduously courted by Admiral Putyatin's expedition as a hoped for trading partner.

The Frigate Pallada is a vivid snapshot of this moment in history, both for its depiction of China and Japan at their respective economic and political takeoff points, and its description of an imperial Russia expanding its interests into the Pacific and world economy. In its first diplomatic duel with the upcoming United States, Russia would come second, but it would use "hitchhiking imperialism" to gain treaties with both China and Japan, after other countries had done the groundwork. The city of Shanghai, in its eleventh year under foreign domination as a treaty port, comes alive in *The Frigate Pallada's* gritty accounts of Chinese and foreign daily life in the concessions. Goncharov's epic travelogue has lessons, perhaps, for the modern reader, as Russia finds itself again in a Crimean conflict, and Asian trade relations are of paramount importance.

Sven Aarne Serrano *(librarian@royalasiaticsociety.org.cn) is a California-born resident in Shanghai, who has lived in China since 2008 and is currently serving the RAS China as a Council member and Librarian for its collection of rare books and documents. He studied History at UC San Diego and Indiana University before earning an MA at San Francisco State. He taught English in Japan at Setsunan and Kindai Universities in Osaka for many years before taking up a History teaching appointment at Shanghai High School International Division(SHSID). He is the curator of the former WWII Japanese internment camp for Allied Civilians, the Longhua Civilian Assembly Center, located on the campus of SHSID.*

REFERENCES

1 Ilyishev, A.V., Saplin V.I. (2004). "The Mission of E.V. Putyatin. The 150th Anniversary of the Establishment of Russo-Japanese Relations". Archived from the original on July 4, 2007. [accessed 1 July 2022]

2 Central Naval Museum, St. Petersburg, Russia Public Domain https://commons.wikimedia.org/wiki/File:FrigatePallada.jpg [accessed 1 July 2022]

3 Goncharov, Ivan A. the *Frigate Pallada*, (St.Martin's Press, New York, 1987) p. 6

4 Lim, Susanna Soojong, *China and Japan in the Russian Imagination*, (London, Routledge, 2013) p.66

5 Lim, p.68

6 McOmie, William W., Russians in Nagasaki 1853-54—Another look at some Russian, English and Japanese sources, Acta Slavica Japonica, v. 13 1995 p. 43

7 Englelhardt, B. editor, Travel Letters of I.A Goncharov from his around-the world-expedition in *Literaturnoye Nasledstvo*, 22-24 (1935) p.407

8 McOmie, William W., 'Bakamatsu through Russian Eyes - The Letters of Voin Alexandrovich Rimsky-Korsakov,' *Nagasaki University Humanities Study Report*, 48 (1995) 35-53, (p. 40)

9 McOmie, Bakamatsu, p.41

10 Goncharov, Ivan A. the *Frigate Pallada*, (St.Martin's Press, New York, 1987) p. 235-6

11 Goncharov, p. 240

12 Sit, V.F.S., Cremer, R., Wong, S.L. (1991). *Entrepreneurs and Enterprises in Macau: A Study of Industrial Development*. Hong Kong University Press, Hong Kong, p.11

13 Goncharov, p. 240

14 Goncharov, p. 242

15 Goncharov, p 244. Admiral Putiatin, Commodore Perry, and Vice-Consul Cunningham would be involved in a tug-of-war over coal resupply for the Russian ships, as the Americans had bought up local stocks for their own fleet. Cunningham's superior, Minister Humphries, allotted one load of American coal for the Russians, but at Perry's urging, blocked the delivery of a second.

16 Goncharov, p. 284

17 https://commons.wikimedia.org/wiki/File:Putyatin_in_Nagasaki_1853.jpg [accessed 5 July 2022]

18 McOmie, William W., The Russians in Nagasaki, p.49

19 Goncharov p. 340

20 Goncharov p. 340

21 Goncharov p. 340

22 Goncharov, p. 349

23 Goncharov, p. 250

24 Grunëy, Andrew Valterovich, *Russian Colonization of Alaska: From Heyday to Sale, 1818–186*. University of Nebraska Press, p.148

25 Goncharov, p. 357

26 Goncharov, p. 358

27 Goncharov, p. 359

28 Goncharov, p.352

29 Goncharov, p.365

30 Goncharov, p.364. In the following year tensions between this Imperial Army Camp and the foreigners using the Promenade

will boil over, leading to the Battle of Muddy Flat on April 4, 1854, which saw a force of British and American sailors, augmented by armed foreign residents of Shanghai attack the Imperials with the deaths of 300 Chinese and 4 foreigners reported.

31 Goncharov, Ivan. p. 370
32 Goncharov, p. 371
33 Goncharov, p. 373
34 Goncharov, p. 371
35 Bojanowska, Edyta M. , World of Empires The Russian Voyage of Frigate Pallada, p. 67
36 'Russian Frigate Diana'. Gallipolis Journal, Gallipolis, Ohio. 31 May 1855. p. 1
37 https://www.russianartandculture.com/frozen-wine-and-cabbage-soup-ivan-goncharovs-audacious-voyage-to-japan-and-the-creation-of-oblomov-russias-laziest-literary-character/ [accessed 1 July 2022]
38 Dudyshkin, Stepan, *Otechestvennye Zapiski,* 1(1856), p.50
39 Alexander Druzhinin from Tyunkin, K. N. *Commentaries to Frigarte Pallada. The Works of I. A.Goncharov in 6 Volumes* Ogonyok's Library. Pravda Publishers. Moscow, 1972. Vol. 2, pp. 327–342
40 Treaty of Shimoda, https://www.ru.emb-japan.go.jp/RELATIONSHIP/MAINDOCS/1855.html#7 [accessed 1 July 2022]
41 Lensen,George, 'The Historicity of Fregat Pallada', *Modern Languages Notes* 68, 7 (1953): 463
42 Ehre, Milton, *Oblomov and His Creator: The Life and Art of Ivan Goncharov*, (Princeton University Press, Princeton, 1973), p.144
43 Goncharov, Ivan A. *The Frigate Pallada,* (St.Martin's Press, New York, 1987)
44 Bayley, John, 'Oblomov's Travels,' *The New York Review of Books,* March 3, 1988
45 McOmie,William, 'The Russians in Nagasaki 1853-54 - Another Look at Some Russian, English, and Japanese sources,' *Acta Slavica Japonica*, I3 (1995), p.43
46 Lim, Susanna Soojung, p. 85
47 Bojanowska, Edyta, A World of Empires—the Russian Voyage of the Frigate Pallada (Cambridge Mass., Harvard University Press, 2018) p.19.
48 Bojanowska, Edyta. P. 20

SECTION 3

Stories of the Cities

'[In] Came Pu Yi in His Prince of Wales Suit with a Pink Carnation in His Buttonhole'

CUTTING THROUGH THE HAZE: REASSESSING IMAGES OF SHANGHAI GIRLS IN CIGARETTE ADVERTISEMENTS, 1910-1940

By Julie Chun

Abstract

Early twentieth-century Shanghai calendars or yuefenpai (月份牌) featuring images of the 'Modern Girl' (摩登女子) and the 'New Woman' (新女性), have captured the imagination of viewers past and present as iconic symbols of the city's glamourous past. Ravishingly attired in qipao and presenting a beguiling smile, the colourful illustrations of young women evoke well-recognised 'Orientalist' images that continue to be used in China to this day. Due to their popular appeal, much has been written and published about this genre of posters, which formed an important part of Shanghai's visual culture. Previous studies of yuefenpai have positioned the stylish Chinese women wielding cigarettes primarily as an advertising strategy to push cigarette sales for male consumption. However, the decades from 1910 to 1940, when these advertisements were created and circulated, were also a time of social, economic and political instability fraught with ambivalence within China, exacerbated by tensions arising from foreign encroachment and domestic ideological shifts. What layered and alternate stories do the images of the yuefenpai reveal beyond their emblem as icons of pretty Chinese women? What do these images reveal about the historical conditions in which they were created, produced and consumed? In the light of recent scholarship in the fields of social sciences and corporate history, this article traces the visual coupling of women and tobacco and examines the ways in which the images reflected the changing times and society. By casting a renewed gaze upon the historical images, this paper reveals unexpected encounters of contestation and subversion by men and women who were both agents of their choices as well as fodder for gender profiling and the construction of stereotypes.

An Iconic Image

About six months ago, as I was strolling past the small shops in Yu Garden in Shanghai, I noticed a flood of visually similar packaging.

Figure 1: Hand lotion packaged using tobacco advertisement designs from 1920-30
Yu Garden, Shanghai. Photo by Julie Chun, 2022

Inexpensive lotions, embossed with replicas of the iconic Shanghai calendar girls, were being sold as 'Old Shanghai Snow Flower Cream'.

A few weeks later, I came across these same products at a weekend outdoor market in central Jing'an district and a few months thereafter, I stumbled upon boxes of biscuits bearing similar images in an upscale supermarket in the Pudong New Area. These nostalgic illustrations are easy on the eyes of young and old, as well as attractive to both foreign and local beholders, thus creating a visual gravitational pull. The girls showcased on the packaging are youthful and elegant with petal-tinted cheeks and inviting smiles. Their voluminous jet-black hair is carefully styled, and their slim figures sheathed luxuriously in gorgeous *qipao* dresses. These are images that momentarily transport the viewers to a captivating era when Shanghai was known as the 'Paris of the East'.

These images are an homage to the Shanghai Girls that graced illustrated calendar posters, more familiarly known as *yuefenpai* (月份牌). The advertisements and calendar posters were created, distributed and sold by product manufacturers and dealers in China in the early

Figure 2: Biscuits packaged with tobacco advertisement designs from 1920-30
Ole Supermarket, Pudong New Area, Shanghai. Photo by Julie Chun, 2022

decades of the twentieth century, the period of foreign concessions and internationalism in Shanghai, when material and visual culture flourished through commercial exchanges with the outside world. The illustrated posters and calendars promoted a wide range of commodities, including digestive tonics, powdered milk, cosmetics, toothpaste, alcohol, insect repellent and most famously, cigarettes. Aside from paper-based advertisements and illustrated calendars for cigarettes there were also cigarette cards, but, due to limitations of time and space, cigarette cards will not be discussed here.[1]

The hegemonic presence of cigarettes in China gained wide awareness with the mass dissemination of calendars and advertisements, which advocated the allure and glamour of smoking culture. Former analyses of *yuefenpai*, have emphasised the production process of these advertisements; there are ample books and articles that trace the historical precedents of print culture in China and how text and later, accompanying images, were transferred and appropriated for use in advertising as foreign goods entered the Treaty Ports of Ningbo, Xiamen, Fuzhou, Guangzhou and Shanghai after 1842. While I will touch upon the historical aspects of tobacco usage in China, as well as the introduction of cigarettes into Chinese society, my purpose is to examine the ways in which the cigarette campaigns reflected the thoughts and attitudes of China's changing society and culture, a topic that deserves renewed attention.

Incursion of British American Tobacco (BAT) into Shanghai

How did cigarettes, which are a distinctly foreign import, come to dominate the Chinese social landscape? Cigarette, meaning 'diminutive cigar', is the French word for chopped tobacco leaves that are rolled in paper and smoked. From the 1860s to the 1910s, the global cigarette industry was monopolised by the markets in Turkey and Egypt, which exported to Britain, the United States and anywhere else a foothold could be established. Considered an inferior and cheaper product than the cigar, cigarettes were associated with effeminate qualities and shunned by elite gentlemen's societies and clubs in the US and Europe, where the cigar evoked high society, wealth, class and refinement.[2] Perhaps the snub was due to the cigarette's slim size compared to the robust, hulking form of the cigar. Or perhaps it was due to its association with the 'Other', the foreign cultures of Egypt and Turkey where men wore robes and tunics rather than the three-piece suits that were signifiers of masculinity in America.

The commercial rise of the US cigarette industry began with the incorporation of the American Tobacco Company (ATC) in January 1890, when a business partnership was formed in New Jersey between James B. Duke, Lewis Ginter, the Kinney Brothers Tobacco Company, Goodwin & Company and W.S. Kimball & Company. The ATC had an expansionist agenda, steered by Duke, who came from Durham in North Carolina and was already a leading figure in the tobacco industry. Although one of ATC's brands, Pinhead, entered China around 1890 via the Shanghai commissioning agency Mustard & Co, James Duke sought to extend his ambitions to 'conquer the rest of the world' by concentrating on business opportunities in East Asia after he recognised the immense market of China's 430 million potential customers.[3] The story of the mass distribution and marketing of cigarettes in China began in 1902, when ATC joined forces with the British Imperial Tobacco Company to form British American Tobacco (BAT) and established multiple subdivisions and factories across China.

In Shanghai, BAT's main office was located in the former British Concession, in the premises of what today is 175 South Suzhou Road. In 1906, it set up a massive manufacturing factory complex and a creative advertising agency in present day Pudong New Area, and then a packing factory on present day Yulin Road, Hongkou District in 1907. Although BAT's main global headquarters were in London, where they remain, Duke served as the Chairman of both companies. It was a joint venture in name only, as BAT was largely helmed by American experts from the tobacco-growing regions of North Carolina and Virginia, with many young male American recruits sent to Shanghai and BAT's numerous subdivisions in China.[4] From the international Treaty Port cities to far-off outposts in Guangdong, Shandong, Anhui and Henan provinces, BAT's ambitious entry and expansion in China represents one of the most successful business endeavours of the twentieth century.

Tobacco in China

As a New World crop, tobacco was originally cultivated in the Americas and brought to Asia by Portuguese traders in the 16th century, from where it came to be grown and harvested in southern China. The use of dried tobacco leaves slowly integrated into Chinese society in the form of snuff, or was smoked in long pipes or water pipes. It was used for recreational and medicinal purposes, and even for repelling insects. According to historian Carol Benedict,[5] it is likely that water pipes were brought into China's southern ports by Indian traders in the 18th century, while the concept of smoking shredded tobacco rolled in old newspapers was was introduced to China from the 1830s by Filipino traders.

As a non-essential crop, tobacco gained status as an auxiliary product for those who were above the hunger and poverty level. Whether used as snuff or smoked in pipes, tobacco became a distinctly leisure activity, associated with rest and relaxation. Initially popular with lower-class men and women, the consumption of tobacco soon gained an elite appeal. Unlike peasants, who used tobacco indiscriminately, consumption by aristocrats was segregated by gender and space. While men could consume tobacco in public, or indeed in any place they wished, aristocratic women were limited to enjoying tobacco in the private space of their rooms.

The 'inner quarter' is a Chinese euphemism for a woman's private chambers. Whether it was a wife or one of many concubines, the inner chamber was the place where women resided, worked and slept, or where they conducted business if they were courtesans or prostitutes. During the Qing Dynasty, the practice of smoking tobacco and opium in a long pipe was regarded as an invitation to, and an aid to, sex. Thus, the act of smoking in private quarters came to embody undertones of eroticism, a concept that would later become pervasive in BAT's cigarette advertising campaigns and emulated in advertisements for other consumer products.

As Benedict notes the consumption of tobacco in China continued despite official bans, which were enacted on numerous occasions. The Korean author of *Simyang Changye* (Letters from Shenyang)[6] recorded in 1638 that, 'There is a prohibition [of tobacco] in the capital [of Shenyang], but it is still used without restriction because it is desired by everyone'. Introduced, cultivated and sold throughout China without stigma, as a new form of cash crop, tobacco was accepted in society as an exotic, modern arrival from distant foreign lands. The appeal of its novelty, and its addictive quality, entrenched the use of tobacco in China.

According to Benedict, during the late Qing Dynasty, the water pipe, rather than the long tobacco pipe, became emblematic of the

Figure 3: Late Qing Dynasty beauty ca. 1900, Shandong Province ookami_dou on flickr. Posted by Lu Tianqi on Pinterest

upper class and signified the gentility of a noble woman.[7] Indeed, a basic internet search using the key words 'Qing Dynasty women with water pipe' yields an abundance of images of beautifully groomed Chinese ladies photographed in studios with water pipes as visible accoutrements in luxurious interior settings.

The carefully crafted images of young women with elegant water pipes placed on a table or held in their hands visually assert their high status, which is further reinforced by the size of their tiny bound feet. With no chores or domestic duties to attend to, the young ladies in these portraits are poised and groomed, exuding an aura of luxury, comfort and wealth. However, we must not forget that these are staged images, constructed in a controlled environment. The women would not ordinarily have appeared in such finery, with such perfectly coiffed hair and powdered makeup. The photo is, therefore, far from mundane, since it was likely commissioned to give to a matchmaker to find a suitable husband, or perhaps to be used as a courtesan's calling card.

Notably, in addition to her elaborate attire and elegant pose, the young woman is surrounded by objects of sophistication and discrimination, such as ink paintings, artisan-crafted furniture, and teacups. For all her finery, none which may actually belong to her, the image of youth and beauty is purposefully linked to the water pipe, which according to photo historian Régine Thiriez,[8] was usually included at the subject's request. The use of a water pipe contrasted directly with the more old-fashioned long pipe, which by this period was associated with the smoking practices of peasants and the elderly.

These opulent photographs circulated in society to indirectly advertise the refined use of tobacco, to associate it with an aura of decadence, and to appeal to the leisurely male gaze. The combination of an alluring young woman as muse and her association with a product to be consumed were to become a powerful visual stimulant as objects of desire for men, who wished to possess them, as well as for women, who wished to fashion themselves after them.

The shift to the refined, filtered flavour of machine-rolled cigarettes brought about a decrease in the use of water pipes. By the time BAT came to be formally established in China in 1902, the American journalist and advertising mogul Carl Crow observed that 'cigarettes have almost entirely replaced the old-fashioned water-pipe in China'.[9]

After the introduction of cigarettes into China, sales figures climbed from 1.24 billion units of cartons in 1902 to 12 billion in 1916, with BAT achieving a company valuation of $20.75 million USD and net profits of $3.75 million USD.[10] By 1937, over 80 billion cigarettes were being sold in China, despite numerous boycotts of foreign goods. BAT's lucrative success was not only derived from the volume of sales, but also from the favourable tax policies of the Treaty of Nanjing. All foreign enterprises benefited tremendously from these, which stipulated that imports were exempt from tariffs and additional levies, including domestic transit tolls. Between the production of low-grade tobacco in China as well as importation of the premium, grade yellow or bright leaf tobacco from North Carolina and the eventual cultivation of bright leaf in China, BAT was able to monopolise and exploit the supply chain to its advantage. As the industry leader, the company dominated cigarette sales in China, amassing annual growth ranging between 61% and 82% from the 1910s until the annexation of the business by the Japanese in 1941.[11]

Image Formation in Cigarette Advertising

Annual calendars in China were, and still are, used to decorate homes and shops. In order to increase the lifespan of paper-based advertisements, many advertising posters, also known as 'hangers', came with the added-value feature of a calendar; generally covering a year but some covered two. These were distributed as Chinese New Year gifts by companies to customers as auspicious greetings and tokens of thanks. According to the art historian Francesca Dal Lago, a calendar poster was included with the purchase of a 50-pack carton of cigarettes. As such, they also became a marketing ploy, a gift-with-purchase to encourage people to buy in greater bulk during the gifting season.[12]

In 1915, BAT expanded its advertising department composed of American, British, Japanese, German and Chinese artists.[13] The visual potency of their lithographic prints was far superior to the rough-hewn, black-and-white woodblock prints being used in China for textual advertisements. In addition, the range of colours and modern composition used in their prints heightened naturalistic realism and accentuated the poster's glamourous novelty, one not seen before in China.

At BAT's Shanghai agency, high-level Chinese artists were recruited from the ateliers of master painters and professional art academies, while apprentices with no training were often hired through the family connections of company artists. Much as with its factory production, BAT's advertising department operated as a standardised assembly line, where the apprentices painted the backgrounds while the more experienced artists drew and painted the human figures. According to the art historian Ellen Johnston Laing,[14] the division of labour confined some Chinese artists to mostly working on colour illustrations, while others were responsible for black-and-white newspaper ads. The younger apprentices were relegated to drawing the cigarette packages in the adverts, and some were tasked with hand-writing the English inscriptions, which proved to be a challenge since many could not read or write what they were copying. For commissioned works, the artists were provided exact specifications and were not permitted to deviate or add their own creative or artistic touches. This explains, in part, why many of the commercial illustrators have received little or no attention in the canons of Chinese art history and remain relegated to the genre of design rather than fine arts.

Unlike most jobs, where employees were expected to remain in their positions until they resigned or were fired, the Chinese artists in Shanghai's advertising industry were free agents, taking on work at multiple firms. According to Laing, 'artists could accept commissions from other businesses and often moved from one firm to another … In addition to in-house advertising departments, independent advertising agencies under foreign and native management sprang up to provide services to smaller companies that could not afford their own advertising departments'.

Since artists free-lanced, and went from one job to another, they also opted to take short cuts by appropriating the designs and formats they had created for one brand to use at another. Prior to the acknowledgment of copyright, the artists believed that the designs and illustrations they created belonged to them, rather than the company. This practice had to have been a source of frustration for

BAT executives since original designs and concepts were often reused by the Chinese artists; not only for competing cigarette brands but also for other commodities such as tonics, alcohol, and face creams. These practices often made the advertisements' compositions indistinguishable from one another, with some featuring the same models. Moreover, as photography came into wider use, many of the *yuefenpai* were painted from photographs taken from American mass media. This process of mimicry heightened the repetitive appearance of the images in circulation, achieving a sense of visual redundancy as well as familiarity.

CONSTRUCTING THE CIGARETTE BRAND

In China, prior to the arrival of European and American companies, the modernist idea of associating a corporate identity to the product was transmitted by Japanese businessmen. Established under the Mitsui Trading Company, the Murai Brothers Tobacco Company from Kyoto was the largest cigarette manufacturer in East Asia prior to the arrival of BAT. Having established a base in Shanghai as early as 1897,[15] Murai cigarettes were marketed under the Peacock brand, emblazoned with a distinctive logo of the exotic bird from the distant land of India.

This move was novel in China, since tobacco was an undifferentiated agricultural crop. Yet for cigarettes, the practice of forging a brand had been a fundamental business model used since the 1860s by the Egyptians.[16] Packaged in a compact, portable box, the foreign cursive lettering of the Murai Brothers Co. Ltd. name was visually melded to the image of the peacock to create a memory association. Some two-thirds of the population in China was illiterate at the time, and very few were able to read the English letters, thus, the foreign script became as exotic as the image of the alluring bird.

Since posters were created through the process of lithography, later

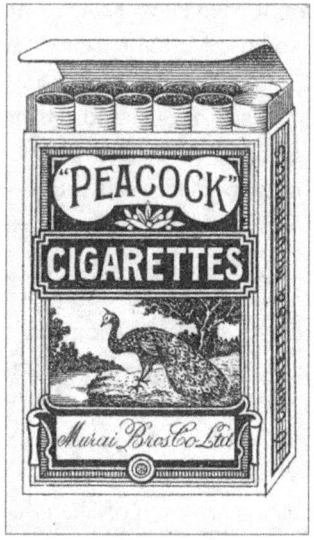

Figure 4: Murai Brothers Co. Ltd. Peacock brand cigarette, ca 1897-1904; Photo by cigcardpix on flickr

Figure 5: Artist Zhou Baisheng, Nanyang Brothers Tobacco Company Ltd., 1920s
Images from Classic and Vintage Print

versions could be reproduced weeks, months and even years after the first print run. The subsequent practice of reprinting can make it difficult to precisely date the month or year of the *yuefenpai*, or even to identify who had created it. One Murai advertisement that featured a tastefully dressed Modern Girl in a languid pose holding a cigarette, was not created by Murai at all, but by BAT, who in 1904, had taken over the Murai Brothers Tobacco Company.[17]

BAT was able to exercise creative liberties in China. It was the first agency to depict women, specifically Chinese women, in the act of smoking, with a cigarette in hand. This was over a decade before cigarette advertising agencies could attempt such a move in Great Britain and the US, due to conservative societal attitudes against women smoking.[18]

BAT's main competitor, the Nanyang Brothers Tobacco Company, founded in Hong Kong in 1905,[19] took advantage of the 1915 National Products Movement in China by deploying the 'New Woman' (新女性) as a symbol of patriotism to advocate the notion that beautiful, modern ladies supported native products, including Chinese-brand cigarettes. By linking young mothers to national efforts, the Nanyang Brothers Tobacco advertisement celebrated stylish mothers as virtuous Chinese beauties surrounded by chubby babies and healthy children.

While it has been argued by historians such as Karl Gerth[20] that displays of wifely domesticity linked women's moral sensibilities to the support of national causes, another plausible reading, by both male and female viewers, was the desire of married women to remain sexy and attractive in the eyes of men, especially to wealthy husbands who could afford extramarital affairs or to take in multiple women. According to the historian Gail Hershatter,[21] it was customary for the wealthy men of Shanghai to keep a wife, a concubine and several mistresses. For example, D. V. Woo (Wu Tongwen), who, in his famous residence, Green House, was able to keep his wife and mistress on separate floors of the immense mansion.

The practice of keeping a concubine, a vestige of premodern Asian tradition, was still very much alive in the age of modernity in China. In fact, concubinage did not become illegal until 1950, a year after the Chinese Communist Party came to power.[22] The male-centric acceptance of keeping mistresses during the Republican era underscores the prevailing lack of basic social and legal rights for women in China, even during the age of modernity when women had supposedly been liberated to be the 'Modern Woman'.

Consequently, cigarette advertisements featuring voluptuous mothers sent competing and ambiguous messages to conservative women, who were not passive observers of posters and calendar pictorials. In the aftermath of the 1919 May 4th Movement, the wives who formed the Women's National Products Association (妇女国货会) proclaimed that Chinese women who used imported products were considered prostitutes for degrading their bodies with corrupt foreign goods and betraying the national economy, and thereby the nation.[23]

Ironically, BAT's earlier cigarette adverts, which featured mothers and children, did not prompt the same indignation, possibly because the portrayal of women in earlier *yuefenpai* were presented as appearing traditional and aligning with the style favoured by the members of the Women's National Products Association. Yet, the fact that these Chinese mothers in BAT's advertisements were also promoting foreign cigarettes seemed to have gone completely unnoticed.

Paradoxically, in the aftermath of the 1934 Women's National Goods Year, when gender was directly linked to patriotism and national products, there was a sharp increase in the wide-spread use of the sexy mother with child/children image in cigarette advertising campaigns. Throughout the 1930s and into the early 1940s, domestic companies including the Nanyang Brothers Tobacco Company, the Qingdao China Shandong Tobacco Company, the Harbin Qiulin Tobacco Company and the Fengtian Taiyang Tobacco Company all used such

Figure 6: British American Tobacco Company advertising its range of cigarettes, ca. 1910
From: Museum of Foreign Brand Advertising in The ROC (MOFBA)

imagery.

Despite the formation of anti-cigarette societies and the publication of articles and editorials about the damaging health effects of smoking cigarettes (and opium) that began appearing frequently in Chinese newspapers,[24] one notable and attractive aspect of cigarettes was that they symbolised equality since anyone, old or young, wealthy or poor, Chinese or foreigner, male or female, had access to them. In Shanghai, cigarettes of varying quality and price range, in tin packs, foil boxes or even individual sticks, could be bought at the thousands of tobacco-and-paper convenience stores (烟纸店) throughout the city. According to Benedict, the cigarette adverts were targeted at 'particular social groups in distinct locales, [from] Shanghai's new professional salaried class, petty urbanites, and factory workers…dockworkers and boatmen' to promote a democratic society of smokers. Indeed, there was a brand, a flavour and a price point to suit any willing consumer.[25]

LOCALISING THE BRAND

BAT manufactured an assortment of brands to meet wide-ranging customer demand. Aside from Pinhead and Peacock, there was also Pirate, Atlas, and Chienmen amongst others, but its proprietary brand was Ruby Queen. Simultaneously packaged as Da Ying (大英), literally meaning 'Great England', Ruby Queen was not the company's highest grade nor its most expensive brand, but its main selling point was that it was made with 100% bright leaf tobacco. Ruby Queen and Da Ying were to become the best-selling brand in China, due to its mid-range price and mystique of an occidental aura.[26]

Zheng Bozhao (郑伯昭) is one name that has not received due attention. According to an extensive study published by historian Nan Enstad,[27] Zheng was the 'single most significant entrepreneur in the branding and marketing of Ruby Queen cigarettes'. Born in 1863 in what is today's Zhongshan City in Guangdong Province, Zheng joined BAT in 1905, only three years after the company was established in Shanghai. He first earned trust as an interpreter, since many of BAT's foreign executives were unable to speak or understand Chinese fluently. By 1912, Zheng had been promoted to a new position in charge of the distribution of Ruby Queen cigarettes, for which he achieved phenomenal success using his strong *guanxi*, the cultivation of reciprocal relations, with business associates from his native Guangdong Province. It was Zheng who renamed the brand

Ruby Queen as Da Ying to underscore the cigarette's unmistakable British association in the aftermath of the wide-spread 1905 anti-American product boycott. It was also Zheng's idea to brand Ruby Queen in English lettering and Da Ying in Chinese characters so that, despite being the same product, the packaging captured the differentiated customer bases of locals and foreigners.

Zheng's success also resulted from his foresight in fully exploiting brand appeal. Rather than cramming the company's various cigarette brands together under a single advertisement banner, as BAT and its competitors had previously been prone to do, Zheng requested that Ruby Queen be singled out.

Figure 7: Artist Ding Yuxian, BAT's Ruby Queen cigarette advertisement, ca. 1920s

When he and his sales team visited cigarette dealers and retailers, they staged parades and opened street kiosks to give away free cigarettes and calendar posters. More importantly, they hired cheap labourers to plaster Ruby Queen and Da Ying posters across the city's walls. Inundating public spaces with advertisements wasn't new to China, but BAT's high-quality colour illustrations were unprecedented. According to Enstad, Zheng's ingenious move constituted 'BAT's earliest changes in branding to satisfy Chinese customers'; an important strategy that would be later redeployed with BAT's Hatamen cigarettes.

Inevitably, Zheng Bozhao became an influential force at BAT. In 1921, with the company's backing, he established the Yongtaihe Tobacco Company, Ltd., a subsidiary that helped achieve two items on BAT's agenda. The first was to hold onto Zheng, so that he would not create a company of his own and pose direct competition. The second was to create the public perception of a Chinese cigarette company, but whose profits would still be channelled to BAT. The development of an inexpensive, low-grade cigarette, specifically a Chinese national brand called Hatamen (哈德门), followed the same calculating tactics

Zheng had established with Ruby Queen.

Launched in 1924, Hatamen was a direct response to the fever-pitched National Products Movement and anti-foreign sentiment resulting from the May 4th Movement of 1919. The Hatamen brand's perceived support of nationalism and accessible price swiftly won over customers and critics alike with a marketing strategy that proved innovative, starting with its name. Hatamen is a reference to Chongwenmen (崇文门), the inner city gate in Beijing, constructed in 1419 and later demolished in 1968. The Arrow Tower of Chongwenmen was destroyed by British artillery in 1900, during the Boxer Rebellion.[28] The ill omens of this historical conflict with the British appeared to have been ameliorated when the western side of Chongwenmen was later turned into an embassy district, home to many foreigners. Thus, as a name, Hatamen was a metaphor for restored relations with the British.

There was another element to the Hatamen name-play that aimed to appeal to men's sexual urges. The women featured in these adverts were consistently young and alluring. In Chinese concubinage, the term *zhai dou* (宅斗) was used to refer to the resident ingénue, while *gong dou* (宫斗) was a term for palace or harem intrigue. Hatamen was actually pronounced as *ha-dou-men* (哈斗门) with 'ha' also being a slang word, meaning to adore or be infatuated with someone. The brand conflated the erotic association of girls as 'gates' (门) to infatuating or adoring intrigue.

Hatamen followed on the heels of a previous 'domestic national' brand developed in 1922 by Zheng's Yongtaihe. The cigarette, named Shuang Shi (双十) or 'double ten', was an ingenious reference to the tenth anniversary of the founding of the Chinese Republic on 10 October 1912. Given the Chinese penchant for auspicious numbers, what could be more nationalistic than a brand called 10.10 released to memorialise the tenth year of the Republic? While considered Chinese brands, BAT oversaw all aspects of the production, distribution and advertising at the Yongtaihe Tobacco

Figure 8: BAT's Hatamen cigarette ad

Company. Sinicised brands such as Shuang Shi and Hatamen ensured that foreign vestiges of BAT remained invisible in localised cigarette markets. The enduring appeal of these two brands still exists today despite the dissolution of BAT in China. When cigarette production came under the state jurisdiction of the China National Tobacco Corporation (CNTC) in 1982, the brands Hatamen and Shuang Shi were revived. Shuang Shi has come to be identified with 'double happiness' and is given to guests at weddings in China. It is the largest brand by volume and according to the CNTC website, 'aims to replicate its domestic success in international markets'.[29]

Public Personas, Private Desires

While cigarette companies gave complimentary calendar posters as gifts with purchases around the Chinese New Year period, excess calendars were sold on the mass market. With an eye on profit, however small that may have been, hawkers found ingenious ways to sell the calendars as home decorations. As the historian Leo Ou-Fan Lee[30] has written in his studies of Shanghai's urban culture, the cigarette company's calendar posters became a 'fixture of daily urban life'.

Yet, where would these posters actually have been hung in the home? Very few published sources provide concrete answers to this issue. Just as now, in the early decades of the twentieth century, Chinese homes varied greatly in size, from large mansions to humble communal residential homes, known in Shanghai as *lilong*. While there are spacious single dwelling homes in China, which have grown in number over the years, they are still fewer in number than the one or two-bedroom flats in high rise apartment complexes throughout the mainland.

From my experience of being invited to the homes of many Chinese friends, colleagues and acquaintances in Shanghai and Beijing, as well as lodging in guesthouses in the remote provinces of Guizhou, Fujian and Gansu, I've noticed that contemporary calendars tend to be hung predominantly in bedrooms rather than living rooms. While smaller calendars can be found on desks or the kitchen counter, hanging calendars, especially ones featuring contemporary models or scantily attired pop stars, tend to be hung in the private quarters of the bedroom. Similarly, *yuefenpai* are often hung in the bedrooms of memorial homes that have been converted to public museums.

The bedroom was and still is a place of private sanctuary, a place of rest but also of sexual pleasure. The alluring gaze of fashionably dressed women obviously caters to the male gaze. Yet, no study has explored the relationship of the female gaze to these images. If a woman was married and her husband was a dedicated smoker, he would most likely have received the complimentary calendar with his New Year's purchases, which either he or his wife would then have used to decorate the bedroom. If a wealthy woman was a heavy smoker, she would also have received the calendar poster. If a woman was an occasional smoker or even a non-smoker of modest means, she would be able to buy a calendar of her choice from a street vendor, since the cost was relatively inexpensive.

The advertising agent Carl Crow noted, 'we once produced a large, lithographed hanger for an American cigarette company which sold readily at 25 cents [$3.70 today], actually a few cents more than the cost of production. Chinese buy these hangers as works of art and use them to decorate their homes and see nothing especially objectionable in the fact that they may advertise a cigarette or a brand of cod liver oil'.[31]

The changing images of seductive young women portrayed in *yuefenpai* served a dual purpose: as a visual aid for men's sexual fantasies, and as an aspiration for women seeking to become modern, whether that meant keeping up with changing trends or finding her own sense of liberation. A Chinese observer lamented in 1912 in *Shenbao*, the first Chinese newspaper,[32]

> I have seen Western-clothed prostitutes in rickshaws, with cigarettes in their hands, spewing smoke incessantly along the journey. Whatever the style of clothing the courtesans wear, respectable women soon imitate. Now that smoking cigarettes is so fashionable, probably in a few months time, respectable women will also be smoking.

The distinction between a proper woman and a debauched one in possession of a cigarette was not the cigarette itself, but rather the space she occupied when smoking it. The gendered designation of space that had begun with tobacco consumption in water pipes also carried over to cigarettes, maintaining that men could smoke everywhere, but cultured and elite women were only permitted to do so within the confines of their home and bedroom. So, when a wife, a female or a professional courtesan lit up a cigarette in public the woman's ability to partake in what was an exclusively male privilege granted them a commensurate standing, even if that satisfaction was limited to the duration of the smoke.

Over time, as more and more women began to boldly smoke in the public domain, the anxiety and disgust of men and conservative women germinated to discriminate against the women who openly defied social conventions. While there is no consensus as to what defined the 'Modern' or the 'New Woman', certain characteristics were key to the construction of their stereotypes. A 'Modern/New Woman' wore her hair short and bobbed and refused to bind her feet. She embraced western attire, flapper dresses and even masculine suits, and participated in sports like a man.[33] She smoked cigarettes in full public view as a sign of her defiance of tradition and came to be admonished by even the most progressive of revolutionaries, such as the essayist Lu Xun, himself a lifelong smoker. In 1930, he decried the image of the 'Modern Woman' presented in calendars as decadent and counter-revolutionary, claiming,[34]

Figure 9: Zheng Mantuo (1888-1963) Advertisement for Nanyang Brothers Tobacco Company, ca. 1927

> Today…calendar posters are popular with ordinary people in Chinese society. The women in calendar posters are sick. Not only are calendar painters unskilled but the subjects of their paintings are disgusting and depraved. China has lots of women who are strong and healthy, but calendar painters only draw sickly ladies so weak that they could be knocked down by a gust of wind. This kind of sickness does not come from society. It comes from the painters.

The depravity brought on by the 'Modern Woman' is exemplified in the cigarette advertisement designed by Zheng Mantuo where two Chinese women in the latest western dress, with legs exposed, are merrily dancing in close contact with one another.

While Zheng was considered a high-level

commercial illustrator, he nonetheless had to follow the requirements of the advertising agencies. Chinese scholars like Xinmei Tan[35] have nothing but praise for Zheng, whom she believes championed China's cause by painting patriotic cigarette advertisements for the Nanyang Brothers Tobacco Company. Yet, Zheng, like Hang Zhiying, who painted numerous portraits of topless Chinese women, recognised that higher profits came from commissions which requested depictions of nudity, sex and taboo subjects.

Certainly, there would have been a wide range of complicated responses to female representations in *yuefenpai*, which were divided not only amongst men but even more so amongst women, although preserved personal accounts remain difficult to locate. While conservative women baulked at the debauched imagery of the 'Modern Woman', Benedict[36] notes that liberal-minded women embraced the cigarette by associating it with intellectual activity, specifically poetry, literature and even keeping current on popular culture. When a courtesan smoked a cigarette in the company of men, it signalled her cultured status as one equal in knowledge to men. Intellectual women were invited to partake in tobacco and cigarettes with male colleagues precisely because they could keep pace with them. According to Benedict, it was the educated, urban women who 'increasingly participated in political movements and social reforms efforts that marked the New Policies Era'. The blatant affront of women smoking in public was one of the most powerful signs of personal emancipation for the many women who felt oppressed by traditional society.

Figure 10: China Fuchang Cigarette Company (中国福昌煙公司) ca. 1920s
Shanghai Propaganda Poster Art Centre. Photo by Julie Chun, 2019

The fact that certain women were able to cross over into the space of men led to criticisms and attacks on those who fashioned themselves to take on the role of a man by, for example, supporting themselves, having a profession or being comfortable in the company of men. Communities of women united by sexual dissidence and non-normative desires also expressed that to be modern was to explore one's sexuality and to defy socially-accepted heterosexual standards. The conventional 'two sisters' image of women in adverts promoting alcohol, tobacco and cosmetics became laden with overtones of sexual ambiguity and promiscuity.

As the years progressed from the 1920s to the 1940s, subtle and even direct voyeuristic connotations of lesbian eroticism increased, as did the appearance of women who cross-dressed as men. The growing body of queer studies, such as those by Gender Studies Professor Tze-Lan D. Sang, reveal that 'the growing visibility, or increasing discursive production, of female same-sex desire in modern Chinese culture in the 1910s and 1920s reflected Chinese women's changing economic, social, and political status—above all, upper and middle-class women's entrance into wage labour, women's unprecedented participation in public life, and women's relative economic independence from the patriarchal family'.[37]

These societal shifts, which were exacerbated by the anxiety born of foreign occupation and the ideological division between the Guomindang and the Communists added to the ambivalence of the times, which was reflected not only in the images of the *yuefenpai* that dominated the landscape of Shanghai's public and private realms, but also were written in the literature of the era by female novelists, such as Lu Yin, Ling Shuhua, Ding Ling, Yu Dafu, and Zhang Yiping.

FACTORY GIRLS

Of all its diverse modes of factories, BAT was the single, largest employer in Shanghai in the early twentieth century. According to Nan Enstad,[38] there were hundreds of American and British citizens working for the company, but low-wage Chinese employees far exceeded them in number. By 1918, twenty-five thousand Chinese labourers worked in BAT's cigarette factories, and by the mid-1930s, Enstad[39] writes that there were approximately two million Chinese farmers cultivating bright leaf tobacco in the three main provinces of Shandong, Anhui and Hunan. According to estimates by the economist Thomas Rawski, the number of labourers in cigarette factories increased at an annual rate of 26 to 30 per cent during those years while cigarette production expanded at a rate of 20 per cent per year.[40] There was contraction in growth during the foreign goods boycott years, but as soon as the protests subsided, BAT's production and sales growth continued to surge.

What had not received much attention until Enstad's discovery of Qian Meifeng's 1963 interview transcript at the Economic Research Institute at the Shanghai Academy of Social Sciences,[41] was that women, including young girls, made up two-thirds of the workforce in tobacco factories in China. Qian herself was only nine years old when she began working in BAT's Hongkou District cigarette packing factory. Young girls were considered to have nimble fingers, and their age justified the basest of low wages, which, according to historian Sherman Cochran, was merely 0.20 to 0.50 yuan per day;[42] a fact confirmed by a foreign manager of the Pudong plant, who reported in 1932 that the amount the girls received was not enough to sustain a living. Furthermore, the opportunities for advancement at the factories were low or non-existent. In 1903, James Duke, who never visited China, stated that his company hired women because it was 'all light, easy work'; a false claim given the reality of twelve to eighteen-hour workdays.[43]

The girls were often recruited from the then poor region of Zhejiang Province and often lived with relatives or in ghettos near the factories. According to Qian, Chinese male and female supervisors regulated disciplinary regimes, including the segregation of the sexes, and distinguished different jobs with colour-coded uniforms. Free cigarettes were used as a form of reward. The practice of hiring mostly female factory workers was common throughout many factories in Shanghai, including at BAT's most significant competitor, the Nanyang Brothers Tobacco company. They went as far as to only hire young girls with connections to the company owners' hometowns. Gender discrimination was rampant. Women had to wear uniforms while men did not, and while men received 50-100 free cigarettes a week, female workers only received 50 cigarettes a year, which they sold to tobacco shops to supplement their livelihoods.[44]

The dire working conditions, uncovered by Enstad, included physical beatings of the girls and an unhygienic environment in which some mothers ended up delivering babies in factory toilets. Tensions finally erupted into protests and strikes by the female workforce, who sought better working conditions. Enstad lists fifty-six strikes by female workers at cigarette factories between 1918 and 1940. In 1928, the factory girls made history by negotiating with BAT's upper management to form a union and to bargain collectively. This was a full seven years before tobacco factory workers in America gained similar rights. Despite this small victory, the Chinese girls had to protest continually and organise regular strikes to avoid dismissal without due cause and to get compensation for job-related injuries, six weeks paid maternity leave, health benefits, and company-funded schooling for the children of mothers who worked at the Pudong factory. Black-and-white photos of factory girls in sordid work environments are a world away from the glamourous depictions of the 'Modern Women' in *yuefenpai*, yet ironically, it was in the space of the very same factories where cigarettes were produced and packaged that young women - specifically young girls - rose to the occasion and sought justice, and a path towards basic human rights.

In Conclusion

To be 'modern' in Shanghai during the 1910s to 1940s signified both liberty and oppression for women. There was the freedom for a woman to transform herself physically by cutting her hair, donning western attire and smoking cigarettes in public like a man. Yet, the social norms that governed how filial and pious women were to behave, especially in distinctly male spaces, remained deeply constrained. Most women had little choice but to turn to the private space of the bedroom to smoke, to gaze upon the images of the beauties presented in *yuefenpai* and to project her desires and fantasies. As historian Susan Buck Morss[45] has asserted, Chinese modernity was constructed as a cultural imaginary.

Regarding the *yuefenpai*, did cigarette advertisements empower women? In certain ways, I believe they did. The images provided housewives and young women with the opportunity to smoke as equals with their husbands and other men; tragically so, as the ill effects and health hazards of smoking were little known at the time. Most importantly, however, the cigarette brought the discourse of the 'Modern Woman' into full view, as images of smoking women were plastered all over urban cities and rural provinces. There is obviously no denying that the images exploited women by conjuring false perceptions of wealth and beauty, but these were also subtly and directly contested and challenged by defiant women who fought against convention. The story of the cigarette in China reveals an intricate web of complexity and complicity that still awaits further unravelling.

China is now the world's leading producer and consumer of cigarettes. Today, the state-owned tobacco industry produces 2.2 trillion cigarettes annually, and over 300 million men and 20 million women in China have become regular smokers.[46] As in the early decades of the twentieth century, product placement in films and the fashion industry is once again being used to entice young girls to smoke and to associate cigarettes with glamour, modernity and independence. The narrative of cultivating the desire for cigarettes continues, albeit with trendy and lavish updates. No doubt, the pull can be alluring. Much as was the case a century ago, to smoke a cigarette is to assert rebellion, independence, youthfulness, and short-lived beauty in the face of impending death.

Acknowledgment

I'd like to thank George Godula for sharing a pivotal book with me and providing images and factoids from his website *The Little Museum of Foreign Brand Advertising in the ROC*. I would also like to acknowledge Fudan University PhD candidate Edward Allen for our discussions about Hatamen, and I express my gratitude to the urban researcher Xu Ming of Urban Archeo for assisting me in locating the present site of BAT's factory in Pudong.

Julie Chun *(julie.arthistory@gmail.com) is an American art historian, based in Shanghai since 2011. She has lectured and taught East Asian art history in global programs at the Shanghai University of Finance and Economics, Donghua University and the CIEE at the East China Normal University. Since 2013, she has served as the Art Focus Convenor of the Royal Asiatic Society in China (artgroup@royalasiaticsociety.org.cn) where she devotes her time to expanding the public's understanding of artistic objects, past and present. As a regular contributor to* Yishu Journal of Contemporary Art, *her reviews and criticisms have also been published in academic and art journals, both in China and internationally.*

References

1. For an analysis of the depictions of Chinese women on cigarette cards, see Gao, Jie. 'Refining modern beauties: The evolving depiction of Chinese women in cigarette cards, 1900-37' *East Asian Journal of Popular Culture*, vol. 4, no. 2, June 2018, pp. 237-254.
2. Milov, Sarah, *The Cigarette: A Political History* Harvard University Press, Cambridge and London (2019)

3. From an interview with James B. Duke in a British tobacco trade journal. Re-quoted in Enstad, Nan, *Cigarettes, Inc.* (2008), p. 13, pp.23-25
4. Cochran, Sherman, *Big Business in China: Sino-Foreign Rivalry in the Cigarette Industry 1890-1930* Harvard University Press, Cambridge, MA (1980), p.14
5. Benedict, Carol, *Golden-Silk Smoke: A History of Tobacco in China, 1150-2000* Berkeley and Los Angeles: University of California Press (2011), p. 134
6. 'Simyang changgye' (Letters from Shenyang, 1637-43), *Kaiguo Shiliao (Historical Materials on the Founding of the Country)*, 3:7 (1970)
7. Benedict, Carol provides an extensive study of the use of water pipes in China in *Golden-Silk Smoke* (2011)
8. Thiriez, Régine, 'Photography and Portraiture in Nineteenth-Century China', *East*, p.126
Asian History, 17–18 (June–December), pp. 77–102
9. Crow, Carl, *Four Hundred Million Customers*, Halcyon House, New York (1937), p.5
10. Cochran, Sherman, *Big Business in China* (1980) p. 11
11. Cox, Howard, 'Learning to Do Business in China: The Evolution of BAT's Distribution Network, 1902-41', *Business History*, vol. 39, no. 3 (1997) pp. 30-64
12. Dal Lago, Francesca. 'Crossed Legs in 1930s Shanghai: How 'Modern' was the Modern Woman?' *East Asian History* (19 June 2000), pp. 103–44
13. Laing, Ellen Johnston, *Selling Happiness: Calendar Posters and Visual Culture in Early Twentieth-Century Shanghai*, University of Hawai'i Press, Honolulu (2004), p.68
14. Laing, Ellen Johnston, *Selling Happiness* (2004), pp.68-69
15. Benedict, Carol, *Golden-Silk Smoke* (2011), p. 135
16. Shechter, Relli, 'Selling Luxury: The Rise of the Egyptian Cigarette and the Transformation of the Egyptian Tobacco Market, 1850-1914', *International Journal of Middle Eastern Studies*, vol. 35, no. 1, February (2003), pp. 51-75
17. Benedict, Carol, *Golden-Silk Smoke* (2011), p. 202
18. Tinkler, Penny, 'Red Tips for Hot Lips: Advertising Cigarettes for Young Women in Britain, 1920-70', *Women's History Review*, vol. 10, no. 2 (2001), 251

19. Cochran, Sherman, *Big Business in China* (1980), p. 56
20. Gerth, Karl, *China Made: Consumer Culture and the Creation of the Nation*, Cambridge and London: Harvard University Press (2003)
21. Hershatter, Gail, *Dangerous Pleasures: Prostitution and Modernity in Twentieth-Century Shanghai* Berkeley, University of California Press (1997)
22. Li, Yuhui, 'Women's Movement and Change of Women's Status in China', *Journal of International Women's Studies*, vol. 1, issue 1, (January 2000), p. 31
23. Gerth, Karl, *China Made* (2003)
24. Benedict, Carol, *Golden Smoke* (2011), p.217
25. Benedict, Carol, *Golden-Silk Smoke* (2011), p. 132
26. Benedict, Carol, *Golden-Silk Smoke* (2011), p. 166
27. Enstad, Nan, *Cigarettes, Inc* (2008), pp. 157-165
28. The History of the Hataman gate: <https://archive.ph/20130628182104/http://www.bjlyjszx.com/news/2013-05-03/1713963939.htm>, pp. 157-165
29. China National Tobacco Corporation (CNTC) website <https://www.ctbati.com/en/brands/our-products.php> [accessed 25 September 2022]
30. Lee, Leo Ou-fan, 'Shanghai Modern: Reflections on Urban Culture in China in the 1930s', *Public Culture*, 11:1 (1 January 1999), pp. 75-107
31. Crow, Carl, *Four Hundred Million Customers* (1937), p. 44.
32. *Shenbao*, 22 June 1912, p .9
33. Benedict, Carol, *Golden-Silk Smoke* (2011), p. 222
34. Translated in Cochran, Sherman, 'Marketing Medicine and Advertising Dreams in China, 1900-1950' in *Becoming Chinese: Passage to Modernity and Beyond*, ed. Wen-hsin Yeh University of California Press (2000), p.62
35. Tan Xinmei, 'Research on Calendar Design Philosophy of Zheng Mantuo', *Advances in Social Science, Education and Humanities Research*, volume 144 (2007), pp. 368-372
36. Throughout her book Benedict, Carol presents this case of tobacco/cigarette consumption and intellectual women and courtesans in *Golden-Silk Smoke* (2011)
37. Sang, Tze-Lan D., *The Emerging Lesbian: The Female Same-Sex Desire in Modern China*, University of Chicago Press (2003)
38. Enstad, Nan, *Cigarettes, Inc* (2008) p.122

39. Enstad, Nan, *Cigarettes, Inc.* (2008) p. 101
40. Rawski, Thomas, Economic Growth in Prewar China (Berkeley: University of California Press, 1989), p. 355.
41. Enstad, Nan, *Cigarettes, Inc* (2008), p. 120, p. 127
42. Cochran, Sherman, *Big Business in China* (1980), p. 25
43. Tiley, Nannie M., *The Bright Tobacco Industry, 1860-1929*, Chapel Hill: University of North Carolina Press, (1948) p.45
44. Enstad, Nan, *Cigarettes, Inc* (2008), p. 136, pp. 138-139
45. Morss, Susan Buck, *Dialectic of Seeing*, Cambridge, MA: MIT Press (1991) revised ed.
46. Benedict, Carol, *Golden-Silk Smoke* (2011), pp. 240-241

SWEET DREAMS: THE KIESSLING CAFÉ, CHINA'S FIRST CROSS-PROVINCIAL CONFECTIONERY CHAIN

By George Godula

Abstract

One will not find a Chinese person in Tianjin who isn't familiar with the famous Kiessling Café and Restaurant. Likewise, others with an interest in China, be it as tourists, business travellers, expats, authors or researchers will have come across its emblematic name. The iconic Kiessling Café and Restaurant was founded around the turn of the twentieth century in Tianjin (then spelled Tientsin) by restaurateur Albert Kiessling. Its confectioneries, cakes, ice cream and Western dishes earned it a rightful place in the hearts and bellies of Tianjin's foreign and Chinese communities, and it operates to this day on Jianshe Road, Heping district.

Throughout the eatery's tumultuous history, spanning three epochs from the Qing Dynasty to the Republic of China to the People's Republic of China, it was frequented by emperors, presidents, politicians, authors, actors, socialites, criminals, Nazi double agents and ordinary Westerners and Chinese alike.

The history of the Kiessling is ultimately the story of an immigrant family enterprise, that, against all odds, in a foreign land and through famine, floods, earthquakes, wars and regime changes, persevered to become not only one of the most beloved foreign institutions in China but, at its peak, also the largest and most significant enterprise of its kind in the Far East. Its legacy is a true testament to German and Austrian "Gastfreundschaft" (hospitality) and their legendary food and confectionery culture.

The Founding Years 1906-1913

Karl Albert Kiessling was born on 11 June 1879, in Haselbrunn-Plauen, Saxony, Germany. His wish to study theology and become a priest could not be fulfilled, because his four elder sisters had to be married off first, so he instead learned to be a baker, confectioner and cook in Dresden.[1] Driven by an urge to shed the pettiness of the home land ('Die Engherzigkeit der Heimat abzulegen') as he later wrote in a letter

Figure 1: A Kiessling & Bader thirtieth anniversary photograph taken on the roof terrace in 1937. From the private archive of Mrs. Schmitt-Englert.

to future partner Bader,[2] he sailed on the ocean liners of the German Ostasien Reederei from 1901 as a ship's cook and confectioner. In 1904 he signed off from seafaring in Hong Kong and worked as a confectioner in various restaurants. From the German Consul there, he learned of the growing German community in Tianjin, North China. Kiessling moved there around 1905 and found employment at a Greek bakery 'Karatzas'. After a few years at Karatzas, he decided to start his own business, which was incorporated in late 1906 under the name 'A. Kiessling Confectioner & Baker'. The founding year is confirmed in a letter from Albert Kiessling to Friedrich Bader and by former employees.[3][4] The shop itself opened to the public in early 1907, as verified by a 1937 photograph whose inscription describes a gathering of the staff of the main Tianjin branch as the 30th anniversary of the Kiessling.

The original Kiessling was located on the corner of Rue Dillon and Rue de France in the Tianjin French Concession, opposite the French Post Office, and appears in the 1909 *Rosenstock Directory*.[5] Although not the first Western restaurant, bakery or patisserie in Tianjin, the Astor House Hotel with dining options had opened as early as 1863,[6] the business was soon popular. According to his son, Albert worked very hard and managed well.[7] He got up at 5am every morning and would be the first person to work in the shop and the last person to leave at night. The Rotary Club member, nicknamed 'Kiss', developed a wide circle of friends and was reported to be fluent in German, Chinese, English and French. Originally only a bakery, Kiessling's soon expanded to become a European restaurant and a confectionary shop in the style of a Viennese 'Konditorei', or patisserie, and included a roof terrace. The business was thriving, and, in 1911, Albert Kiessling married Maria Olga Pohle from Leipzig in Shanghai.[8]

EXPANSION IN TIANJIN 1913-1919: FRIEDRICH BADER JOINS AS PARTNER
In a surviving letter, dated 18 April 1913, Albert Kiessling offered

fellow German Friedrich Bader an equal stake in the company:⁹ the partnership was established the same year. Most notably Herr Kiessling mentions in the letter that 'my business, which has now existed for 5½ years, has become too much for me to manage alone'. The letter gives a glimpse of the scale Kiessling had already achieved during the first few years of the business. Besides Kiessling himself, it had one other German employee, one Pole and 19 Chinese. He enthusiastically wrote:

> We produce Wedding, Christening, Birthday, Plum, Madeira etc. cake, other gateaux, St. Honorex, mille feux and other French cakes and puddings, have large revenues with self-produced pralines, fondant marron glacé, candied fruit, caramelised pineapples, walnuts, dates, etc., different Macrons and Mürbteiggebäck [..} Dessertstückchen, Blätterteig-Törtchen in large amounts, then current bread, Kranz-, Butter- and Streusel-, Apple, Cheese Ecken etc. to fulfil each and every wish [...] We have many orders from outside of Tianjin, mostly Beijing. We daily bake 700 pounds of bread. Revenues vary with approx. 4-5000 dollars per month, it's not easy to exactly determine it but ultimately, I earned more than 20,000 dollars in the last few years. I love such advantageous opportunities abroad and which would never be offered back home.

Convinced by Kiessling's glowing letter, Herr Bader joined the enterprise the same year and its official name was changed to Kiessling & Bader (起士林点心铺), although it was mostly still referred to as 'Kiessling's' by Westerners and 'Qǐ shì lín' (起士林) by Chinese patrons. Friedrich Bader was born on 17 May 1884, in Künzelsau, Württemberg. Like Herr Kiessling, he originally wanted to learn a different profession, in his case engineering, but ultimately became a baker and confectioner just like his business partner. His journeyman years took him to the German city of Lindau in 1904, Scotland in 1905, London in 1906, Maastricht in 1907, America until 1912 and then, finally, China in 1913. His main contribution to the partnership was the mechanisation of work processes, for which his penchant for tinkering and handicrafts particularly qualified him. He was also the main driver behind Kiessling & Bader's diversification into a wide-ranging food production, dining, consumer retail and trading enterprise.

Raw materials were not only sourced domestically in China but imported from all around the world. Chocolate arrived from Switzerland, butter from New Zealand, flour from the USA and Europe, and wines and liqueurs from France. The bakery rails and other production equipment were ordered at the Leipzig sample fair and modified according to the company's requirements. Porcelain came from Bavarian specialist companies, and the silver from Württemberg.[10] According to his grandson, Herr Bader not only brought a much-welcomed entrepreneurial spirit but also a vast network of valuable contacts in China and from around the world to the joint-venture. For example, he reports that his grandfather hired four royal court eunuchs - three for the café and one as a private gardener.[11]

After the start of the First World War, tensions rose between the Austrian and German population and the other occupants of Tianjin's foreign concessions, first and foremost with the French. In 1915, a physical altercation occurred at Kiessling's between French soldiers and Herr Kiessling, and on 12 June the *Peking Daily News* reported that: 'Kiessling's German confectionery shop in the French Concession at Tientsin has been closed by order of the French Consul'.[12] Albert Kiessling and Friedrich Bader were forced to apologise and were given

Figure 2: Albert Kiessling, his wife Olga and their children, Werner and Lotti. From *Kiessling - Legend spanning a century* (Tianjin People's Publishing House, 2011)

three days to move their business to the nearby German Concession, where they established what would become their most iconic branch along the main thoroughfare of the Kaiser Wilhelm Strasse. The new, art nouveau building they moved into was situated across from the German Club Concordia and was considerably larger than the previous premises. It eventually had 350 seats in the café and 200 more were added in the roof garden each summer. A small orchestra of elderly musicians, under the leadership of Herr Schneider on violin, played Viennese waltzes every afternoon.[13]

It appears the move was organised very quickly, with German efficiency, and was followed by the addition of outside catering to Kiessling's services. The restaurant was quick to embrace the modern idea of catering and developed an excellent reputation, providing meals for receptions by foreign missions, hosting up to 2,000 people a night, using only their own plates and utensils. Only one month after being expelled from the French Concession, *The Army & Navy Register* reported that for the 4th of July celebration in 1915, 'delicious refreshments were served throughout the entertainment to the hundreds of guests under the management of caterer Kiessling'.[14] In fact, throughout the war, Kiessling's remained a must for elegant afternoon coffee or tea among all Westerners, even the British. After all, Kaiser Wilhelm II, whose statue, reimagined as revered German knight Roland, stood adjacent to Kiessling's, was still Queen Victoria's grandson.

Figure 3: Kiessling & Bader on Woodrow Wilson Street, Tianjin, as it looked in the 1930s and 40s. From Gary Nash, The *Tarasov Saga* (Rosenberg Publishing, 2002)

Chinese sources claim that Republic of China President Yuan Shikai celebrated his birthday at Kiessling's with a fabulous mountain-like, multi-layer cake. This stirred politician Li Yuanhong to order an even larger cake for his birthday, which apparently was a metre high, a metre wide and colourfully embellished.[15] The Father of Modern China, Dr Sun Yatsen, is also rumoured to have visited the Kiessling. Whether true or not, the fact that Chinese officials, celebrities and members of the upper class did regularly frequent the Kiessling helped to popularise it among the native population of the treaty port and to nurture their fondness for foreign-owned enterprises. Even some twenty years later, Konrad Stingl, originally from Konstanz in Germany and an employee at Kiessling & Bader in Tianjin from 1937 to 1941, wrote that 'through smart advertising it had become custom in Tianjin to gift one's Chinese friends and business partners a cake for Chinese New Year, which was also followed by wealthy Chinese. For this occasion, it was not uncommon to receive orders for 200 to 300 large cakes for the price of 20-30 Marks, all with caramel work'.[16]

The mythical aura Kiesslings held over Tianjin's native population was described by Chinese author Han Suyin, '"Kiesslings", said a golden sign, and in front of two windows full of mouth-watering pastry I gazed at chocolate shapes of Father Christmas, and angels, bears and ducks. I remember my elder brother writing of this shop as the best pastry shop in the whole of China. "We went to Kiessling's" implied social acceptance'.[17]

THE END OF WORLD WAR I, REPATRIATION AND RETURN 1918-1921

At the end of World War I, the 'Strasse' was renamed Woodrow Wilson Street after the victorious American President. In their letters, German prisoners of war in Tianjin, such as one writing on the 14th of December 1918, described 'how mean the enemy behaved after the armistice' and that 'windows and display cases at the Kiessling were broken and the establishment was looted and almost destroyed'.[18] As a result of the German defeat in Europe, on 15 March 1919, *Millard's Review of the Far East* reported that 'Kiessling's coffee and ice cream parlours were closed on Sunday by the Chinese Authorities in the ex-German Concession in Tientsin, but, although the front doors are battered up, a small trade is carried on by the back entrance'.[19]

Soon after, German inhabitants of Tianjin were forced to repatriate. After much back and forth, Albert Kiessling was eventually deported from Tianjin on 3 April 1919, and sent home aboard the steamship Antilochus.[20] His wife Olga was exempt from repatriation because she was pregnant at the time. Herr Bader managed to go underground and hide among the Chinese.[21] Evidently, Kiessling had tried to evade deportation by claiming to be a Swiss national. The *Shanghai Times* reported on 28 February 1919, 'All kinds of stories are current about Kiessling, whose clientele has included in it a surprisingly large number of allied people, but from inquiries made it seems unlikely that Kiessling will be able to work his "Swiss Nationality" bluff on anybody'.[22] Kiessling's absence from Tianjin would not last very long. On 9 August 1919, the *North-China Daily Herald* wrote that 'Herr Kiessling has sent a letter from Germany to Tientsin in which he announces his intention to return to the port at an early date. The N.C. Daily Mail hears that he has even named the steamer in which he proposes to travel'.[23]

And, lo and behold, in 1921 Herr Kiessling returned to Tianjin with a new recruit in tow, Walter Reichel from Dresden. Like Kiessling, Reichel had earned his master's certification in fine pastry and candy making in Germany.[24] Presumably on the same ship as Albert, his sister Fräulein Emmy Kiessling also came to Tianjin in 1921 to support the expansion of Kiessling & Bader. Besides the return of many Germans to Tianjin, another movement that would shape the city for decades was the influx of White Russian refugees that flooded into China after the Russian Revolution and into the early 1920s. Soon Russian girls staffed the patisserie of Kiessling & Bader whilst Chinese waiters attended the restaurant.[25]

Golden Years in Tianjin 1921-1933

After Albert's return, Kiessling & Bader soon opened a branch in Beidaihe during the summer months. This summer resort town, about 250 kilometres northeast of Tianjin, was a popular holiday spot. Their products were sold through the firm of Moyler Powell & Co, as an advertisement from the *Peitaiho Directory 1924* reveals.[26] Through his strong relations with the German community in North China, Friedrich Bader was able to establish Kiessling's as a supplier to the newly opened Jinpu Railway Line in 1923. With the extension of the railway line, Kiessling & Bader's fame spread all over China.

It was truly a golden time for Tianjin, which had risen to become the second largest treaty port in China, second only to Shanghai and equally immortalised in countless memoirs and biographies. Famed

Chinese writer Eileen Chang lived in Tianjin as a child from 1922 to 1928. She vividly recalled joyful times at the Kiessling in her literary debut *What a Life! What A Girl's Life*. In it she wrote, 'My aunt didn't like my brother, so she would grab me and take me to the Kiessling to dance every night. I would sit at the table with the white cream on the cake in front of me raised up to my eyebrows. I ate the whole piece, and gradually dozed off in the reddish dusk'.[27]

Not only did the foreign population increase significantly, but also many Chinese celebrities from nearby Beijing now lived in the coastal city. Besides the aforementioned Yuan Shikai, the 'Last Emperor' Pu Yi also moved there in 1925. Brian Power, in his memoir of *The Puppet Emperor*, recalls how Pu Yi, the Empress or his favourite concubine, and three or four Pekinese dogs on tangled leads would regularly arrive at Kiessling's with much fuss:[28]

> People sitting at the marble-topped tables in K&B stopped chatting. Some of them stood up and began to clap. Herr Kiessling, a fat double-chinned man, rushed with surprising speed towards the swing-doors, followed by Herr Bader. The trio of two violinists and a cellist, seated by some potted palm trees, faltered and then broke off playing. There was a buzz of excitement. "The Emperor", someone said. "The Emperor!", people repeated down the length of the café. More people stood and joined in the clapping. "This is indeed an honour, Your Imperial Majesty", chorused Herr Kiessling and Herr Bader as they bowed and then collided with each other in their eagerness to usher their distinguished visitors to a table. At the head of the imperial party came Pu Yi in his Prince of Wales suit with a pink carnation in the button-hole. He was followed by the secondary, consort, Elegant Ornament, with a Pekinese under each arm. After them came Woodhead[A], who nodded condescendingly to some friends, and last of all a lady in waiting with the four Pekinese pups. Herr Kiessling clicked his fingers at the trio. Their leader was Herr Schneider, a short, pale-faced Austrian with a small moustache and sad, dark eyes. He raised the bow of his violin, bowed to his colleagues and they continued with the

---

A   a prolific British journalist

Viennese waltz 'Gold and Silver'. Woodhead gave the order, hot chocolate and pastries. Herr Kiessling repeated to the head-waiter and his assistant, who raced to the kitchen. Herr Bader, a small, bald-headed man, hovered behind Pu Yi's chair, keeping a nervous eye on the Pekinese.

In her biography of Russian immigrant Olga Yunter, Stephanie Williams confirms similar stories when she writes, 'Kiessling & Bader Café, the most popular and fashionable place for coffee. Originally the place had been a bakery, but it had expanded to include a restaurant and a magnificent confectionery shop. Its cakes were legendary. You could choose to drink Russian tea or German beer, American soda or French wine, and eat freshly made chocolates. Even the last Emperor of China Pu Yi and the Empress, both of whom spoke English, were frequently seen there to have coffee'.[29] Like its dishes, Kiessling's patrons could not have been more diverse. Side by side with the Emperor were seated the US Marine 'Leathernecks', far away from the prohibitions imposed in the USA from 1920 to 1933, who reportedly very much enjoyed Kiessling's German beers, some brewed domestically in Qingdao, others imported from Bremen in Germany.[30]

Figure 4: A Kiessling & Bader street cart showing both Tianjin locations ca. 1938. From *Kiessling - Legend spanning a century* (Tianjin People's Publishing House, 2011).

After Emmy Kiessling, one of the next key hires at Kiessling & Bader was Erna Kluge in 1926. She was a German born in Tianjin whose father had been a supplier to Kiessling's. Already as a young adult she was fluent in German, English, French and Chinese. Erna worked closely with Kiessling's sister Emmy, who was in charge of the salesgirls, the shop and all outgoing orders. In her memoir, Erna, emphasises how kind the Kiesslings, as well as Herr Bader and his wife, were to her. After Herr Reichel's first five-year contract ended, he went to Germany on vacation. The trip, including train fare and six months leave, were paid for by Kiessling & Bader. Herr Kiessling asked him to bring back another 'Konditor Meister" or Master Pastry Chef, and he dutifully returned with Wilhelm Scheel, a native of Stendal in Saxony-Anhalt and former classmate of his at pastry and confectionery finishing school.

The working culture was very congenial. Erna was particularly enthusiastic about her first staff Christmas Party at Kiessling & Bader, where on top of many characteristic confections like 'a Stollen, a plate with cookies, candies, and marzipan', she received an envelope with a month's salary and even a brand-new, fur coat fitted for her. Another employee at the party was the recently arrived Wilhelm Scheel, with whom she would soon fall in love. 'Wilhelm was short, had steel grey eyes and brown wavy hair—a rather handsome man', she raves in her biography.[31] After about a year of Erna joining Kiessling & Bader, Fräulein Kiessling got married and left, leaving Erna to take her position. Emmy Kiessling's new husband was an Austrian by the name of Robert Töbich. He had been an engineer onboard the Austrian war ship "Kaiserin Elisabeth," which was once positioned in Far Eastern waters. On 2 November 1914, the vessel was sunk by its crew before they were taken captive by the Japanese. After his release in 1920 Töbich worked for the China American Engineering Corporation in Tianjin.[32]

A print advertisement from 1924 reaffirms how well-known and sought-after Kiessling & Bader had become, as well as how innovative their business expansion across the country through the relatively new channel of distance selling was, 'Kiessling & Bader forward their famous delicacies to Peking and all parts of China by Parcel Post'.[33] By the 1930s, the delivery of confectioneries in galvanised boxes had expanded to Africa, Australia, Japan, Hawaii, the United States and other countries. An 8-page German language mail order catalogue shows how wide the choice of packaged consumer goods had become.³⁴

Business was booming and so a White Russian girl, Nina Tarasov, was hired shortly before Russian Easter 1927. The sales staff now consisted of Erna and four Russian girls including Nina, growing to five or six during the busy holiday periods. Kiessling & Bader was a very busy place. Except for Chinese New Year Day and Christmas Eve when they closed at 5 in the afternoon, it was open for business every day of the year from 8 in the morning until 1am, and sometimes later.³⁵

Kiessling's fame spread across China, so much so that, in 1928, the 'New Kiessling Cafe' or Kǎisīlìng (凯司令珈琲館) opened at 1001 Bubbling Well Road (now Nanjing West Road) and became the talk of the town as the first Chinese-run, Western-style coffee house in Shanghai. It turned out the founders were the former pastry chef Lin Kangmin (林康民) of Kiessling & Bader in Tianjin together with a partner Deng Baoshan (邓宝山). Albert Kiessling just happened to be in Shanghai when the copy-cat café opened and protested strongly through the German Consul; he wanted its Chinese owners prosecuted but they ultimately avoided this by transferring ownership to another company.³⁶ Eileen Chang located several scenes of her novella *Lust Caution* in the New Kiessling café³⁷ and, to add insult to injury, the Kaisiling still exists today on Nanjing West Road, making it the longest-standing coffeehouse in Shanghai in its original location.³⁸

The golden years were soon to come to an end as in 1929 a disaster set off a chain of events that brought significant transformation to Kiessling & Bader. On 13 August 1929, Friedrich Bader's wife and baby died during a difficult birth.³⁹ The shocking death triggered another major change in the previously tight family enterprise: Albert Kiessling's wife Olga moved back to Germany in October 1929, together with son Werner and daughter Lotti, to settle in her hometown. She would never return to China.⁴⁰

Wilhelm Scheel's initial five-year contract ended in the summer of 1930, but instead of staying with Kiessling & Bader, he set off to Mukden, Manchuria with Erna Kluge, where they married and founded the Café Royal.⁴¹ Sad but not distraught, Albert and Friedrich, both now without wives, continued managing the business with pastry chef Reichel until 1933, another pivotal year in the history of Kiessling & Bader.

EXPANSION TO NANJING AND SHANGHAI UNDER NEW OWNERSHIP 1933-1937
In 1933 Friedrich Bader returned to Germany, living in Munich-Geiselgasteig until his death on 18 May 1967. Before leaving China, he and Kiessling decided to retire and sell their treasured Kiessling & Bader's.[42]

Robert Töbich is listed as part of the business for the first time in *The North-China Hong List 1933*,[43] although the *Rosenstock Business Directory* of the same year still lists Kiessling and Bader as proprietors.[44] The actual ownership transfer document in the Chinese company registry is dated 5 April 1935, and seems to have been signed retrospectively after the business was handed over in 1934.[45] Either way, the new owners were Albert Kiessling's brother-in-law Robert Töbich, his sister Emmy and the long-time pastry chef Walter Reichel. Despite the ownership change, the contract stipulated that the name 'Kiessling & Bader' was to be kept.[46] The Austrian Töbich was not a restauranteur or confectioner by trade but brought with him experience in engineering, business management and a flair for Viennese café culture. This often caused the enterprise to be later referred to as 'Austrian-owned', although Reichel was German and an equal partner.

With the ownership change, Nina Tarasov was given more responsibilities. She described Reichel and Töbich as 'both pleasant men, with Töbich the up-front manager, very people-oriented and a great motivator, while Reichel was the main behind-the-scenes production manager'.[47] The company expanded under the new ownership and, at its peak, had around 300 employees throughout China, with up to 10 White Russian sales girls and chefs renowned Asia-wide for their international-grade desserts, dishes and breads. 10-12 course lunches and dinners were sold at up to 600 to 800 servings a day. 'The richness of the selection surpassed any conceivable scale known in Germany' wrote Konrad Stingl and continued:

Figure 5: A 1939 letterhead, listing Reichel and Tobich as owners. From the Museum of Foreign Brand Advertising in the Republic of China (MOFBA) collection

Wedding, birthday and other festival cakes such as for New Year for the Europeans and Americans, Indians on different days and Chinese New Year for the local population, were produced. Easter was celebrated on separate days for the Europeans and the White Russians and so was Christmas. For Valentine's Day caramel hearts were manufactured [...] Heavy American-style fruit cakes were especially suitable for export to South-China, Japan and the Philippines. Another top seller was Dutch Hopjes which became legendary among the Chinese as medicine.[48]

Meanwhile, the year 1933 was a restless one for the former Kiessling employees Wilhelm Scheel and Erna Kluge-Scheel in Mukden. 'The combined military and economic position of Japan in Manchuria made it most difficult for foreign business to exist, and the future for us there was uncertain. One foreign business after another closed and moved south' wrote Erna.[49] Thus, Wilhelm left for Nanjing in 1934 to look for a house suitable to hold a bakery, a restaurant and living quarters. After a building was secured, Erna, their child and their business partner Herr Zaudig soon followed. The family had not lost contact with Kiessling's and its new owners and so, through a franchise model with Wilhelm as partner, their new confectionery opened under the name of Kiessling & Bader the same year.

After its opening and initial advertising as the 'only foreign bakery in Nanking', patrons promoted the business by word of mouth, and it grew rapidly. 'The name Kiessling & Bader helped too since it was well-known all-over China', Erna recalled. All foreign embassies ordered cakes from them. Even Chiang Kai-shek and his wife were customers, as Erna confirmed, 'They often sent their servants to us to pick up orders for them'. As in Tianjin, Kiessling & Bader's Nanjing branch catered to all nationalities:[50]

> Croissants and Bûche de Noël for the French, plum pudding, English fruitcake and scones for the British, Paska and Kulich for the Russians, Boterietters for the Dutch, Stollen and Lebkuchen and Marzipan and Hutzelbrot and all sorts of fancy Torten and pastries for the Germans

Figure 6: The first Shanghai location operated by the Scheels's on Bubbling Well Road

Back in Tianjin, Albert Kiessling remained involved in the business as an advisor. After stepping away from the day-to-day operations, he went on a journey around the world. The *North China Daily News* reported on 8 May 1935, 'Mr. A. Kiessling, senior partner of Kiessling & Bader, has returned to Tientsin after being away for nearly a year which was spent travelling in the United States and Europe'.[51] After his return he continued to live in Tianjin and invested his money in, among other ventures, the Art Deco Leopold Building and the German American Hospital.[52]

The business continued to grow. On 22 December 1935, a paid editorial in the *North China Daily News* appeared promoting Kiessling & Bader's famous 'Christmas Fruit Cake, German Currant Cake, Ginger Bread, Santa Clauses and everything your heart desires' in the newly opened Shanghai branch at 1617 Bubbling Well Road.[53]

On 28 October 1936, the same newspaper reported that Kiessling & Bader had re-opened their Shanghai branch at 1255 Bubbling Well Road.[54] In 1936 Kiessling's also opened a wholly-owned branch in Beidaihe. Situated in the Bohai Gulf of the Yellow Sea, it boasted ten kilometres of magnificent white sandy beaches, and, during the peak month of August, the resort welcomed an estimated 10,000 vacationers. Nina was sent to run the branch at Peitaiho Beach from late May to early September, an assignment that became an annual pilgrimage for her and her son until 1939.[55]

On 30 July 1937 the Japanese army occupied Tianjin but, as a firm owned by allies of the Japanese, the Kiessling continued to operate without interruption. Ironically, sales even increased through the supply of Japanese army rations.[56] Also, upper-class Chinese continued to frequent the establishment, such as well-known banker Bian Baimei. According to his diary, his favourite restaurant in the 1930s was the Kiessling, leading him to be there several times a week for bread, dessert or afternoon tea, business lunches or dinners.[57]

In early 1937, Kiessling & Bader's business in Nanjing had grown so much that the Scheels began contemplating expansion. But, while an architect began drawing up plans for a new building, the Japanese army was steadily closing in on Nanjing. Negotiations with the architect were soon postponed and the Scheels evacuated, first to Guling and then, following a short return, over to Hankou and eventually Hong Kong.[58] Herr Zaudig stayed behind and witnessed their beloved store bombarded and burnt down amidst the Rape of Nanking on 13 December 1937. The German 'Oskar Schindler of China' John Rabe, who documented the Japanese atrocities in Nanjing, wrote of the fate of the Kiessling & Bader branch: 'It is not until we toured the city that we learned the extent of destruction. We come across corpses every 100 to 200 yards. The Japanese marched through the city in groups of ten to twenty soldiers and I watched with my own eyes as they looted the café of our German baker Herr Kiessling'.[59] Herr Zaudig barely escaped Nanjing with his life, but managed to flee to Shanghai.[60]

The War Years in Tianjin and Shanghai 1937-1945

Having lost everything in Nanjing, the Scheels started again from the bottom and in August 1938 leased a building opposite the race course (now People's Park), on Shanghai's busy main thoroughfare, at 72 Bubbling Well Road. Even though Shanghai was by then crowded with foreign bakeries, confectioneries and coffee shops, it did not take long before they were once more thriving.[61]

Despite Japanese rule, business in Tianjin continued to flourish. An advertisement in the *Tientsin Marines* magazine from December 1938, shows that around that time a second branch of Kiessling & Bader was established in Tianjin's French Concession at 4 Rue Gabriel Deveria (Road 24)[62] Furthermore, both Konrad Stingl and the son of Robert Töbich, Heinz, mention a branch in Beijing during the late 1930s or early 1940s, although no further details could be found or verified.

The outbreak of war in Europe in 1939 shocked the foreign communities in China, and, to make matters worse, Tianjin was ravaged by a flood that same year which destroyed many of the city's businesses. Interestingly, citizens of the warring European nations, the Germans and the British, for example, as well as the Germans and the Russians, seemed to live happily together in spite of the fierce war raging between their countries. There was very little animosity evident. Kiessling's went on hiring Russian girls, and the Russian staff bore no resentment to their bosses. Konrad Stingl writes how, during that time in Tianjin, 'different nations lived in harmony and peace'. An exceptionally memorable event he recalls was the 1940 Thanksgiving dinner organised by the American Consulate General, for which catering was managed by Kiessling & Bader: 'All leading businessmen and diplomats of Tianjin were invited to it, and Germans, British and French met and talked although their countries were at war with each other in Europe. As the central decoration of the event, I produced a large turkey made of sugar. The Consul General's wife thanked me profusely and even introduced me to her husband'.[63]

In May of 1940, the Scheels went on vacation to Germany and Kiessling's Tianjin sent one of their pastry chefs, Bruno Wolf, to help with the business while they were away. But like everywhere in China, life had become difficult in early 1940s Shanghai. The *North China Herald* reported an assassination on 20 July 1940, when Samuel Chang, a leading Chinese journalist who frequented the café 4-5 times a week, was shot by two gunmen inside Kiessling & Bader's on Bubbling Well Road. A Polish citizen Mr. V. Krason was also killed when he grappled with the assassins.[64] Similarly, darker figures began to appear in Tianjin. For example, Nazi Germany's Consul-General in Tianjin and former personal adjutant to Hitler, Fritz Wiedemann lived in Tianjin from 1941 to 1945. As a socialite and opportunistic spy, he 'enjoyed his women, his schnapps, his thick German beer and Kiessling Cafe's fresh bread and Wiener Schnitzels'.[65]

Still, business in Shanghai was flourishing, so much so that an architect was hired in 1942 to construct a large three-story building at 225 Hart Road (now Changde Road), close to the German Lutheran Church School and the German radio station.

On the ground floor was the store, the candy and fancy cake-making department, the bread and pastry rooms and the big ovens. The jams and juices were cooked outdoors. On the second floor was the kitchen and the restaurant, which could seat one hundred and sixty-five people. The long wall of this restaurant had a narrow balcony fitted with small tables for two. On the third floor were two apartments, one for pastry chef Herr Wolf and his wife Olga, the other for the Scheels. Above the apartments was the roof garden, which extended the length and breadth of the building. Every fitting and furnishing was custom-made. To top it off, a four-piece orchestra played either on the roof garden or in the restaurant.[66]

To match the décor, new uniforms for the sales girls were made. They were rose colored with the beige initials 'KB' stitched on the front shirt pocket. The waiters and servant boys wore black pants with white jackets, and the cooks white uniforms. Since they also kept the small business on Bubbling Well Road, the Shanghai staff now numbered about one hundred and fifty people.[67]

It was at this location that the paths of Eileen Chang and the 'real' Kiessling's would cross once again. After studying in Hong Kong, she returned to Shanghai in 1942 and lived in room 60 of the Eddington House on 195 Hart Road with her aunt. Here she completed her most important novels. The newly-opened, second Kiessling & Bader location was just downstairs on Hart Road. Eileen fondly recalled how 'next to our house is the Kiessling Café, which moved from Tianjin during the war (sic). I would wake up at dawn to the smell of the freshly baked bread and a fragrant aura of grandeur burst into the air'.[68]

Despite, or perhaps because of the horrors of war, the foreigners and upper-class Chinese who could afford it continued to frequent

Figure 7: The Shanghai main branch opened in 1942 on Hart Road, adjacent to Eddington House, visible on the left.
From *Kiessling - Legend spanning a century* (Tianjin People's Publishing House, 2011)

Figure 8: The Grand Opening of the Shanghai branch was held 19 July 1942, and one of the owners, Herr Reichel (second from the right) from Tianjin attended. From the *Shanghai Sunday Times* 9 August 1942

the Kiessling locations in Shanghai and Tianjin. Their children, reared during these grim times, were especially sentimental whilst recounting their joyful experiences at the beloved confectionery in numerous memoirs. It is fascinating to compare how each of the authors remembers a different drink, sweet or dish to be the 'most famous', a testament to how wide-ranging and international Kiessling & Bader's menu really was.

One illustration comes from Isabel Sun Chao, born in 1931 to a wealthy Chinese family in Shanghai, who wrote, 'Li Gege took me window-shopping on Bubbling Well Road, and then to the popular Kiessling Café. I'd just taken my first bite of chestnut cake when the actress on the cover of Muma's booklet entered the café. She made her way past the glass counters filled with éclairs, macaroons and profiteroles, and sat down at our table between Li Gege and me'.[69] Adeline Yen Mah, born in 1937 recalled from her time in Shanghai, 'I

Figure 9: The Kiessling & Bader logo, listing both Shanghai locations ca. 1942. From the MOFBA collection

remember drinking hot chocolate and eating pastries at the sparkling Kiessling Restaurant, while a music trio played Strauss waltzes and Beethoven romances'.[70]

Likewise in Tianjin, Angela Louisa Cox Elliott remembered; 'It was a wonderful restaurant & I have eaten there many times and was given their chocolates. The best cakes, pastries - Peking Dust, my mother's favourite (whipped cream with ground chestnuts) and beautiful decorations of goodies for Xmas & Easter. Birthday cakes were always ordered from Kiessling's. It was such a treat to have a meal [...] ice cream & such - sundaes/banana splits or sodas'.[71]

As a German-owned enterprise, Kiessling's operated throughout the war with no Japanese interference, but the defeat of Japan and Germany would also mean the eventual defeat of Kiessling's.

THE END OF THE ORIGINAL KIESSLING & BADER: NATIONALIST AND EARLY COMMUNIST RULE 1945-1970

As with most German businesses during the Third Reich, the relationship between Kiessling's and the regime was ambivalent. Both Robert Töbich and Wilhelm Scheel are confirmed to have been early NSDAP (Nazi) party members.[72] Likewise, Konrad Stingl wrote in 1949 that 'one should not forget that the Nazi flag flew on the roof of the Kiessling's in Tianjin for 12 years' and that 'many other things were done wrongly'. At the same time, however, Erna Kluge-Scheel gives a detailed account of how the Shanghai branch continued to work with Jewish enterprises during the war:

> The long arm of Adolf Hitler expanded even to us in Shanghai and the party came out with a new ruling. The Germans in Shanghai were no longer permitted to buy from or deal with Jews. Wilhelm did not see any reason why he should discontinue dealing with those who had served him well. He came to an agreement with them. We would place our orders by telephone, the merchandise would be delivered by Chinese people, and the bills would show a Chinese firm's name. That was the way we continued trading with them and Wilhelm's practice was never discovered.

Nevertheless, immediately after the German loss in World War II, all

Germans in China had their bank accounts frozen and businesses and private properties were confiscated, including those of all Kiessling & Bader companies in Tianjin and Shanghai. For some time, the Kiessling was still able to do business, with Erna reporting that 'the American hospital and the army personnel continued to purchase from us. Little by little, though, business slowed down and we had to dismiss a few employees. In 1945 Herr Zaudig was repatriated. The pastry chef Herr Wolf and his wife returned to Tianjin as the business in Shanghai no longer had enough work for him.'[73]

In the fall of 1945, Erna and her husband Wilhelm were visited by American officers in uniform and given three days to turn over the main branch on Hart Road to the American authorities. They were allowed to sell their inventory and stay in their apartment on top of the restaurant for the time being. The rest of the building was converted to a mess hall to accommodate military hospital personnel. For the third time in only a few years the Scheels had lost their livelihood, and Erna recalled in desperate words how 'Our Chinese employees took possession of the original bakery on Bubbling Well Road. They just stepped in and took over. We were helpless; we had no rights and had been proved wrong in hoping to keep that store. Another terrible blow - to think that our own people would do that to us. We never once expected that'.

Wilhelm briefly accepted a job in the kitchen of the American Military Hospital, but, in 1947, he left for Germany with his wife and then emigrated to the US in 1951. The 1947 *Shanghai Telephone Directory* lists the name Kiessling & Bader on Changteh Road but no longer the Nanjing Road location.[74] On 23 September 1947 the *Chinese-English Intelligence* reported that, 'Kiessling & Bader, a Germany confectionery and bakery, will henceforth be operated by the Municipal Bureau of Foreign Affairs. Thirty percent of the net profits will be handed over to the Alien Property Administration which will provide two persons to take charge of all accounts and also the stock'. Prices were set by the US Army and settled in US dollars in both the Shanghai and Tianjin locations.[75] Interestingly, the Rue Gabriel Deveria (now Changchun Road) branch was still operated by Töbich and Reichel, who tried everything in their power to regain ownership of all their properties across China and avoid deportation. Not everything changed though, David C. Hulme in his 1946 book *Tientsin* states: 'The Kiessling and Bader bakery and restaurant, just a couple of blocks south along Victoria Road from Ewo Street, remained one of Tientsin's finest places of relaxation'.[76]

In April 1947, Robert Töbich's shares were indeed returned and Kiessling's main branch in Tianjin temporarily reopened under the old owners after he had successfully argued that he was Austrian and not German, thus exempt from the seizure of assets. The ruling was based on a loophole that went back to 1938, when, after the annexation of Austria, the Kuomintang government gave all Austrians in China the same rights as other nationals whose countries did not maintain active treaties with China.[77] However, according to Chinese researcher Zhou Licheng of the Tianjin Municipal Archives, the authorities soon received a letter from a Kiessling's employee in Shanghai named Wang Lianping (王连平) tipping them off that Töbich had been an NSDAP party member.[78] The Shanghai Municipal Archives also recorded the following, 'At the age of 14, Wang Lianping went to Kiessling's in Tianjin as an apprentice. Later, he continued to work for them in Shenyang (sic)[B] and Nanjing. Since 1938, he has worked for Kiessling's in Shanghai'. Töbich's proved party membership, independent of nationality, now allowed his prosecution under the denazification acts. On 28 August 1947, the Tianjin Central News Agency reported that Töbich and Reichel were deported and their property irrevocably seized by the Tianjin Nationalist Government.[79] The ownership transfer document, stored in the Tianjin Municipal Archives, shows the former Kiessling & Bader accountant Pestonjee J. signing on behalf of majority owner Töbich on 26 September 1947. Robert Töbich, his wife Emmy and their son Heinz moved to Vienna. Walter Reichel travelled via Asperg to Kirchheim unter Teck, where he lived with his wife Betty and daughter Renate.[80] Their employees, both Chinese and Russian, were sorry to see them go, gave them a big farewell party and saw them off at the railway station. They had been good employers and were well liked.[81]

The firm continued to operate under the Kiessling & Bader name, and Nina and the Russian salesgirls kept their jobs, 'the new Chinese bosses were kind and polite to the staff and life at Kiessling's went on with little change for some time'. But, in 1948, Nina followed the trend when she sold all her possessions and left Tianjin, eventually migrating to Canada. The new Chinese owners of Kiessling's were saddened by her departure. She had worked there for 22 years and was

---

B   Scheel's 'Café Royal' in Mukden

like an institution. According to her biography, 'the management gave her a good bonus and loaded her up with boxes of chocolates, cakes and biscuits'. After the founding of the People's Republic of China in 1949, Kiessling's was taken over by the Tianjin Municipal People's Government and henceforth operated as a state-owned enterprise.[82]

Albert Kiessling himself was excluded from repatriation because of his special status in the city and his connections with both the Nationalist and later the Communist authorities. Throughout his life in Tianjin, he was a great and highly respected benefactor to inhabitants of all nationalities. He was a supporter of the German Club, donor to the Church, schools, and associations, as well as an investor in the German-American Hospital. According to his son 'he always had an open ear and hand for his Chinese employees' and 'they would have walked through fire for him'. Over the years he gave many loans to people in need, many of which he never asked to be repaid.

In 1952 he was still an active citizen of Tianjin but had suffered a stroke, leaving him paralysed on one side. Impoverished and in poor health, Albert Kiessling left China, his home of 48 years, as part of the very last repatriation organised by the German government in the same year. He arrived in Hamburg on 22 December and travelled on to Bietigheim where he spent his last few years with his son Werner and his family.[83]

Tragically, he lived to hear how his life's work, the Kiessling in Tianjin, was merged with the former Victoria Restaurant in 1954. The joint-enterprise continued under the name of Qishilin but was moved to the Victoria's Art Deco premises on Jianshe Road. This building had no connection with the original Kiessling's whatsoever. Soon after, the pioneer of East Asia's first and longest-lasting confectionery empire, Karl Albert Kiessling, passed away; on 11 January 1955, aged 75. Although he was gone, his spirit lived on in China. Pamela Youde, writer and wife of former Hong Kong Governor Edward Youde wrote that in the 1950s and early 1960s '...for a while

Figure 10: Albert Kiessling in his later years. From *Kiessling - Legend spanning a century*.

one could almost forget that one was in Communist China: staying in a European-style villa overlooking the sea and having a chocolate sundae or iced coffee at Kiessling's, a branch of the former Austrian-owned bakery/restaurant Kiessling & Bader in Tianjin and a rare survival of past times'.[84]

After the founding of the People's Republic of China, the Qishilin continued to receive important, national leaders, including Mao Zedong, Liu Shaoqi, Zhou Enlai, Deng Xiaoping, Nie Rongzhen, Deng Yingchao, Liao Chengzhi, as well as Cambodian Head of State Sihanouk and many other Chinese and foreign dignitaries. During the years of the Cultural Revolution, beginning in 1966, the bourgeoisie and foreign-sounding Qishilin was renamed the "Workers, Peasants and Soldiers Canteen" (工农兵餐厅).[85]

REVIVAL OF THE KIESSLING RESTAURANT 1970s -TODAY

Brian Power was one of the first, former Tianjin residents to return to the city of his birth in 1975: there he discovered Kiessling & Bader's café, democratically renamed 'The Tientsin Canteen' (天津西餐厅). He dined there but called the tourist attraction in the former Racecourse Road 'a make-believe Kiessling's'. 'The real one', he wrote, 'was a stylish building a mile away on the former Woodrow Wilson Street'.[86] It was not until some long-standing employees of the restaurant successfully petitioned Premier Zhou Enlai in the politically more moderate years of the early 1970s that the crude name was changed back to Qishilin Restaurant (起士林餐馆). Soon after, Qishilin opened two branches on Dali Road and Nanshi Food Street, respectively, and also resumed the branch in Beidaihe.[87]

Tragically, amidst the Tangshan earthquake of 28 July 1976, the iconic Kiessling building on the former Woodrow Wilson Street was destroyed and subsequently torn down.[88] Its name and spirit however proved once more to be indestructible. The *JAL Guide to the People's Republic of China* boasted of its legacy, writing in 1980, 'The main street of Beidaihe has a number of charming shops. The No. 96 Kiessling Bakery is the sole surviving Chinese branch of the Kiessling German Bakery. It bakes breads, pastries, cakes and biscuits of all varieties and, according to connoisseurs, has the best ice cream in the country. The original owners, Kiessling and Bader, are long gone, but their influence remains. The Chinese like to joke that the bakery is a fine example of "making foreign things serve China"'.[89]

In 1985 the new management of the Qishilin invited Dr Werner Kiessling and his wife to Tianjin for the first time since his departure as a child in 1929; there they attended a banquet with then Vice-Mayor Liu Jinfeng.[90] In October of the same year, Erna Kluge-Scheel also went on a trip to China. When visiting Shanghai, she was able to locate her family's former Kiessling & Bader branch opposite the old race course. The bakery shop had been expanded and did not look the way they had left it, but when she entered, she wrote:[91]

> A short friendly man approached us and recognised me. When he welcomed us in Chinese my eyes filled with tears. His name was Liang and he was just fifteen years old when we left in 1947. His brother, Wang was our No. 1. cake baker. Wang had retired a year earlier and Liang planned to retire the next year. Liang served us ice cream and I bought some coffee cake for our group for breakfast. I left the bakery that day with mixed feelings. It was in Shanghai that we started again for the third time and had our greatest success in business. Shanghai represented the "yin yang" of our lives.

Unbeknownst to Erna, Liang's brother Wang is almost certainly the 'Wang Lianping' who had tipped off authorities in 1947 about Töbich's Nazi party membership, ultimately causing his and Reichel's ownership of Kiessling & Bader to be confiscated without compensation. Apparently, as a reward, the brothers were given the smaller Shanghai Nanjing Road branch and were allowed to continue to operate it under a different name.[92] A truly bitter and even more tragic conclusion, than previously realised.

When Nina Tarasov's son Gary Nash visited Tianjin in 1988, he also found the Kiessling of old; now housed in the former Victoria Café. According to him, 'it still possessed some of the old-world charm of the Victoria and had an excellent Russian borscht on the menu'.[93] Around the same time in 1989, Robert Boulanger in his book *China* reported that in the Beidaihe location 'even the old German patisserie Kiessling, which is a branch of the main shop once famous in Tianjin, is still there'.[94]

In 1990, Qishilin entered a new era of rapid expansion, opening many confectionery outlets across Tianjin. In 1994, even a Qishilin

Hotel (北戴河起士林大饭店) was established in Beidaihe, with the first modern Beijing branch later opening its doors on 18 December 1998.[95] Back in Shanghai, the decrepit row of old buildings which housed Kiessling & Bader's Bubbling Well Road branch was demolished in the mid-1990s and is now the site of the Radisson Blu Hotel. The former Shanghai Kiessling & Bader building on Changde Road stood until 2001, when it was torn down to make way for the Jing'an Swissotel. Beside it, Eileen Chang's former residence still stubbornly stands. Now called the 'Changde Apartment', it houses a bookshop and a small café in commemoration of the coffee shop 'downstairs' that Eileen wrote about so ardently.[96]

Conclusion

In March 2001 the Baihua Literature and Art Publishing House published the book *There is a Qishilin in Tianjin* (天津有个起士林) by author Wen Shu (文淑).[97] Rather than a historical account it was a reimagined novel, loosely based on the Kiessling history but full of invented facts and made-up dialogues. This work of fiction is the single source of most of the false information about the Kiessling circulating today: that, for example, Kiessling was royal chef to Kaiser Wilhelm II and came to Tianjin during the Boxer-Rebellion or that Yuan Shikai was an investor. Conveniently, the book also pushed back the founding date to 1901. In 2001, the Vice Mayor of Tianjin, Xia Baolong, organised a celebration for the apparent 100-year anniversary of 'Tianjin's first foreign restaurant'. As part of the festivities, Dr Werner Kiessling was once more invited to his former hometown with his wife and daughter as guests of honour at 'The First China Western Style Food and Drink Culture Festival'. Dr Kiessling was awarded honorary citizenship of the city by the administration of Tianjin.[98] Since then, the Qishilin has proudly listed 1901 as its founding date on its logo, prominently displayed on all its products and marketing materials and throughout the main building and branches. It is a forgivable error, considering how devotedly its new owners continue to foster cross-cultural understanding through international food culture and to promote Herr Kiessling's name to this day.

As of 2022, Qishilin does not maintain any shops in Shanghai. However, together with the main branch and the hotel in Beidaihe, the chain boasts close to 100 patisserie locations across the provinces of Beijing, Tianjin, Hebei, Shaanxi and Shandong. And, just like in the

Figure 11: The Kiessling logos, as used by the Chinese owners today.

early 1900s, Qishilin continues to distribute its packaged pastries and chocolates via distance selling: the only difference being that it is now called 'e-commerce'.

Albert Kiessling, who is long forgotten in his home country of Germany, might very well be the most prominent foreigner to have ever started a business in China, as his name and portrait continue to be displayed on millions of advertisements and packaged goodies across the world's most populous country.

George Godula is a Shanghai-based entrepreneur and investor. He maintains the 'Museum of Foreign Brand Advertising in the Republic of China' (MOFBA), a private collection of close to 1,000 artefacts, showcasing the captivating history of Western brands advertising and selling in China during the Golden Years, 1912 to 1949.

REFERENCES

1. Werner Kiessling *Kurzbiographie des (Karl) Albert Kiessling*, 17.03.1991, private archive Schmitt-Englert, p. 1
2. Letter from Albert Kiessling to Friedrich Bader, 18.04.1913, private archive Schmitt-Englert
3. Erna Kluge Scheel *The Strength to Persevere* (Fairway Press, 1998)
4. Konrad Stingl "Konditorei in China" *Der Konditormeister: Fachzeitschrift des Konditoreihandwerks*, 2.31/32, 24.12.1948, 19f., p.19
5. *Rosenstock's Directory of China and Manila*. Vol. 14, 1909, p. 32
6. See <https://www.historichotelsthenandnow.com/astortianjin.html>
7. Werner Kiessling *Kurzbiographie des (Karl) Albert Kiessling*

8. Werner Kiessling *Biography of Albert Kiessling* Archive of the German club "Studienwerk Deutsches Leben in Ostasien e.V." Wolfgang Müller, p. 3
9. Letter from Albert Kiessling to Friedrich Bader (18.4.1913, private archive Schmitt-Englert) p.1
10. Werner Kiessling p. 3
11. See <http://friedrich-bader-sammlung.blogspot.com/>
12. *Peking Daily News*, 12 June 1915, p. 4
13. Stingl p. 12
14. *Army and Navy Register* 28 August 1915, Vol. LVIII, No. 1832, p. 282
15. *Tianjin Daily* (天津日报), 4.1. 2009 See <http://epaper.tianjinwe.com/>
16. Stingl p. 7
17. Han Suyin *A Mortal Flower* (Triad Grafton Books, 1966) p. 24
18. Haiko Hoffmann *Die Ausweisung der Deutschen aus China; eine Darstellung der Ereignisse auf Grund englischer, Shanghaier Zeitungen vom Oktober 1918 bis April 1919* (Sütterlin & Co., Schwerin/Germany) p. 385
19. *Millard's Review* 15 March 1919, p. 90
20. *The Shanghai Times* 'Antilochus sails for Germany' 4 April 1919, p. 3
21. Werner Kiessling p. 3
22. *The Shanghai Times* 28 February 1919, p. 9
23. *The North-China Herald and Supreme Court & Consular Gazette* 9 August 1919, p. 360
24. Scheel p. 75
25. See <https://www.cshagen.com/tag/kiesslings-cafe/>
26. *Peitaiho Directory* 1924, p. 26b
27. Eileen Chang *Shanghai Evening Post and Mercury* "What a Life! What A Girl's Life", 1938
28. Brian Power *The Puppet Emperor: The Life of Pu Yi, Last Emperor of China* (Peter Owen Publishers, 1986) p. 149
29. Stephanie Williams *Olga's Story* (Penguin, 2006) p. 263
30. Werner Kiessling p.4
31. Scheel p. 101
32. *The Comacrib Directory of China* 1925, p. 149
33. Emil Sigmund Fischer *Guide to Peking and Its Environs Near and Far* (Tientsin Press, 1924)

34. Wolfgang Müller *Kiessling & Bader Sonderpreisliste für Versandt* Archive of the German club „Studienwerk Deutsches Leben in Ostasien e.V."
35. Scheel p. 104
36. Peter Hibbard 'A New Course in History' *Journal Of The Royal Asiatic Society China*, 2013 Vol. 75 No 1, p. 262
37. Eileen Chang *Lust, Caution* (Penguin Books, 2007)
38. See <https://www.kaisiling.com.cn/>
39. *The China Press* 24 August 1929 Obituary p. 17
40. StuDeO. Studienwerk Deutsches Leben in Ostasien e.V. INFO magazine, December 2003, p. 30
41. Scheel p. 112
42. Werner Kiessling p. 5
43. *North-China Desk Hong List* 1933
44. *Rosenstock's Business Directory of China 1933* Millington, Limited, Tientsin Directory p. 28
45. Tianjin Municipal Archives / Figure "起士林"登记申请书 from 老档案中的西餐名店起士林, p. 53. Also published in *Foreigners in Old Tianjin* (外国人在旧天津) (Tianjin People's Publishing House (天津人民出版社), 2007)
46. StuDeO. p. 31
47. Gary Nash *The Tarasov Saga* (Rosenberg Publishing, 2002) p. 89
48. Stingl p. 19
49. Scheel p. 121
50. Scheel p. 124
51. *North China Daily News* 8 May 1935
52. StuDeO. p. 31
53. *North China Daily News* 22 December 1935
54. *North China Daily News* 28 October 1936
55. Nash p. 106
56. Werner Kiessling *Kurzbiographie des (Karl) Albert Kiessling*
57. Kan Li *On The Road To A Modern City: New Transportation Technology And Urban Transformation Of Tianjin, 1860-1937* (unpublished PhD Dissertation, University Of Minnesota June 2020) p. 239
58. Scheel pp. 127-134
59. John Rabe *The Good Man of Nanking: The Diaries of John Rabe* (Knopf Doubleday Publishing Group, 2007) p. 67
60. Scheel p. 137

61. Scheel p. 146
62. *The Tientsin U.S. Marine* 25 December 1938 Vol. 1, No. 1, p. 57
63. Stingl p. 12
64. *The North-China Herald and Supreme Court & Consular Gazette*, July 24th 1940, p. 126
65. See <http://www.cshagen.com/tag/kiesslings-cafe/>
66. Scheel p. 170
67. Scheel p. 171
68. Chang Ailing Collected Works 张爱玲文集, Vol 4, 张爱玲, 安徽文艺出版社, 1992, p. 382 Aurhor's translation of: "在上海我们家隔壁就是战时天津新搬来的起士林咖啡馆,每天黎明制面包,拉起嗅觉的警报,一股喷香的浩然之气破空而来,有长风万里之势"
69. Isabel Sun Chao and Claire Chao *Remembering Shanghai: A Memoir of Socialites, Scholars and Scoundrels* (Girl Friday Books, Seattle, 2018)
70. Adeline Yen Mah *Falling Leaves: The Memoir of an Unwanted Chinese Daughter* (Pearson Education Ltd. 1997) p. 38
71. Angela Louisa Cox Elliott, personal correspondence with the author
72. Scheel p. 185
73. Scheel pp. 207-219
74. *Shanghai Telephone Directory and Buyer's Guide* 1947, p. 5
75. *The Chinese-English Intelligence* September 23rd, 1947
76. David C. Hulme *Tientsin* (Lumix Ltd. 2002)
77. 乾坤寥廓日月长：天津市和平区政协历年文史资料精编 (The sky is long and the sun and moon are long: the compilation of cultural and historical materials of the CPPCC in Heping District, Tianjin over the years), Beijing Book Co. Inc., 2019, article "西餐名店起士林" by 周利成 p. 140
78. See <https://www.archives.sh.cn/shjy/scbq/201407/t20140710_41201.html>
79. *Gong ping bao* (公評報), 1947.08.28, p.1
80. StuDeO. p. 3
81. Nash pp. 172-208
82. *Kiessling - Legend spanning a century* 起士林，跨越世纪的传奇 (Tianjin People's Publishing House (天津人民出版社), 2011)
83. Werner Kiessling *Biography of Albert Kiessling*
84. Beverley Hooper *Foreigners under Mao: Western Lives in China*,

1949–1976 (Hong Kong University Press, 2016) p. 91
85. https://zh.m.wikipedia.org/zh/%E8%B5%B7%E5%A3%AB%E6%9E%97%E9%A4%90%E5%8E%85>
86. Brian Power *The Ford of Heaven* (Peter Owen, London, 1984) p. 211
87. <https://zh.m.wikipedia.org/zh>
88. StuDeO. p. 31
89. Arne J. De Keijzer, Fredric M. Kaplan, and Koku Nihon *JAL guide to the People's Republic of China*, 1980, p. 134
90. StuDeO. p. 17
91. Scheel p. 331
92. 乾坤寥廓日月长：天津市和平区政协历年文史资料精编 (The sky is long and the sun and moon are long: the compilation of cultural and historical materials of the CPPCC in Heping District, Tianjin over the years), Beijing Book Co. Inc., 2019 has the Wang background story
93. Nash p. 270
94. Robert Boulanger *China* (Prentice Hall Press, 1989) p. 282
95. <https://baike.baidu.com/item/%E8%B5%B7%E5%A3%AB%E6%9E%97%E9%A4%90%E5%8E%85/5319895>
96. Map and Google Earth research of historic satellite photos by the author
97. Wen Shu (文淑) *There is a Qishilin in Tianjin* (天津有个起士林) (Baihua Literature and Art Publishing House, 2001)
98. Interview with Hang Ying, <http://news.enorth.com.cn/system/2004/06/23/000807358.shtml>, 2004

1978: A YEAR OF ENORMOUS SIGNIFICANCE

BY JOHN DARWIN VAN FLEET

ABSTRACT

In terms of scale, speed and scope, China's socioeconomic growth over the past four decades is unprecedented in human history. The world widely heralds 1978 as year zero for the start of this period of astonishing development. Three totemic events heralding the era of gaige kaifang (改革开放, Reform and Opening) occurred within a 60-day period toward the end of that year. Deng Xiaoping visited Japan in late October. The 18 impoverished villagers in Xiaogang, Anhui Province, ratified their 'seditious' document promoting individual usage rights by candlelight in late November risking imprisonment or worse in a desperate struggle for survival. And finally the Communist Party of China (CPC) convened the Third Plenary Session of the 11th Party Congress in mid-December. During that same period, on 15 December, Beijing and Washington announced that diplomatic relations would be normalised on the first day of 1979.

FIRST TIME IN HISTORY

> As a country, [China] has gone through change on an unprecedented scale since the launch of market reform in 1978, [...]
>
> Jonathan Fenby, *Tiger Head, Snake Tails*, 2011[1]

> [...] the fastest sustained expansion by a major economy in history.
>
> The World Bank, 2017[2]

> [...] the greatest economic advance the world has ever seen, and the greatest improvement in history in the living standards and life chances for ordinary people.
>
> The Adam Smith Institute, *The Document that Changed the World*[3]

China's explosive socioeconomic development over the past several decades is incontrovertibly a first time in history (FTIH) phenomenon: to paraphrase Churchill, never before have so many risen so far so fast. According to the Maddison Project, China's per capita gross domestic product (GDP), measured on a purchasing power parity (PPP) basis, has risen by about eightfold since 1978.[4] In non-technical terms, China's people have, in aggregate, become eight times wealthier over the course of these four decades.

An eightfold increase is less impressive if others have grown by that much or more, but China's growth has been in a class of its own. The per capita wealth of two other large-population developing countries, India and Indonesia, grew only half as much during the same period. The per capita wealth of a third, Brazil, grew by a factor of only two, one quarter as much as China's growth—reasonable, as Brazil started from a much higher level of per capita wealth. Note that the slope of China's line, indicating faster growth, is the outlier.

Two caveats accompany this point. Some economists suggest that GDP is primarily useful as a gauge of in-country trends, and not so useful for cross-national comparison. And an increasing amount of China's GDP since the 'infrastructure decade" of the 2010s has been inflated by debt. However authorities at the level of Nobel Prize winners in economics and the World Bank have concluded that the aggregate effect of China's comparative growth in recent decades is

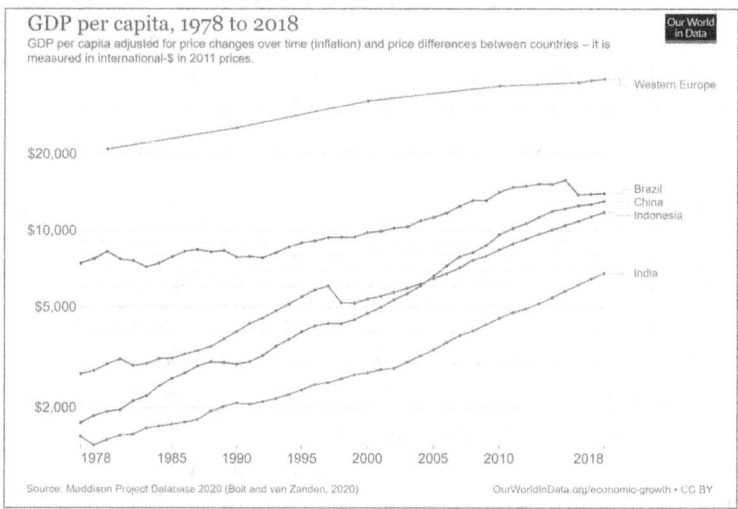

Figure 1: Comparative growth in per capita GDP.

large enough to override these concerns.

China's socioeconomic rise since 1978 is also unmatched by historical precedents. According to economist and Nobel laureate Robert E. Lewis though, we need consider only the past few hundred years:

> [...] up to 1800 or maybe 1750, no society had experienced sustained growth in per capita income. (Eighteenth century population growth also averaged one-third of 1 percent, the same as production growth.) That is, up to about two centuries ago, per capita incomes in all societies were stagnated at around $400 to $800 per year.[5]

Lewis' '1800 or maybe 1750' refers to the dawn of the Industrial Revolutions, before which per capita income was tied closely to agricultural output. Until then, human and animal muscle could produce only so much grain, or mine only so much gold.

For the 200 years until the late 20th century, neither China nor India gained much benefit from the advent of machines and the fossil fuels that powered them—both countries stagnated economically. Great Britain, centrepiece of the Industrial Revolution, took nearly two centuries to gain a five-fold increase in per capita wealth from 1760, while the European continent overall grew by substantially less. (Europeans in those centuries were often occupied with civil wars.) The United States required a century to gain a five-fold increase in its 1850 per capita wealth. Great Britain and the U.S. had only a fraction of China's population at any time—all of Europe had a population of about 200 million people in 1850, about half of China's 400 million. The current number of European inhabitants is now well under half of China's population.[6]

West Germany and Japan enjoyed a roughly tenfold increase in per capita wealth from 1946 until the mid-1980s, but two factors remove them as rivals for China's FTIH status. Each had a population of less than 10% of China's, but more importantly, the late 1940s were extreme outlier lows for both countries. Each had its per capita wealth reduced by nearly half as a result of World War II, as the images of Dresden, Hiroshima and Nagasaki attest.

In the next section, I consider the four tectonic forces that have powered China's astonishing socioeconomic rise since 1978: promising demographics, foreign re-engagement, some wise government policy and, arguably most important, the initiative, courage and entrepreneurship of hundreds of millions of Chinese people. But in 1978, China was an uncommonly poor country. Only some of the countries in Africa, in war-ravaged Indochina and in South Asia had substantially lower per capita wealth figures. India was slightly lower, Eastern Europe, Latin America and the remainder of Southeast Asia all far higher. So as 1978 dawned, in addition to demographics, China had another advantage in support of its eventual FTIH status: an exceptionally low baseline.

A Promising Demographic Platform

While China was an economic basket case in 1978, a closer look reveals a few demographic factors that held promise for the future. As with per capita wealth, comparisons with Brazil, India and Indonesia, the other large-population developing economies over the relevant years, illuminate[7]

Literacy

A 1989 paper by A. John Jowett, *Patterns of Literacy in the People's Republic of China*, tells the story of China's educational achievement, as measured by comparative literacy rates.

> China's educational progress since 1949 appears to have been unmatched among developing countries at comparable levels of income. Success is apparent from the fact that literacy rates have risen from an estimated 20% in 1949 to a recorded 68% in 1982. In neighbouring India and Pakistan literacy rates are 43% and 30%, and the average in the developing world is 50 to 55%.[8]

In 1950, China's literacy rate trailed Brazil's by 30 points. By 1980, China had narrowed the gap to about ten points, and had closed the gap entirely with Indonesia.

One way China increased literacy so much was by educating girls. As late as 2011, only about eight in ten women in India could read, while in China virtually all women could.[9] China's educational progress was largely gender-neutral.

Life expectancy

> China's growth in life expectancy between 1950 and 1980 ranks as among the most rapid sustained increases in documented global history.
>
> Babiarz, et al, 2015[10]

In the first few years of the 1950s, the early postwar period, countries in the developing world had life expectancies at birth (LEBs) far below those of Western Europe and North America, which had LEBs in the mid to high 60s. Brazil's LEB was about 51, China and Indonesia were at about 44 and 42, respectively, and India lagged at about 40.[11]

By the late 1970s, Brazil's figure, from the highest starting point of the four, had climbed 11 points, to about 62; Indonesia's figure had risen 15 points, to about 57, while India's figure had reached about 55, a 16-point increase. But China's figure had climbed farthest in both absolute and percentage terms, by 22 points, to about 66.

LEB measures not only what age people attain, but also information about infant mortality. The United Nations Development Programme uses LEB as one component of the Human Development Index, along with literacy.[12] Another economist and Nobel laureate, Amartya Sen, has repeatedly asserted that LEB and literacy largely explain China leaving India far behind in per capita wealth.[13]

The World Bank and World Health Organization, among many others, credit China's famous 'barefoot doctors' for much of China's dramatic rise in LEB from the 1950s. Reorganised into the Rural Cooperative Medical System (RCMS) in the 1960s and 1970s, the barefoot doctor program has been 'considered an unprecedented example of a successful health care model in a low-income, developing country'.[14]

Pyramids Tell the Story

The 'population pyramid' enjoys wide popularity for its ability to graphically represent population distribution.[15] Compare the 1978 population pyramid for Japan, Asia's most economically advanced economy at the time, with that of the world (see following page).

Japan's pyramid has a narrower base and fatter upper bands, reflecting the higher LEB common in developed economies. In addition, the noticeable bulge around the 30—34 age group represents Japan's baby boom immediately postwar, in the late 1940s and into the early 1950s.

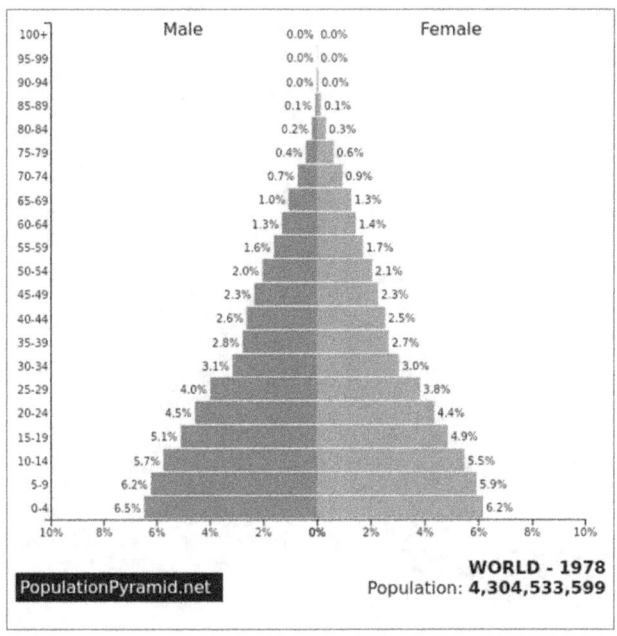
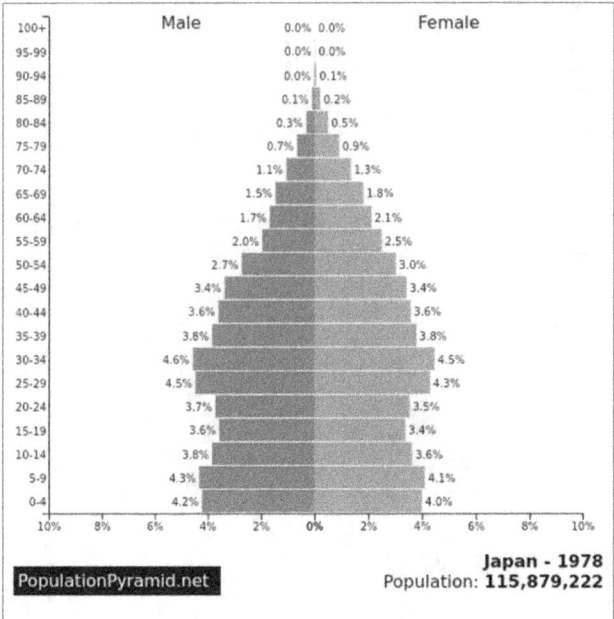

Figure 2 and 3: Population Pyramids, The World and Japan, 1978

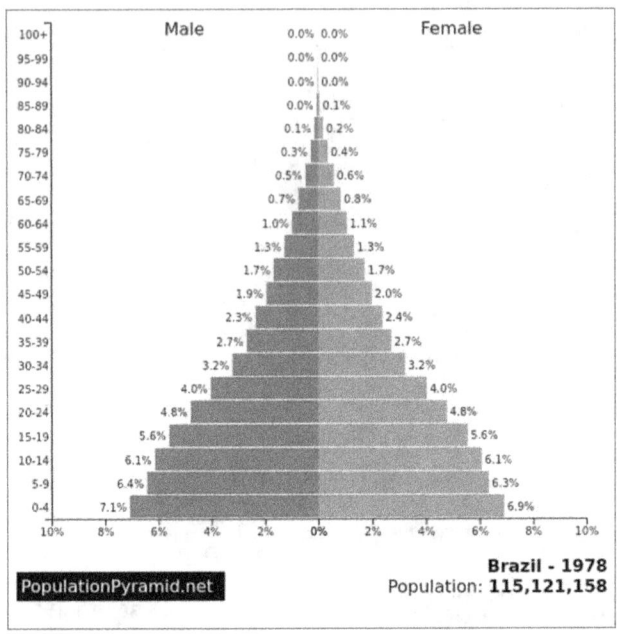
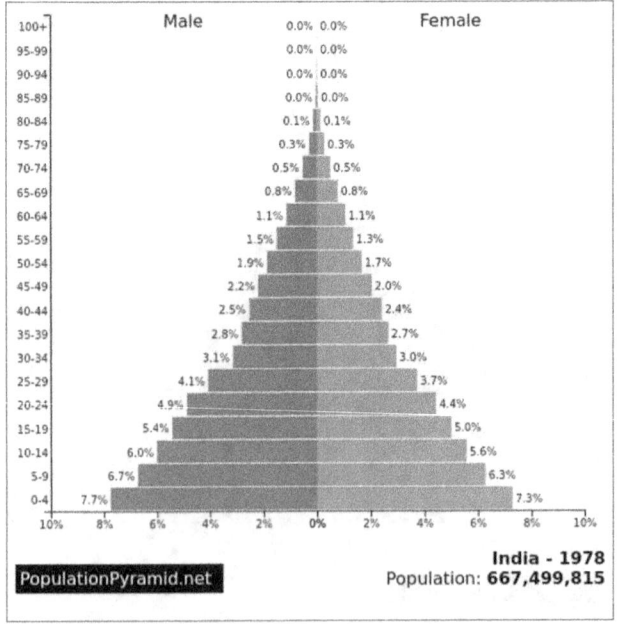

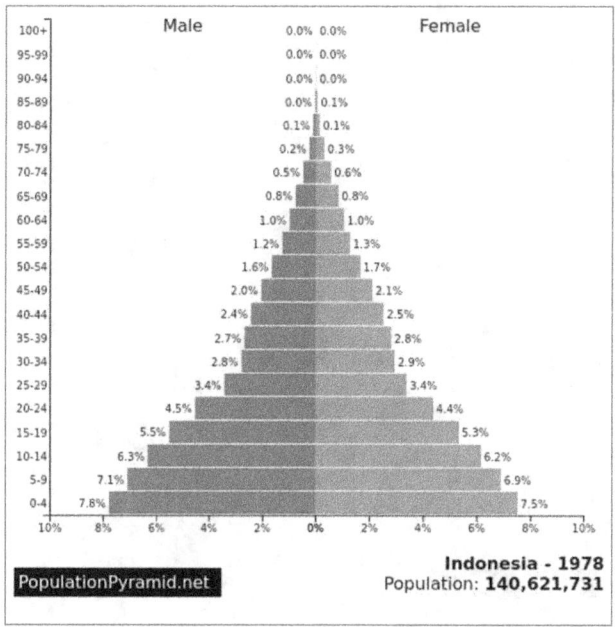

Figure 4, 5 and 6: Population Pyramids, Brazil, India and Indonesia, 1978

Now consider the pyramids above for Brazil, India and Indonesia, three large-population developing countries in the period.

Intuitively for developing economies, the pyramids have much fatter bases and narrower higher bands, reflecting lower LEBs. Compared with the other two, Brazil's pyramid is somewhat narrower at the base, reflecting Brazil's higher LEB.

Finally, consider China's pyramid in 1978 (following page).

China's slopes more steeply than those of the other three large developing economies, reflecting China's higher life expectancy. In addition, China's own baby boom, which started in the early 1960s and continued through the early 1970s, commands attention.[16]

The Demographic Dividend

To become 'the world's factory', a moniker some apply to China even today, the country needed a large labour force of reasonably healthy and literate people.[17] By the time export manufacturing really took off in the 1990s (illustrated in Figure 10), China had by far the largest young labour force of all the developing economies.

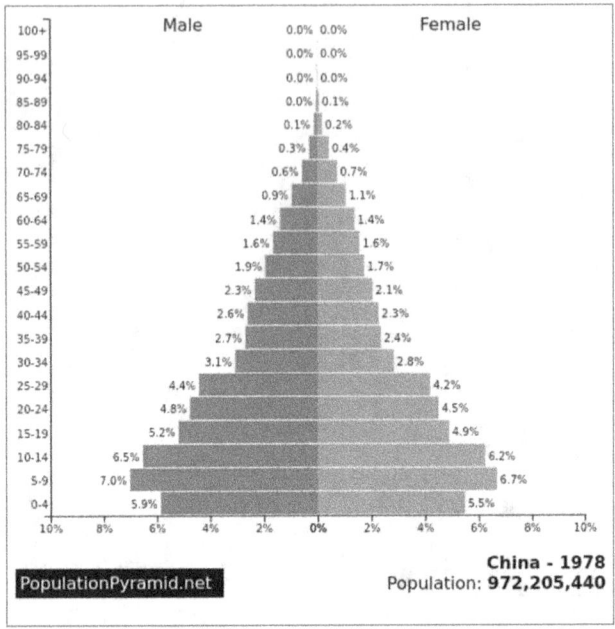

Figure 7: Population Pyramid, China, 1978

Those young people were healthier than their peers in the other large-population developing economies. Their literacy—both genders—rivalled or exceeded their peers.

China's demographic dividend therefore became the first of the four tectonically powerful forces impelling China's FTIH rise.

OCTOBER 1978: MR DENG GOES TO TOKYO

By 1978, Deng Xiaoping and his faction of the CPC had long since realised that they needed help, and a lot of it, to rebuild the economy they'd inherited. They also recognised China's enormous potential, if they could just secure the capital and technological inputs that China itself could not yet generate by itself. (At that point, the Sino-US economic partnership was embryonic at best; diplomatic relations weren't normalised until January 1979.)

They knew of one nearby place where such inputs might be available. Japan had risen from utter dissolution to global #2 in GDP in just three decades, at an annual average growth rate of nearly 10%.[18]

So Mr Deng, then China's top leader, went to Tokyo in October 1978, becoming the highest-level official from the People's Republic of China ever to visit Japan, and the first ever to meet a Japanese emperor.

The dean of China-Japan scholars, the late Ezra Vogel, describes:

> On arriving in Japan, Deng announced that he had come for three reasons: to exchange the formal Treaty of Peace and Friendship documents, to thank Japanese friends who had worked to improve relations between the two countries, and to find the "magic drug" [...] how to modernize.[19]

Figure 8: Japanese Prime Minister Fukuda Takeo welcomes Deng Xiaoping to Japan.[20]

In addition to the treaty documents, China and Japan had other geopolitical matters to address, such as Taiwan and the increasingly tense relations with the Soviet Union. But as Prof. Robert Hoppens writes,

> The importance of the economic program is reflected in Deng's itinerary. In addition to his talks with Prime Minister Fukuda, Deng also toured a Nippon Steel plant, visited a Nissan auto plant, and met with Japanese industrial and business leaders and the leaders of Japan's most important industrial and economic organizations like the Federation of Economic Organizations (Keidanren).[21]

Deng's 1978 milestone was one of many along a long path. Japanese Prime Minister Tanaka Kakuei had visited Beijing six years earlier, meeting Mao Zedong and Zhou Enlai, for the formal signing of the Joint Communique of the Government of the People's Republic of China and the Government of Japan. Normalisation of 'trade, fisheries, aviation, navigation, etc.' followed over the next few years.[23]

China had also famously welcomed US president Richard Nixon for a visit earlier in 1972. Nonetheless, Deng's October 1978 visit to Japan, resolutely focused on accelerating China's modernisation, inaugurated a growth in bilateral trade of about 15% per year from 1978 to 2010, nearly double China's overall GDP growth.[24]

Richard McGregor, author of *Asia's Reckoning: China, Japan and*

Figure 9: Deng Xiaoping's meeting with Matsushita founder and CEO Matsushita Kōnosuke[22]

the Fate of U.S. Power in the Pacific Century, penned an op-ed in the South China Morning Post on the 40th anniversary of Deng's 1978 visit to Japan. Comparing that trip with Deng's famous visit to the United States in January 1979, when Deng donned a gigantic cowboy hat with a smile, McGregor titles his piece, 'Forget Texas, China came out when Deng tipped his hat to Japan'.[25]

China's demographic dividend was the first tectonic force propelling the FTIH phenomenon, in that it was already in place by 1978. Deng's 1978 Tokyo visit, and his subsequent trips to Singapore and the United States, symbolised re-engagement with the global economy, which became the second of the four. In 1980, exports claimed a tiny part of China's miniscule GDP, in both monetary and percentage terms. 25 years later, China was exporting US$1 trillion per year, but more importantly, exports had grown to account for nearly a third of China's total GDP.

November 1978: Entrepreneurship by Any Other Name

In late November 1978, peasants from each of the 18 households in a Chinese village gathered in its largest structure, a dilapidated, mud-floor and dirt-wall house. At night, to shield their impending treasonous act from prying eyes. The village had no electricity, so by candlelight each of the 18 villagers thumb-printed and chopped a

Figure 10: China's exports, 1980–2010[26]

document that proclaimed a new arrangement for their lives. They also pledged that they would care for the children of any of the signatories who might be jailed or executed for signing such a document.

What 'seditious, heretical' document was this? It divided ownership of some of each household's production among the households themselves, after they'd met their collective quota. It created private property, in the form of a portion of the harvest. While this might have seemed far from radical elsewhere in the world, in Xiaogang, this village in eastern Anhui Province, in aggressively communistic 1970s mainland China, privatisation of the means and the fruits of production carried the potential of capital punishment.

So why would the household heads of a village of 150 or so people ratify a document that might become their death warrants? Because the village had teetered on the cliff edge of starvation for decades, and some had fallen into the abyss. Only 18 years before, fully half of the villagers had starved to death during China's great famine, in which roughly 35 million people died throughout the country.[28] China.org, a state media company, illuminates the situation in Xiaogang and elsewhere in Anhui during the famine. Quoting Xiaogang villager Guan Youjiang:

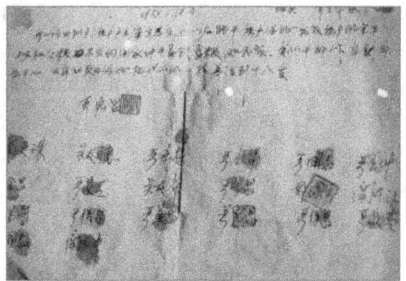

Figure 11: The Xiaogang villagers' 'seditious' document[27]

> Everybody was dying of hunger. The village population was only 120 before 1958 and 67 villagers died of hunger between 1958 and 1960. In Fengyang County [where Xiaogang is located], a quarter of the population died—90,000 in all.[29]

Ratified in darkness, the Xiaogang villagers' document—the revolution-in-reverse plan it codified—worked. The China.org article continues:

> Dividing up the land helped Guan's fellow farmers feed their families. The village was the first in China to implement the household responsibility system, under which land was leased to families in return for delivery of fixed output quotas. In less than a year, villagers increased output by more than enough to meet their own needs and had accumulated a surplus for sale on the market. According to the village committee, grain output increased to 90,000 kilograms in 1979, six times as much as the previous year. The per capita income of Xiaogang climbed from 22 yuan to 400 yuan.[30]

However, no good deed goes unpunished—the neighbouring villages, and then regional officials, inevitably learned of Xiaogang's astonishing leap forward in agricultural productivity, and then discovered the pact with the private property devil. Another villager, Yeng Hongchang, 'was hauled into the local Communist Party office. The officials swore at him, treated him like he was on death row'.[31]

But the era favoured the Xiaogang villagers. 1978 was not 1968. A reformist-minded Wan Li (万里) had been appointed the Party head of Anhui in May 1977. He implemented early forms of privatisation, and eventually approved the Xiaogang villagers' initiative.[32]

In Sichuan, another province devastated by the great famine, Shunshuke described,

> A production contract system was established in 1978, letting peasants freely sell in the marketplace rice and other crops that exceeded the production quotas set by the communes.

The People's Daily [...] reported on the efforts made by Jinyu's ninth production team in December 1978. The reforms in Jinyu then spread across China.[33]

Numerous scholars have described similar entrepreneurial, village-level initiatives around the country, dating back more than a decade. In *How the Farmers Changed China*, Prof. Kate Xiao Zhou writes,

> Contrary to conventional thinking, unorganized increases in rural productivity, rather than any urban economic development, accelerated China's economic development (still overwhelmingly rural). Farmers attempted unorganized decollectivisation or surreptitious grassroots land reform, in many parts of rural China throughout the 1960s and 1970s. Their efforts finally succeeded in the late 1970s and came above ground in 1982 [...][34]

FROM MICROMANAGEMENT TO MARKETS

The household responsibility system (HRS, 家庭联产承包责任制, *jiā tíng lián chǎn chéng bāo zé rèn zhì*), which grew out of these rural initiatives, represented a sea change in policy. On their website, China.org describe the system: 'Households could make operating decisions independently within the limits set by the contract agreement, and could freely dispose of surplus production over and above national and collective quotas'.[35]

In a late 1980s journal article, Prof. Justin Lin states:

> [The HRS] thus spread rapidly to many parts of China. Full official recognition of the HRS as universally acceptable was given in late 1981; at that time 45.1% of production teams in China had already switched to this system.[36]

By the 2000s, the transformative effect of the HRS in the 1980s and beyond was obvious to all. In a 2005 report, the OECD describes it:

> During the reform period, which started in 1978, China made huge progress in meeting its objectives: agricultural production rose sharply, rural industries absorbed a large part of farm labour, poverty fell dramatically, and

the level and quality of food consumption improved significantly. The commune system was replaced by one where individual families lease land from the collectives [the HRS], ensuring that almost all rural households have access to land and are, at minimum, food self-sufficient.[37]

Moreover, the HRS proved to be merely the first step. In a paper published for a Reserve Bank of Australia conference in 2016, noted economist Nicholas Lardy writes,

> China has moved from a system in which almost all important prices were set administratively, with scant attention to underlying supply and demand, to one in which markets determine the prices of virtually all goods and services and, more recently, most factors of production as well. In this increasingly market-driven environment, private firms have become the dominant source of the growth of output, employment and exports.[38]

In 2019, the World Economic Forum put some numbers on the concept.

> The combination of numbers 60/70/80/90 are frequently used to describe the private sector's contribution to the Chinese economy: they contribute 60% of China's GDP, and are responsible for 70% of innovation, 80% of urban employment and provide 90% of new jobs. Private wealth is also responsible for 70% of investment and 90% of exports.[39]

The Xiaogang villagers' nocturnal 'insurrection' is now honoured as another milestone in China's path toward modernisation. China hails the 18 villagers as heroes; the village hosts a memorial museum, where the Xiaogang document, now a national treasure, rests under glass. One may also view a sculpture of the 18 villagers there.

Entrepreneurs, in the common definition, risk their capital and time, hoping for a return on their investment. The Xiaogang villagers, and the tens of millions of others, risked their freedom, even their lives, hoping for the return of a better future for their families. Entrepreneurs

Figure 12: The Xiaogang villagers' iconoclastic act, memorialised in sculpture in the museum in Xiaogang[40]

in any rational definition of the term, they may reasonably look with pride on what their spiritual descendants, in aggregate the private sector, have achieved in China. Their spirit of pioneering initiative was and remains the third of the of the four tectonic forces impelling China's FTIH rise, and perhaps the most important.

DECEMBER 1978: GOODBYE CLASS WARFARE, HELLO ECONOMIC DEVELOPMENT
From 18-22 December 1978, less than two months after Deng Xiaoping had called on Japan requesting economic support, the Communist Party of China (CPC) convened its now-famous Third Plenary Session of the 11th Central Committee of the CPC (十一届三中全会). The session's closing communique famously asserted that, 'From this day forward we renounce class struggle as the central focus, and instead take up economic development as our central focus'.[41]

Figure 13: Unanimous approval of the Communique, 22 December 1978.[42]

187

The tale of how China's leadership had evolved to this point is remarkable and complex, as is that of the subsequent evolution. Zhu Jiamu, an attendee at the session, writes:

> According to Deng Xiaoping, the two years that followed the downfall of the Gang of Four paved the way for the Third Plenary Session. Without those two years it would have been impossible for the Party to establish clear ideological and political lines [...].[43]

Zhou Enlai had been calling for the 'four modernisations' (四个现代化)—industry, agriculture, national defence and science-technology—since 1963.[44]

Perhaps the most famous regulatory initiatives undertaken by the post-1978-Chinese government were the special economic zones (SEZs). Initially four—Shenzhen and two others in the Pearl River Delta, and Xiamen in neighbouring Fujian Province—the SEZs rocketed into international prominence as symbols of China's economic ascent, particularly from the 1990s.

> One primary characteristic was a revolutionary shift towards deregulation. Not only did these areas enjoy lower tax rates, but also, and perhaps more importantly, they enjoyed special institutional and policy environments, allowing them to gain more authority over economic development. Although the rest of China was still dominated by central planning and public ownership, special economic zones were allowed to become more like market economies.[45]

Less well known but more important to China's socioeconomic rise in the 1980s were the township and village enterprises (TVEs) - *xiang zhen qi ye* (乡镇企业). 'Township and village' specified location—the ownership structure could vary, but these initiatives were rural by definition and design. And they had the power to make market-based decisions.

> The peasants took advantage of cheap land and labour, semi-formal or informal fund-pooling, the authority of

the existing rural hierarchy or kinship, of local market and low transaction costs, of central government ignorance, and eroding control over income disparity since the adoption of the household responsibility system, and gradually shifted their resources into rural industry.

Furthermore:

> The economic policies from the central government can be summarised as the following popular slogans then. First, 'controlling better by controlling less' (*fenquan rangli*). The decentralised fiscal and personnel system was designed to increase responsibilities and incentive [...][46]

The Chinese slogan evokes Deng Xiaoping's famous utterance of the era: It doesn't matter if a cat is black or white so long as it catches mice.[47]

Prof. Huang Yasheng of MIT assigns to TVEs the credit for most of China's reduction in poverty since 1980 (by itself a FTIH accomplishment), and for economic development overall until the mid-1990s to the TVEs.

> China's take-off in economic growth starting in the late 1970s, and its poverty reduction for the next couple of decades, was completely a function of its rural developments [...] especially rural industry spearheaded by the rise of township and village enterprises. [...]
>
> [TVEs] raised rural income, absorbed rural surplus labor, and contributed to a decline in the rural–urban income gap in the 1980s. The value-added produced by these rural businesses increased from 6 percent of GDP in 1978 to 26 percent of GDP in 1996[48]

The preeminence of TVEs in China's overall economic development starting in the 1980s is natural, considering that 80% of China's people were still rural in 1980.[49] But the TVE's rapid proliferation and ascent surprised even Deng Xiaoping, as the People's Daily reported in June 1987, 'What took us by complete surprise was the development of TVEs. All sorts of small enterprises boomed in the countryside, as if a strange army appeared suddenly from nowhere.'⁵⁰

Dual Track Regulatory Reform

The SEZs became symbolic of China's globalisation and deregulation from the 1980s, but the less-famous TVEs contributed an outsized portion to China's socioeconomic growth. Similarly, a second aspect of government policy in addition to deregulation, from the 1980s on, hasn't gained the credit it deserves. In *How Asia Works*, Joe Studwell asserts that,

> In a world of bad developmental advice, the Chinese government did not make the mistake of Southeast Asian States and listen like a patsy to the imprecations of the World Bank, the IMF, and the US government to deregulate its economy prematurely. [...] The World Bank's neoliberal prescriptions for financial deregulation were not entertained.⁵¹

Prof. Isabella Weber published *How China Escaped Shock Therapy* in 2021. The shock therapy she refers to was China's successful avoidance of price liberalisation in the 1980s. As the title suggests, Weber outlines how China's leadership steered the recovering economy away from the types of shock therapy that Russia experienced in the 1990s. She illuminates, for example, China's dual-track price system, in which producers sold some of their output to the state at fixed, below-market prices, but retained some of their output for private sale at market prices.

Prof Huang and others point out that it wasn't the concept, but rather the Chinese government's implementation of it, that made it work for China.

> The dual-track price system was neither novel nor Chinese. The Soviet Union tried it many times but failed. The difference is the Chinese leadership committed itself to not ratcheting up the targets and did so credibly. It was the politics of the Deng Xiaoping era, not just the mechanics of the reform, that accounted for the success.⁵²

Weber suggests that, rather than follow a neoliberal prescription from overseas, China's regulators adhered to an ancient Chinese aphorism. 'Seeking truth from facts' was not a mere epistemological principle but an art of government'.[53]

Studwell too outlines how the Chinese government made some wise, strategic 'interventions', starting from the late 1970s. But Studwell casts a wider net. Writing about all of Asia, he asserts that China joined the rest of northeast Asia—Japan, South Korea and Taiwan—in a three-stage strategy for development that defied the World Bank, IMF and U.S. Treasury consensus. The interventions were designed to:

> Create conditions for small farmers to thrive.
>
> Use the proceeds from agricultural surpluses to build a manufacturing base that is tooled from the start to produce exports.
>
> Nurture both these sectors (small farming and export-oriented manufacturing) with financial institutions closely controlled by the government.[54]

How did China escape the fate of the Soviet Union? Weber's book addresses the factional infighting and strategic challenges facing the Chinese government in the decade of the 1980s and the successes it achieved despite these impediments. Studwell suggests an additional approach common throughout north Asia during that decade and the two following.

> Unfortunately, the intellectual tyranny of neoclassical 'efficency' economics—the natural subject matter of rich countries—means that it is all but impossible to have an honest discussion about economic development. Poor states can only be successful by lying. They have to subscribe publicly to the 'free market' economics touted by the rich while pursuing the kind of interventionist policies that are actually necessary to become rich in the first place. [...] Far better to take a page out of Park Chung Hee or contemporary China's book: make public pronouncements about the importance of free markets and then go quietly about your *dirigiste* business.[55]
>
> Multinational business interests have complained bitterly for two decades now that China agreed to the

requirements of World Trade Organization (WTO) accession but has not adhered to those requirements.

Whether those accusations have merit is debatable, but Studwell's book gives us one possible explanation of the phenomenon.

Similar to China's dual-track price strategy, the country had a dual-track regulation strategy—deregulation combined with incremental and historically grounded agricultural, industrial and financial policies. These regulatory strategies, symbolised by the Third Plenary Session in 1978, became the fourth tectonic force, along with the demographic dividend, re-engagement with the global economy, and the innovation and entrepreneurship of the Chinese people themselves, driving China's FTIH rise.

Remembering 1978, Looking Forward

By the end of the century, hundreds of millions of (mostly) rural entrepreneurs and their spiritual and actual descendants would be creating about two thirds of China's total industrial output. China's regulatory strategies, combined with both governmental and private sector engagement with the global economy, and a substantial demographic dividend, and most importantly the initiative and courage of those hundreds of millions of pioneers, worked in concert to produce the FTIH phenomenon.

On a purchasing power parity basis China already boasts the largest GDP in the world. An economic basket case in 1978, an exporter of relatively cheap manufactured goods because of an abundance of low wage labour in the 1990s, China has now become a global leader and technology innovator in uncounted economic categories. They include electric vehicles, 5G, AI, high-speed rail, wind-generated energy, the entire universe of the consumer-smartphone interface, and many others.

While China's fundamental political system has changed little since the 50s, the country and the world economy may look back with gratitude on the symbolic events of 1978, and what they represent. Chinese people may with some justification be proud of some wise strategic decisions made by the government over the course of those decades, as outlined above. They may, with even more justification, be proud of their parents and grandparents, uncles and aunts, who, often at great risk, pioneered economic initiatives that have transformed not only China but the entire world, and that will resonate through to the end of the 21st century at least.

John Darwin Van Fleet (jvf_road@hotmail.com) has lived in Japan for 10 years and in China for 21. He currently serves as Director, Corporate Globalisation, and adjunct faculty, Antai College of Economics & Management, Shanghai Jiao Tong University. A contributor to the Asian Review of Books, Caixin, Nikkei Asia and SupChina, Van Fleet's first book, Tales of Old Tokyo, *was published in 2015.*

REFERENCES

(All websites accessed 4 June 2022)

1 Fenby, Jonathan, *Tiger Head, Snake Tails* (London: Simon & Schuster, 2012), p. 1.
2 2017 archived page quoted in numerous places, including 'China's Economic Rise: History, Trends, Challenges, and Implications for the United States', *Congressional Research Service*, 25 June 2019. https://sgp.fas.org/crs/row/RL33534.pdf
3 Pirie, Madsen, 'The Document that Changed the World', Adam Smith Institute, 15 June 2018. https://www.adamsmith.org/blog/the-document-that-changed-the-world
4 All macroeconomic data in these several paragraphs are from Bolt, Jutta and Jan Luiten van Zanden, 'Maddison style estimates of the evolution of the world economy. A new 2020 update', *Maddison Project Database*, version 2020. https://www.rug.nl/ggdc/historicaldevelopment/maddison/releases/maddison-project-database-2020?lang=en
5 Lucas, Robert E, 'The Industrial Revolution: Past and Future', Federal Reserve Bank of Minneapolis, 2003. https://web.archive.org/web/20071127032512/http:/minneapolisfed.org/pubs/region/04-05/essay.cfm#lucas
6 Various sources, including 'Issues and Trends in China's Population History', Weatherhead East Asia Institute, Columbia University, [n.d.]. http://afe.easia.columbia.edu/special/china_1950_population.htm
7 Pakistan now has more people than Brazil, No. 4 in this list by population, but was far behind Brazil until the 2000s.
8 Jowett, A. John, 'Patterns of Literacy in the People's Republic of China' *GeoJournal*, Vol. 18, No. 4, (June 1989), 417—427. https://

www.jstor.org/stable/41144462

9 Sen, Amartya, 'Quality of Life: India vs. China', *New York Review of Books*, 12 May 2011. https://www.nybooks.com/articles/2011/05/12/quality-life-india-vs-china/

10 Babiarz, Kimberly Singer and others, 'An exploration of China's mortality decline under Mao: A provincial analysis, 1950–80', Asia Health Policy Program Working Paper No. 40, Walter H. Shorenstein Asia-Pacific Research Center Stanford University, 26 January 2015. https://papers.ssrn.com/sol3/papers.cfm?abstract_id=2850698

11 Life expectancy figures from United Nations, Department of Economic and Social Affairs, Population Division (2019). World Population Prospects 2019, Online Edition. Rev. 1. https://population.un.org/wpp/Download/Files/1_Indicators%20(Standard)/EXCEL_FILES/3_Mortality/WPP2019_MORT_F07_1_LIFE_EXPECTANCY_0_BOTH_SEXES.xlsx

12 'Human Development Report 2020: 'The next frontier: Human development and the Anthropocene' United Nations Development Programme, 15 December 2020. https://hdr.undp.org/content/human-development-report-2020

13 Tuck-Primdahl, Merrell, 'Amartya Sen on India and China', World Bank, 21 June 2013. https://blogs.worldbank.org/developmenttalk/amartya-sen-india-and-china

14 Wang Fang and Liang Yuan, China's Rural Cooperative Medical Scheme: a type of health insurance or a type of health cooperative?', *Primary Health Care Research & Development*, Volume 18, Issue 2, (March 2017), pp. 194—199. https://doi.org/10.1017/S1463423616000153

15 Population data in this section are from the United Nations, Department of Economic and Social Affairs, Population Division. World Population Prospects: The 2019 Revision. (Medium variant); and several others, via PopulationPyramid.net. Graphics are available under Creative Commons license. https://www.populationpyramid.net/sources

16 China's total fertility rate (TFR), the common measurement for a population's birth rate, dropped by 50% from 1970 to 1980, as is apparent from the noticeably narrower population band for the 0—4 age range. The dramatic decline suggests that the one-child policy was largely unnecessary, but that's a separate discussion.

17 'China is the world's factory, more than ever', *The Economist*, 23 June 2020. https://www.economist.com/finance-and-economics/2020/06/23/china-is-the-worlds-factory-more-than-ever
18 GDP growth (annual %)—Japan, World Bank national accounts data, and OECT National Accounts data files. https://data.worldbank.org/indicator/NY.GDP.MKTP.KD.ZG?locations=JP
19 Vogel, Ezra F, *China and Japan: Facing History* (Cambridge: The Belknap Press of Harvard University Press, 2019), p. 338.
20 China Daily via RG21, 22 October 2013. http://rg21.jp/?p=611
21 Hoppens, Robert, 'Deng Xiaoping Visits Tokyo, October 1978 and February 1979', Wilson Center, History and Public Policy Program, 18 May 2020. https://www.wilsoncenter.org/blog-post/deng-xiaoping-visits-tokyo-october-1978-and-february-1979
22 Chen Wei, *Fengyu Tongzhou, Jiwang Kailai* (in Chinese) (Matsushita Electric (China), 2018), p. 6.
23 Kim Hong N., 'Sino-Japanese Relations Since the Rapprochement', *Asian Survey*, Vol. 15, No. 7 (July 1975), pp. 559—573. https://www.jstor.org/stable/2643340
24 Marukawa Tomoo, 'Bilateral Trade and Trade Frictions between China and Japan, 1972-2012', *Eurasian Geography and Economics*, 53(4) (August 2012), pp. 442—456. https://www.researchgate.net/publication/264084166_Bilateral_Trade_and_Trade_Frictions_between_China_and_Japan_1972-2012
25 McGregor, Richard, 'Forget Texas, China came out when Deng tipped his hat to Japan', *South China Morning Post*, 1 December 2018. https://www.scmp.com/week-asia/opinion/article/2175446/forget-texas-china-came-out-when-deng-tipped-his-hat-japan
26 Data from the World Bank, via Macrotrends. https://www.macrotrends.net/countries/CHN/china/exports
27 Wang Ke, 'Xiaogang Village, birthplace of rural reform, moves on', *China.org.cn*, 15 December 2008. http://www.china.org.cn/china/features/content_16955209.htm
28 Yang Jisheng, *Tombstone: The Untold Story of Mao's Great Famine*, transl. by Mosher, Stacy and Guo Jian, (London: Allen Lane, 2008), p. 1.
29 Wang Ke, Xiaogang Village.
30 Wang Ke, Xiaogang Village.
31 Kestenbaum, David; Goldstein, Jacob, 'The Secret Document

that Transformed China', *All Things Considered*, National Public Radio (NPR), 20 January 2012. https://www.npr.org/sections/money/2012/01/20/145360447/the-secret-document-that-transformed-china

32 Becker, Jasper, *Hungry Ghosts*, (New York: The Free Press, 1996), p. 261.
33 Tabeta Shunshuke, 'Cradle of China's farm reforms shines without spotlight', *Nikkei Asia*, 10 March 2019. https://asia.nikkei.com/Economy/Cradle-of-China-s-farm-reforms-shines-without-spotlight
34 Zhou, Kate Xiao, *How the Farmers Changed China: Power of the People*, (Boulder, CO, Westview Press, 1996), pp. 4—5.
35 '1983: Household Responsibility System', *China.org.cn*, 16 September 2009. http://www.china.org.cn/features/60years/2009-09/16/content_18534697.htm
36 Lin, Justin Yifu. 'The Household Responsibility System Reform in China: A Peasant's Institutional Choice', *American Journal of Agricultural Economics*, Vol 69, Issue 2, May 1987, p. 410. https://onlinelibrary.wiley.com/doi/10.2307/1242295
37 OECD Review of Agricultural Policies—China. Organization for Economic Cooperation & Development, 15 November 2005. https://www.oecd.org/china/oecdreviewofagriculturalpolicies-china.htm
38 Lardy, Nicholas. 'The Changing Role of the Private Sector in China', Conference paper for *Structural Change in China: Implications for Australia and the World*, Reserve Bank of Australia, 17—18 March 2016. https://www.rba.gov.au/publications/confs/2016/
39 Guluzade, Amir, 'The role of China's state-owned companies explained', *World Economic Forum*, 7 May 2019. https://www.weforum.org/agenda/2019/05/why-chinas-state-owned-companies-still-have-a-key-role-to-play/
40 Wu Nanlan, 'The Xiaogang village story', *China.org.cn*, 6 March 2008. http://www.china.org.cn/china/features/content_11778487.htm
41 Schell, Orville; Delury, John, *Wealth and Power: China's Long March to the 21st Century*, (London: Hachette, 2013), pp. 281—282.
42 Zhu Jiamu. *The Tune of China*, (Diamond Bar, CA: Portico Publishing, 2016), p. 176.
43 Zhu Jiamu, *The Tune of China*, p. vii.

44 'At the Science and Technology Work Conference held in Shanghai, Premier Zhou expounded the significance of modernization of science and technology' (in Chinese). *People's Daily*, January 1963. https://web.archive.org/web/20160214201234/http://rmrbw.net/read.php?tid=302475

45 Lin, Justin Lifu; Tao Ran; Liu Mingxin, 'Decentralization, Deregulation and Economic Transition in China', *Law and Economics with Chinese Characteristics: Institutions for Promoting Development in the Twenty-First Century*, Oxford Online, May 2013. https://sticerd.lse.ac.uk/dps/decentralisation/china.pdf

46 Zou Wei, 'The Changing Face of Rural Enterprises', *China Perspectives* 50, November-December 2003. https://doi.org/10.4000/chinaperspectives.773

47 Huang Panyue, ed. 'Development, not ideology, is the hard truth', CGTN Insight via China Military Online, 29 June 2021. http://eng.chinamil.com.cn/2021special/2021-06/29/content_10056085.htm

48 Huang Yasheng, 'How Did China Take Off?', *Journal of Economic Perspectives*, Vol 26, No. 4, Autumn 2012. pp. 147—170. https://dspace.mit.edu/bitstream/handle/1721.1/121058/jep.26.4.147.pdf?sequence=1&isAllowed=y

49 'Urban population (% of total population)—China', *United Nations Population Division. World Urbanization Prospects, 2018 Revision.* https://data.worldbank.org/indicator/SP.URB.TOTL.IN.ZS?locations=CN

50 Zheng M. 'The Importance of TVE's in China's Early Economic Reforms', Course notes for Economics 274: China's Modern Economy. Washington & Lee University, 27 January 2017. https://econ274.academic.wlu.edu/2017/01/the-importance-of-tves-in-chinas-early-economic-reforms/

51 Studwell, Joe, *How Asia Works*, (London: Profile Books Ltd, 2013), p. 184

52 Huang Yasheng, How Did China Take Off?

53 Weber, Isabella. *How China Escaped Shock Therapy: The Market Reform Debate*, (London: Routledge, 2021), p. 164.

54 Gates, Bill. 'Can the Asian miracle happen in Africa?' *GatesNotes: The Blog of Bill Gates*, 8 December 2014. This condensation by Studwell fan Gates doesn't appear in Studwell's book, but in my opinion it nicely summarises the three interventions.

55 Studwell, Joe, *How Asia Works*, pp. 224—225.

CHINESE OPERA MEETS POPULAR CULTURE: A STUDY OF LI YU'S FAMILY TROUPE
By Yufeng Lucas Wu

Abstract

*Li Yu*李渔 *(1611-1680) was a famous Chinese opera (xiqu* 戏曲*) theorist, director and playwright active in the late Ming* 明 *and early Qing* 清 *Dynasties. His family troupe, which existed for no more than six years, was an anomaly in Chinese history: a family troupe organised by a literatus for commercial purposes, which became widely sought after at the time. An exploration of the performances of Li Yu's family troupe and the routes they took, using both literary and non-literary sources, provides insight into the social environment of theatrical performances during that time, and also how Li Yu's works combined both the refined culture preferred by literati and a more 'vulgar' culture represented by the general public.*

Li Yu and His Family Troupe

Li Yu was a productive writer. He left a multitude of works including nineteen *chuanqi* dramas (such as *Ten Plays* 笠翁十种曲), works imitating the style of the Song Dynasty art form *huaben*话本 (*Silent Resistance* 无声戏, and *Twelve Towers* 十二楼), novels (including *The Story of a Palindrome* 合锦回文传 and *The Carnal Prayer Mat* 肉蒲团), *Casual Expressions of Leisure Activities* (闲情偶寄) a monograph on the aesthetics of life (which included gardening, china collection, food, horticulture, keeping fit and Chinese opera), and other poems and essays.

Today his work has been recognised all over the world and examples are exhibited in museums in China, Japan, France, the UK, and the US. Modern audiences were introduced to Li Yu's work, as well; adapted versions of his plays have been performed recently in China. The *Carnal Prayer Mat* was also adapted for the cinema, and was the basis for the highly successful Hong Kong film *Sex and Zen.*

Born in 1611, Li Yu demonstrated a gift for poetry at a young age. He passed the county-level examination, earning the title of Xiu Cai (秀才) at twenty-five, but was unable to make any further progress after that. On the road to the Imperial Examination in the capital, he faced challenges amid the social turmoil which resulted after the Ming Dynasty collapsed, and was replaced by the Qing. As can be seen in his works, Li Yu was deeply affected by the scourge of war, and he railed against the rule of the Qing Dynasty. He decided to abandon his pursuit of a bureaucratic career and live in seclusion instead. However, without stable economic resources, Li Yu lived a poor life and even had to seek help from his friends and relatives. His financial situation worsened after his father's death and he had to live like a 'wandering monk', which was never what he had wanted for his life. A poem he wrote in 1667, when he was invited to the Gansu area, illustrates his feelings: 'Be advised that I am only constantly being a guest, and I will not be called a wandering monk'[1].

In order to make ends meet, Li Yu moved to Hangzhou, a commercial centre in the lower reaches of the Yangtze River (the Jiangnan region 江南) in 1651, where he began to write for a living.

He once claimed that he was an expert at two things: having discerning taste in music and literature, and designing gardens[2]. Garden design did not pan out as a career, as it required a huge investment and promised little profit, so he chose to start a career in show business instead. It was rare for a literatus in ancient China to make a living by giving commercial performances, which highlights the value of his life story.

During his first year in Hangzhou, he finished *Fragrant Companion* (Lian Xiang Ban 怜香伴), a lesbian love story which was his first *chuanqi* work, a new genre of *zaju*, or variety theatre, which had developed in the Ming Dynasty. After that, he produced *Misguided by a Kite* (Feng Zheng Wu 风筝误) and *Desired Love* (Yi Zhong Yuan 意中缘) over the next two years. At the same time, he produced many many works of traditional Chinese opera.

From a letter he wrote to a friend, we can see how fast Li Yu worked as a playwright

> This work is now half completed, and it can be brought into rehearsal. From today, I will be working on the beginning of the next scene. It will definitely be completed by the end of this month, and then it can be performed right away [3]

Li Yu was known not only for his productivity, but also for the sublime quality of his works, which were widely circulated. Due to this great

Figure 1: A contemporary portrait of Li Yu.[5]

popularity, it was said that 'There is not one person in China, regardless of their gender or age, who does not know Li Yu'[4]. Li Yu, once a failed scholar, rose to become a star of Chinese popular culture, with his published works selling well, and his financial situation greatly improved.

While dedicated to playwriting, Li Yu did not stop making connections all over China as a member of the literati. He was friends not only with other literati but also with government officials. In the four years following his arrival in Hangzhou, he established contact with the Supervisor of Hangzhou's Nanguan area, Danzu 澹足; Zhejiang Governor Qin Shizhen 秦世祯; Zhejiang Surveillance Commissioner Tong Guoqi 佟国器; Magistrate of Renhe County Zhang Nenglin 张能麟, and other local officials.[6] His friendship with these bureaucratic elites also paved the way for his troupe's future performances.

Although he had huge successes in China's developed publishing market and in theatrical productions, his works were also widely pirated, which greatly affected Li Yu's income. As a result, he decided to move to Jinling 金陵 (today's Nanjing 南京), which was at the time China's publishing capital (and unfortunately also the capital for literary piracy). To better publicise his works and expand public awareness of them, Li Yu decided to establish his own troup composed of family members. It made its debut in Nanjing.

Unlike nobles who created family troupes to show off their wealth and refined taste, Li Yu developed his for three reasons. Firstly, as a gifted poet, he had long cherished the idea of establishing a troupe to perform his plays. Moreover, at the time it was not only fashionable to found such a troupe but also advantageous to be able to entertain government officials, nobles and other literati to gain influence and recognition. Lastly, in addition to its social functions, Li Yu's family troupe earned revenue for him, which was not a focus for other troupes kept by wealthy literati.

Li Yu's family troupe was organised as early as 1666-1667 when he successfully acquired Actress Qiao 乔姬 and the gifted Actress Wang 王姬: One played male roles and the other female roles - and both served as Li Yu's concubines. As Actress Qiao said

> That means from today on, I have my perfect partner, just like the female phoenix who has finally met the male phoenix. Please let her play the male roles and me the female roles. Other roles can be played by our sisters here. From now on, when you, our master, write any opera, we should not let the actors or actresses spread it to others without permission: we can perform it with our door closed.[7]

Female entertainers in the late Ming era were widespread in literati culture, and they were often concubines for wealthy men as well. Their low legal status, as well as their excellence in literature and the arts made them appropriate candidates to join a performing troupe. With the inclusion of these two actresses, the company had solid foundations and developed steadily.

There is no specific data about the size of the troupe. But careful examination indicates that there may have been seven members. Among them, Actress Qiao, Actress Wang, Actress Cao (曹姬), and Actress Huang (黄姬) enjoyed a higher status and formed the mainstay of the troupe[8]. Records of the performances of Li Yu's family troupe also frequently referred to them as "The Four Actresses" (四姬). For example, Gu Jingxing 顾景星, one of Li Yu's friends in Wuhan wrote in *Reply to Li Yu on the Moon Lake* 月湖答李渔, 'Li Yu came with four actresses, one of them happened to be sick at that time'.[9] Li Yu also wrote in one of his poems, 'Four actresses of mine were coming with me, and they were fairly good at singing'.[10]

My textual analysis allowed me to follow the history of members of Li Yu's family troupe. In 1666, Actress Cao, also Li Yu's concubine, accompanied him travelling around the capital where they performed, and then travelled to Shanxi and Lanzhou. In 1666, Actress Qiao was presented to Li Yu in Shanxi as a 'gift', and in the next year he added two more actresses (one of them was Actress Wang) in Lanzhou. In 1668, he added Actress Huang. These four were the mainstay of the family troupe. Later, they were joined by Actress Zhou (周姬), and during Li Yu's trip to Guangdong, he added another actress who played supporting roles (no name was noted). Poems and books about Li Yu and his troupe support the existence of these seven people.[11]

In 1672, Actress Qiao became ill and died in Hubei. Actress Wang passed away in the capital the following year. Losing the two actresses playing the leading male and female roles was a heavy blow. Some other actresses were expelled by Li Yu for jealousy or indiscretion in subsequent years. The family troupe was finally disbanded in 1674.

This analysis shows that Li Yu was comfortable in many settings and roles, the best evidence being that he could mingle among the powerful and wealthy without obstacles.[12, 13] Meanwhile, he also displayed ingenuity in business, as his *chuanqi* works and novels were popular with both lower-class labourers and literati, requiring him to start his own publishing house 'Jieziyuan Shufang' 芥子园书坊, a move unusual at that time.[14]

SHOW BUSINESS IN LATE MING AND EARLY QING DYNASTIES

The development and the function of Li Yu's family troupe was subject to social and economic conditions of the times. The existence of commercial theatre required a relatively developed economy, and the ability to travel safely and conveniently. They also required a favourable and flexible political environment that permitted creativity to develop unhindered.

ECONOMIC ENVIRONMENT

From the middle of the Ming Dynasty, continuous population growth and consistent technological and economic improvement meant that grain and other cash crops were grown on an expanding scale. The commercialisation of food and textile production accelerated the transformation of the national economy, turning cottage industries into production centres,[15] and giving rise to early capitalist industry and commercial ventures[16]. These changes provided the material and economic environment for vigorous cultural innovation and the growth of leisure activities.

At the same time, the creation of plantations for a variety of cash crops boosted long-distance trade. Improved national transportation networks forged closer connections between commercially developed cities and towns on a national scale[17-19]. With the emergence of mercantilism and the rise in the status of merchants, the traditional hierarchy of 'scholar, farmer, worker, merchant' was challenged. More and more farmers and migrants flooded into commercial centres. As more such centres developed, a new class of upwardly mobile citizens began to appear and, with them, the literati.[20]

This provided optimal conditions for the development and success of Li Yu's family troupe.

CULTURAL ENVIRONMENT

Theatrical performances were very popular during the Ming and Qing Dynasties, with demand for performances having developed since the mid-Ming period.[21] Theatrical productions organised for ordinary citizens generally took place in teahouses, restaurants, temples, and guild houses. Teahouses and restaurants began to put on public performances by the end of the Ming Dynasty, mostly to entertain customers as they dined. Performances at temples, especially small local temples such as the Town God Temple (Chéng Huáng miào 城隍庙) and God of Earth Temple (Tǔ Dì miào 土地庙), were to entertain both the deity and the masses. They featured narratives of loyalty, filial piety, chastity, righteousness, and karmic retribution. With the development of the economy, these temple productions, especially in the Jiangnan area, took place increasingly at temple fairs (miào huì 庙会) which combined religious worship, performances, and commercial activities. In comparison, guild house performances were more private, generally featuring prayers for prosperous business and safe voyages in the future and the celebration of festivals or events. The audience were mostly members of the guild.

The above three performance locations targeted ordinary businessmen, citizens and lower-class labourers. Judging from the repertoire of Li Yu's troupe, their performances were not suitable for temples or guild houses. And it is noticeable that teahouses or restaurants in China, especially in the Jiangnan area, did not have resident troupes until 1680.[22] Therefore, it was not likely that Li Yu's family troupe performed at teahouses, temples, or guild houses.

During this period, wealthy businessman, government officials and literati began to pursue spiritual advancement and aesthetic enjoyment. Consumption shifted from daily necessities to more highbrow interests. As individuals began to distinguish between refined and 'vulgar' culture, the most prominent manifestations of this luxury consumption were the private performances held in halls or gardens of wealthy landowners' homes. Family troupes travelled from place to place to stage private performances.

Travelling became popular among literati in the late Ming Dynasty, as seen in the many travelling works published after the Wanli 万历 period of the Ming Dynasty.²³ Travel began to appeal to middle- and lower-class literati, who kept sending invitations to each other. During the late Ming and early Qing dynasties, family members of officials and literati began to travel with them.²⁴ Moreover it became a fashionable, and even somewhat competitive, activity to bring young performers along. *Records of the Yangzhou Pleasure-boat* (扬州画舫录)²⁵ described the extravagant behavior of salt merchants along the Qinhuai River, emblematic of the social and cultural trends of the time.

In this sense, Li Yu, followed a business trend trend by setting up his family troupe and taking them on tour, while publicising his works on a broader scale. He could achieve maximum economic and social benefit at minimal cost, and the renown gained from touring helped his career in both his theatrical and publishing careers.

Luxury consumption had become the new trend. And China's 'entertainment culture', comprised of commercial performances and the publication of popular fictions and plays, was mature by the late Ming and early Qing periods.

Li Yu commercial considerations motivated him to cater to the needs of different social classes, which explains the existence of both refined and vulgar elements in his works. Consider *Silent Resistance* and *Twelve Towers* as examples. Both plays were based on the ordinary lives of common people. The plot lines concerned ordinary people living everyday life, or featured a scholar from a poor family.

Their narratives meanwhile featured themes that contrasted with traditional Confucian structures; they were exciting and entertaining to read but not overly vulgar. In this way, his works not only reflected the social reality to a certain extent and thus resonated with readers, but also provided novel reading experiences. Further fuelled by Li Yu's outstanding social skills, Li Yu's career in both literary publication and performance flourished. Some literati described his works as 'extraordinary classics' (yì diǎn 逸典).

Political Environment

Qing Dynasty laws relating to theatrical performance were influenced by the Ming Dynasty to a great degree. Li Yu's family troupe was active until 1674, which mostly fell in the Shùn zhì (顺治)—Kāngxī (康熙)

periods. Therefore, in addition to the relevant Ming Dynasty laws, they also had to obey the "Great Qing Code" (大清律) which was promulgated during the Shùn zhì period.

Owing in part to the perception of people involved in the entertainment business during the Yuán (元) Dynasty, performers were considered to be prone to hedonism and indolence. Drawing on its predecessors, the early Ming Dynasty imposed strict restrictions on theatrical performances and there were many regulations about acceptable themes.[27] Based on relevant literature,[28] five theatrical genres were authorised in the early Ming era, according to law: plays about deities, loyal men and chaste women, filial descendants, and those that promoted good morals, and peace and happiness. At the same time, female entertainers working in cities during the Ming Dynasty ceased to work for state and local government officials and were governed by the Imperial Office of Music (Jiào Fāng sī 教坊司) instead.

In the middle and late Ming periods, the number of bans issued by the imperial court decreased. The political environment became friendlier, as the rulers themselves were often opera lovers, so theatrical performances gradually developed. At the same time, the ban on certain themes was relaxed in the mid- and late Ming Dynasty. For example, in the early Ming Dynasty, emperors or sages was not permitted, but this prohibition was broken by literati in the Jiangnan area, as seen in *Washing the Silken Gauze: Picking Lotus* (浣纱记·采莲),[29] which featured the portrayal of Fuchai (夫差), a King of Wu (吴) in the Spring and Autumn Period.

Although observation of many of the bans decreased to a great extent, no new laws were created to repeal the previous ones. As a result, previous laws still existed, but the rulers during the middle and late Ming Dynasty did not emphasise their importance. These bans were often used as weapons by authorities to combat the scholar-bureaucrats for political purposes. Therefore maintaining a family troupe, and the performance and circulation of operas by either government officials or by the public were illegal at that time. This had little effect on theatrical groups; the creation and performance of *zaju* and *chuanqi* works reached a climax during the end of the Ming period, which, from another perspective, exposed the weak governance of the rulers.

At the dawn of the Qing era, most of the relevant laws were

holdovers from the previous dynasty, but the articles were more specific, and the punishments were more harsh. There were twelve national theatre-related bans in the early Qing Dynasty covering four aspects: performers' rights, the time and place of performances, their themes and content, and the publishing of books[30]. Under the early Qing government, continuing until the first year of the Kangxi period, conditions for theatre performances were similar to those in the late Ming. Numerous prohibitions were issued during the latter part of the Kangxi period, and during the Qianlong period but by then, Li Yu was dead.

Besides national laws, local government bans or instructions also affected theatrical performances. According to *Historical Materials on Banned Fictions and Dramas in the Yuan, Ming, and Qing Dynasties* (元明清三代禁毁小说戏曲史料)[31], there were seven relevant bans or instructions in the middle and late Ming Dynasty (two in Guangdong, four in Jiangnan, one in the capital), but most of them were related to performances involving religious activities or temple fairs. They were issued for three main reasons. Firstly, watching performances was perceived to be indulgent, and therefore and therefore decreased commercial efficiency. Secondly, authorities were concerned that performances instilled poisonous beliefs and undermined social morality. Thirdly, criminal behavior was often in the performances, making it harder to police. In addition, the northern part of Zhejiang province was frequently struck by disasters during the late Ming and early Qing periods, leading to an urgent need to restore agricultural production and social order. These bans or instructions were mostly seen in the Jiangnan area, especially in eastern Zhejiang.

In the late Ming and early Qing periods, these laws did not affect the performances of professional or private family troupes, or maintenance of the latter. As the actresses in Li Yu's troupe were mostly his concubines, travelling with them did not violate any of these bans. It was also for this reason that his troupe's performances, as well as those of the family troupes of other literati, were not prohibited even though bans existed in many places in Shaanxi and Zhejiang. The number and content of relevant bans before 1680 is described in the following table.

By examining the political environment concerning performances in the late Ming and early Qing periods, we see that while some of Li Yu's works were prohibited, most catered to the tastes of the readers

Time of Issuance	Number of Bans		Scope	Punishments	Performable genres
	National	Local			
Early Ming Dynasty	Nine	None	Status and rights of performers, performance venues, contents and themes, book publishing.	Exile, maiming, execution of family members, confiscation of property.	Divine deities, loyal men and chaste women, filial descendants, promotion of positive morals, 'peace and happiness'.
Middle and Late Ming Dynasty	Four	Seven	Fiction and literary styles, scholar-bureaucrats' involvement in the theatre.	Burning and destroying books, flogging.	Almost no restrictions.
Early Qing Dynasty to 1680	Twelve	Two	Status and rights of performers, audience status, performance venues, contents and themes, book publishing.	Flogging, wearing a cangue for at least one month, three year's or more of imprisonment, exile, no salary for six to 12 months, demotion.	Divine deities, loyal men and chaste women, filial descendants, promotion of positive morals.

Figure 2: General opera bans at the national and local levels (Ming Dynasty to Qing Dynasty, before 1680)

but were written in a way that allowed their author to evade legal punishment. In 1674 the Qing government implemented national management and control of play-writing and performances, banning the publication of erotic poems or verses, and prohibiting the offspring of high-class families from performing. Prior to this, the policy environment for literati performances was largely friendly. There were no regulations on performances by literati's family troupes at the places Li Yu visited. This permissive environment, coupled with Li Yu's networking skills with both officials and literati, allowed his troupe to travel around China. In this context, blessed by favourable timing, geographical and social conditions, Li Yu's family troupe was able to tour successfully.

Tours of Li Yu's Family Troupe

During its eight years of formal activity (1666-1674), Li Yu travelled with his family troupe on six tours (once to Gansu and Quanzhou, three times to the capital, once to Fujian and once to Hubei). Although he had intended for the tours to help with both fund-raising and networking, financial success was limited to the trips to Gansu, Quanzhou and Fujian. The rest mostly generated contacts and friendship with local literati and officials, and led to the acquisition of poems they had written.

The troupe's success depended on Li Yu's criteria for performances, as well as his choice of destination. As one of the purposes of touring with his family troupe was to raise funds, he naturally screened the performance venues with care in order to save on travelling costs.

Tour Routes

Analysis of the earliest record of Li Yu's family troupe performing outside of Nanjing was on New Year's Day of 1668, when he celebrated the birthday of Li Shenyu 李申玉, a local officer in Xuzhou, by putting on a new drama *Carefully Married* (*Shen Luan Jiao* 慎鸾交). This is recorded in a couplet:

> Li Shenyu was born on the New Year's Day. We drank wine to celebrate and I had my actresses put on a trial performance of the new drama.[32]

This performance was paid for in poems, not money. After this, the troupe went back to Nanjing and remained for a short time in the Jiangnan area before departing for Fujian.

In 1670, Li Yu brought his manuscript of *Words of My Own* (*Yi Jia Yan* 一家言), a collection of his poems and articles, to Fujian to seek funds.[33] He needed to raise money for the publication of the book, and the performances by his troupe helped to increase his income. This trip can be viewed as the first time his complete family troupe travelled together.

According to mentions in relevant poems and articles, the trip started in Jiangning, followed the Xianxia Ancient Road 仙霞古道 and crossed Xianxia Ridge 仙霞岭 to the south, eventually following the Min River 闽江, downstream, to arrive in Fuzhou 福州 in mid-autumn. Later the troupe returned by the same route. Performances during the trip were mostly held in Jianning county and Fuzhou. Li Yu wrote:

> I begged for money throughout my life, but all I have met were poor people, except on the trip to western Shaanxi, which was barely satisfactory. And the trip to Fujian came the next in line. Other than these two trips, the rest have all been disappointingly unfruitful.[34]

This trip to Fujian turned out to be lucrative for Li Yu. After he returned, he took his troupe to Nanjing and travelled upstream along the Yangtze River into the Hubei area in January 1672. They were stranded in Jiujiang by a storm and performed at the place of Jiang Nianju 江念鞠, the prefectural magistrate of Jiujiang. Li Yu also wrote couplets for a hall newly built for the magistrate[35]. He arrived at Hanyang 汉阳 in February, where a certain Gao Yichen 高翼辰 attended his troupe's performance, and gave him a good amount of money. Li Yu wrote a poem to memorialise the occasion:

> I am a guest in Hanyang, and we are separated by the river, we may not visit each other that much. But every time you paid me a visit, from time to time, I was promised that you will give me something as a gift.[36]

Li Yu arrived at Jingzhou in March, befriending local officials, and putting on performances. He returned to Hanyang that summer and continued to befriend local officials by staging performances.

For all the performances the troupe put on in the Hubei area, Li Yu's goal was to establish friendship and connections rather than make money. According to *Li Yu's Chronology* 李渔年谱 written by Shan Jinheng 单锦珩, over one hundred poems, nearly twenty couplets, and about a dozen letters were compiled into *Words of My Own* at that time.[37] Other evidence includes the letter written by Li Yu and titled

Reply to Gu Chifang (答顾赤方), which states, 'I travelled in Hubei for half a year, earning little money but many poems.'[38] At the end of the summer, Actress Qiao died of an unknown disease causing the troupe to leave Hanyang and return home.[39] No performances were given on their way back.

After review and analysis of these two tours, we can see Li Yu generally followed three criteria in his selection of performance locations.

First, they they had to be prosperous. A place with thriving commerce not only provided more opportunities for earning revenue, but also offered more developed venues. These all created optimal conditions for Li Yu's family troupe to turn a profit.

These locations moreover were accessible by rivers and canals, as water travel was the most economical means of transportation at that time. Li Yu's trips to Fujian, Hubei and the capital Nanjing, were all by water. The troupe was compelled to travel overland when they journeyed to Qin 秦 and Ganquan 甘泉 (in modern day Shaanxi and Gansu)as these places were not located on rivers. However, he must have judged these invitations sufficiently worthwhile to justify the expense.

A third consideration was that *kunqu* (昆曲) opera should be popular and well received. *Kunqu* enjoyed less popularity in places where the Wu (吴) dialect was not spoken and where other, local opera forms competed for audience share; in most of Li Yu's destinations, immigrants and businesspeople from the Jiangnan area congregated. These migrants had relocated due to wars or disasters in the late Ming and early Qing Dynasties and brought with them appreciation for *kunqu*. For example, in Fujian, not only were there public performances of *kunqu* opera, but there were also many private family troupes. Moreover, migrants from Jiangnan were numerous in places such as Jianning and the capital in the north.

It was not possible for Li Yu to rely on his family troupe to sustain his livelihood. It merely supported its daily expenses. As far as we can see from the existing literature included in *Complete Work of Li Yu*, the troupe gave commercial performances only to literati, nobles, or government officials; they were paid for either with money or poems. In other cases, the troupe apparently gave performances intended only for aesthetic recreation and enjoyment. Li Yu's family troupe focused on high-end private performances, which made it distinct from other popular professional family troupes of his time.[40]

Conclusion

The study of the social and cultural environment and positioning of Li Yu's family troupe facilitates our understanding of the particular social and historical environment in which Li Yu lived. The loose policy environment concerning Chinese opera performances and playwriting in the late Ming and early Qing dynasties afforded Li Yu and his troupe great creative leeway. At the same time, the relocation of people from Jiangnan due to war and natural disasters during the late Ming and early Qing dynasties helped expand the influence of *kunqu* opera to more places, including Hubei and Fujian. The booming economy also sharply boosted demand for cultural and recreational activities, which Li Yu was happy to supply.

Li Yu's excellent social skills amongst the upper class also opened doors, allowing him to travel and put on performances, and thereby enhance his fame. Blessed by favourable geographic and social conditions and fortunate timing, Li Yu was able to create and develop a family troupe that became one of the most popular at the time.

Yufeng Lucas Wu (thinseason@gmail.com) *holds master's degrees in Law, and Traditional Chinese Opera and Theatre Studies from Shanghai University, allowing him to draw upon an interdisciplinary mix of historical studies, sociology and anthropology. After working for a couple of years at Shanghai Culture Square, the biggest musical theatre in China, he became an editor at Frontiers Media S.A. His fields of interest include Chinese cultural policy, Chinese literature and culture, especially the form of Chinese Opera known as* kunqu(昆曲).

References

(All translations from the Chinese provided by the author)
1. Li Yu, *Complete Work of Li Yu (vol. 2)*, ed. by Shang Jinheng, 1st edn (Hangzhou: Zhejiang Guji Chubanshe, 1991), p.183.
2. Li Yu, *Complete Work of Li Yu (vol. 3)*, p.156.
3. Li Yu, *Complete Work of Li Yu (vol. 1)*, p.174.
4. Li Yu, *Complete Work of Li Yu (vol. 1)*, p.1.
5. https://commons.m.wikimedia.org/wiki/File:Portrait_of_Li_Yu.png#mw-jump-to-license [accessed 10 July 2022]
6. Shang Jinheng, *Complete Work of Li Yu (vol. 19)*, p.27.
7. Li Yu, *Complete Work of Li Yu (vol. 1)*, p.97.
8. Shen Xinlin, 'Liyu jiashi kao' 李渔家室考, Journal of Ming-Qing

Fiction Studies, 02 (1996), pp.140-148.

9. Gu Jingxing, Baimaotang Ji 白茅堂集 (1902), Ctext <https://ctext.org/library.pl?if=gb&file=105788&page=51&remap=gb> [accessed 22 July 2022]

10. Li Yu, *Complete Work of Li Yu (vol. 2)*, p.183.

11. Shen Xinlin, 'Liyu jinling shiji kao' 李渔金陵事迹考, Journal of Nanjing Normal University (Social Science Edition), 02 (1993), pp.55-60.

12. Shan Jinheng, *Biography of Li Yu* 李渔传, 1st edn (Chengdu: Sichuan wenyi chubanshe, 1986)

13. Yu Weimin, *Li Yu Pingzhuan* 李渔评传, 1st edn (Nanjing: Nanjing University Press, 1998)

14. Huang Qiang, 'On LiYu Being the Master of the Jinling Yishengtang Bookshop', Journal of Chongqing Normal University, 05(2012), pp.5-10.

15. Cheng Shikuang, 'Ming jiangnan zhishui ji' 明江南治水记, in Si ku quan shu cun mu cong shu (Histories Issue 224) 四库全书存目丛书, 1st edn (Jinan: Shandong Qilu Press Co.,Ltd., 1996)

16. Zhang Juzheng,*p* 张文忠公全集, (Shanghai: The Commercial Press, 1935), p. 502.

17. Li Bochong, *Jiangnan de zaoqi gongyehua 1550-1850* 江南的早期工业化1550—1850, 2nd edn (Beijing: China Renmin University Press, 2010)

18. *Quan Hansheng, Mingqing jingjishi yanjiu* 明清经济史研究, 2nd edn (Taibei: Linking Publishing Company, 2019)

19. Matsuura Akira, *Qingdai neihe shuiyunshi yanjiu* 清代内河水运史研究, trans. by Dong Ke, 1st edn (Nanjing: Jiangsu People's Publishing House, 2019)

20. He Bingdi, *The Ladder of Success in Imperial China: Aspect of Social Mobility 1368-1911*, trans. by Xu Hong, 1st edn (Taibei: Linking Publishing Company, 2013)

21. Cheng Guohua, The Study of the Impact on Drama Culture from the Development of Ming and Qing Societies 明清社会变迁对戏剧文化的影响研究 (2008), Xiamen University Institutional Repository <https://dspace.xmu.edu.cn/handle/2288/43301> [accessed 27 July 2022]

22. Fan Jinmin, 'Mingqing diyu shangren yu jiangnan wenhua' 明清地域商人与江南文化, in *Urban Industry and Local Culture in the Yangzi Delta* 江南的城市工业与地方文化, ed. by Li Bochong Zhou

Shengchun, (Beijing: Tsinghua University Press, 2004), pp. 101-110.

23. For more details, see Zhou Zhengyu, 'Cong mingren wenji kan wanming lvyou fenqi ji qi yu dilixue de guanxi' 从明人文集看晚明旅游风气及其与地理学的关系, *Fudan University Journal (Social Science)*, 01 (2005), pp.72-78.

24. For more details, see Gao Yanyi, 'Mingmo qingchu funv de shenghuo kongjian' 论明末清初妇女的生活空间, *Jindai zhongguo funvshi yanjiu*, 03 (1995), pp.21-50.

25. Li Dou, '*Yangzhou huafang lu*' 扬州画舫录, ed. by Pan Aiping, (Beijing: China Pictorial Press, 2014)

26. For more details, see Wu Renshu, *Pingwei shehua wanming de xiaofei shehui yu shidafu* 品味奢华 晚明的消费社会与士大夫, ed. by Wang Fang (Beijing: Zhong Hua Book Company, 2008).

27. Wang Liqi, *Yuan ming qing sandai jinhui xiaoshuo xiqu shiliao* 元明清三代禁毁小说戏曲史料, ed. by Wang Liqi (Shanghai: Shanghai Guji Chubanshe, 1981), pp.12-15.

28. Yu Ruji, 'Libu Zhigao' Issue 99 礼部志稿 卷九十九, in *Qingding Siku Quanshu (Histories)* 钦定四库全书 史部, Wikisource < https://zh.m.wikisource.org/zh-hans/禮部志稿_(四庫全書本)/卷099 > [accessed 03 Aug 2022]

29. Liang Chengyu, 'Huan sha ji' 浣纱记, in *Liushi zhong qu* 六十种曲, ed. by Mao Jin, 2nd edn (Beijing: Zhong Hua Book Company, 2007)

30. A Gui, Da qin lv li (Issue 17,18,34) 大清律例 第17, 18, 34卷, (Beijing: Zhong Hua Book Company, 2015)

31. Wang Liqi, pp.90-95.

32. Li Yu, *Complete Work of Li Yu (vol. 1)*, p.236.

33. Shang Jinheng, *Complete Work of Li Yu (vol. 19)*, p.69.

34. Li Yu, *Complete Work of Li Yu (vol. 1)*, p.163.

35. Li Yu, *Complete Work of Li Yu (vol. 1)*, p.245.

36. Li Yu, *Complete Work of Li Yu (vol. 2)*, p.190.

37. Shang Jinheng, *Complete Work of Li Yu (vol. 19)*, p.83.

38. Li Yu, *Complete Work of Li Yu (vol. 1)*, p.210.

39. For more details, see Zhu Qiujuan, 'Li Yu jiaban xinian' 李渔家班系年, *Nanjing University of Science and Technology Journal (Social Science)*, 04 (2008), 28-33.

40. For more details, see Yang Huiling, '*Studies on the Opera Troupes of Families in Ming and Qing Dynasties*' 戏曲班社研究 明清家班, (Xiamen: Xiamen University Press, 2006)

SECTION 4

Reviews

SCOTTISH MANDARIN: THE LIFE AND TIMES OF SIR REGINALD JOHNSTON

BY SHIONA AIRLIE
HONG KONG, HONG KONG UNIVERSITY PRESS, 2021
REVIEWED BY FRANCES WOOD

Reginald Fleming Johnson (1874-1938) spent the first 30 years of the 20th century in China. He served as a Colonial Officer in Hong Kong and Weihaiwei, later working for the Boxer Indemnity Fund, but is best-known as the tutor to Puyi, the last Emperor of China. It was a period of political confusion and a time when the past and present co-existed uneasily, as the new, modern government of the Republic of China attempted to control the mediaeval, territorial battles of rival warlords. Foreign incursions had reached a peak in 1898, the year that the young Johnston arrived in Hong Kong as a cadet in the British Colonial Service. Germany had claimed Qingdao, Japan demanded Port Arthur and, not to be outdone, the British claimed Weihaiwei as a naval port, leasing it from 1898 to 1930

Johnston became widely known as the tutor of the last Emperor of China from 1919 to 1924, an episode that he recorded in his memoir *Twilight in the Forbidden City* (1934). His appointment was due to a recommendation from Li Jingmai (1876-1938) a son of the modernising Viceroy Li Hongzhang. Li Jingmai, a Shanghai businessman and royalist, had apparently fled to Weihaiwei in 1911 during the confusion of the revolution, and stayed there with Johnston, then a young Colonial Officer, for a few weeks. Li was close to Xu Shichang who served as President of the Chinese Republic from 1918 to 1922 - despite the brevity of his tenure, he was the longest serving President of the warlord era. Xu Shichang approached Sir John Jordan at the British Legation and Johnston was offered the chance of a secondment from his post as District Officer in Weihai to the Peking palace.

Puyi was no longer the Emperor but he still lived in the Forbidden City, was carried across the courtyards in a palanquin, dressed in imperial yellow robes and attended by eunuchs. The appointment of a foreign tutor was one example of the contradictions that characterised China in the early years of the Republic, introducing a potentially radical element into the conservative court. Johnston himself compounded the contradiction during his first meeting with Puyi, when he dressed in top hat and tails and bowed three times, whilst thirteen year-old Puyi in his yellow silk robe held out his hand, western-style.

The events are well-known, enhanced by Bertolucci's film *The Last Emperor* when the good-looking and elegant Peter O'Toole played Johnston who, by this time, was a stoutish, red-faced, middle-aged man. Johnston taught his young pupil English, arithmetic, history, geography and 'small amounts' of politics, botany, art, poetry 'and even astronomy'. Famously realising that the child suffered from headaches, he managed to bring an ophthalmologist into the palace who diagnosed myopia and prescribed the glasses that Puyi wore thereafter. Soon, one of Puyi's cousins, twelve year-old Pujia, joined the classes. Though Johnston managed to achieve friendly relations with Puyi's Chinese tutors, he soon developed an antipathy towards the crowds of eunuchs in the palace. He attempted to stem the flow of palace treasures that were being smuggled out for sale by the eunuchs, and to address the corruption of the imperial household. Eventually Puyi himself dismissed all the eunuchs in 1923.

Johnston was still employed by the palace in 1924 when Puyi, threatened by warlord fighting, left the Forbidden City. As Johnston negotiated fruitlessly with the British Legation, Puyi was offered sanctuary in the Japanese legation, setting off on the path that led to Tianjin and then Manchukuo. Though they maintained a correspondence and Johnston occasionally visited Puyi in Tianjin, the close friendship between pupil and tutor was a thing of the past.

Apart from this interlude, Johnston spent almost all of his time in China as a Colonial District Officer in the interior of Weihai, supported by his fellow Scot and life-long friend Sir James Stewart Lockhart, the Commissioner in Weihai. He worked alone as a local magistrate and wrote several substantial books on his travels in China, Chinese Buddhism and on Shandong province. He also wrote a couple of anti-missionary diatribes, shocked by missionary intransigence and their desire to 'change Chinese society'. He ended his career in the Colonial Office, succeeding his friend and mentor Stewart Lockhart as Commissioner in Weihai and presiding over its rendition to China in 1929. Wearing the obligatory top hat and tails, he received the folded union flag as it was lowered from the mast and presided over speeches and ceremonial duties in pouring rain; gestures and weather that anticipated the ceremonies in Hong Kong in 1997.

In 1931, on his return to London, he accepted the post of Professor of Chinese at the School of Oriental Studies (SOS, the forerunner of SOAS) but immediately applied for leave to return to China for five months with the Universities China Committee, which administered the Boxer Indemnity Fund. The little time he spent at SOS was not happy. Evangeline Edwards, who succeeded him but clearly thought she should have had the post in the first place, was an ex-missionary and very hostile to Johnston and Stewart Lockhart and their friends, such as the artist and writer Chiang Yee. But Johnston was also an absentee Professor. Towards the end of his tenure in 1935, he had bought a Scottish island and that was where he wanted to be. It is said that SOS resorted to inserting appeals in the personal column of *The Times* begging him to attend his classes.

Airlie's book is immensely detailed and meticulously researched and yet she ends by concluding that 'to the very end, he was an enigma'. She makes it clear that he went abroad partly to escape his family: a drunken father who died bankrupt and a hopelessly spendthrift mother. At that time, his father's bankruptcy could have ended his career. Both his siblings emigrated and Johnston was lucky that the scandalous news never reached Hong Kong. He made life-long friends at Oxford and in the Colonial Service but seems to have been happy living at a distance, maintaining contact by letter. His letters contained interminable in-jokes about characters he had invented: Mrs Walkinshaw, 'a most remarkable lady woman female creature', the Quork with her green umbrella and inability to keep her knickers on, and the drunken Earl of Dumbarton. Cecil Clementi, a fellow student at Oxford and Governor of Hong Kong from 1925 to 1930, was so sickened by these characters that he threatened to move out of their shared house in Kowloon in 1900, and one has some sympathy.

These female caricatures and the almost deliberate avoidance of society ran counter to Johnston's relationships with women. He met Eileen Power, a remarkably distinguished mediaevalist, in 1921 at his villa 'Cherry Glen' on the outskirts of Peking. They became engaged in 1929, although they never married. He took great pleasure in teasing the local missionary ladies in Weihai who disapproved of such unchaperoned visitors as Eileen Power and the novelist Stella Benson, who came to stay without her husband. At the end of his life, he met

Mrs Elizabeth Sparshott. The fact that she was married caused a fatal rift between Johnston and Stewart Lockhart. Divorce in those days was, like bankruptcy, enough to end a career. Disapproving, Stewart Lockhart refused to see her so Johnston refused to visit his life-long friend and mentor on his death-bed.

Johnston was named in Mrs Sparshott's divorce and they lived together openly in his Scottish island home with the villagers referring to her as 'Mistress Snapshot'. When Johnston died in 1938, Mrs Sparshott immediately sold the island and tried to sell 'Cherry Glen' but discovered that it had been looted and ruined; she burnt all his 'vast stacks of papers' and gave his precious library to the institution he had disliked, SOS. It is thought that his most precious possessions, such as gifts of porcelain and jade from Puyi, including a huge sable coat, were destroyed in a warehouse fire during the Blitz. This undignified end to the trappings of his eventful life is more tragic than enigmatic.

Although Johnston's considerable and varied achievements survive in his writings and in Airlie's meticulous research, many aspects of his personal life remain a puzzle. An upright Colonial administrator with a passion for top hats and morning coats as well as Buddhism, who openly defied Christian missionaries, an apparently loyal and devoted friend who refused to visit his colleague and mentor on his death-bed because of a woman, he was, as Airlie notes, an enigma.

Frances Wood *studied Chinese at the universities of Cambridge, Peking and London. She worked in the SOAS library before moving to the British Library as Curator of the Chinese collections. Her books include* The Blue Guide to China, Did Marco Polo Go To China, The Silk Road *and* No Dogs and Not Many Chinese: Treaty Port life in China 1843-1943.

CHIANG YEE AND HIS CIRCLE: CHINESE ARTISTIC AND INTELLECTUAL LIFE IN BRITAIN, 1930–1950

EDITED BY PAUL BEVAN, ANNE WITCHARD, AND DA ZHENG
HONG KONG, HONG KONG UNIVERSITY PRESS, 2022
REVIEWED BY DUNCAN HEWITT

If relations between Britain and China can sometimes feel like they are becoming increasingly distant these days, this edited volume provides a timely and fascinating reminder of a largely forgotten but important encounter between a small group of Chinese intellectuals and the British public, and intelligentsia, in the 1930s and 40s - one which helped to change perceptions of China in the UK, and which is particularly relevant at a time of growing emphasis on the study of the historical role of migrants in western societies.

The eponymous Chiang Yee (Jiang Yi 蒋彝, 1903-1977) was a remarkable renaissance man, who came to Britain in June 1933 after falling out with the KMT government, for which he had worked as a magistrate in his native Jiangxi province. Despite knowing hardly any English when he arrived in London, within two years Chiang, who had studied painting with his artist father as a child, had published a book in English on Chinese art, taken a teaching job at the School of Oriental Studies, and had his works featured in a major exhibition of Chinese art in London.

Within another year, he had published the first of what would become the Silent Traveller series - a collection of charmingly written and very personal observations, in English, of his travels to various parts of Britain - from London to the Lake District and Edinburgh - all illustrated with his own whimsical drawings and paintings. One of these, *The Silent Traveller in Oxford*, was briefly Britain's best-selling book in November 1944. Chiang also wrote a book on Chinese calligraphy, provided illustrations for books by other authors, and wrote several successful illustrated books of his own for the children's publisher Puffin Books - one of which, *The Story of Ming*, about a panda at London Zoo, sold more than a quarter of a million copies in the 1940s.

He also published what was probably the first book on Britain's experience of World War II, *The Silent Traveller in War Time*, which was released in December 1939, and featured Chiang's drawings of people in gas masks and other iconic wartime images.

During the war, Chiang Yee was much in demand as a speaker on China's plight under Japanese occupation, and was invited to talk about Chinese culture on BBC radio. He also produced books at the request of both the Chinese Ministry of Information, which had an office in London at the time, and the British government, including one based on the Chinese journalist Hsiao Ch'ien's (Xiao Qian 萧乾) experience of travelling on the 'Burma Road.' And he still found time to score a spectacular success with his striking stage set and costume designs for *The Birds*, one of the first ballets performed at London's Sadler's Wells Theatre, by the precursor of the Royal Ballet Company, in 1942.

Much of Chiang's initial success in establishing himself in the UK was thanks to his friendship with Shih-I Hsiung (Xiong Shiyi 熊式一), a fellow Jiangxi native who, after working as an academic, writer and translator in China, moved to London in the early 1930s and set up home in Hampstead. Here, Hsiung and his wife Dymia (Cai Daimei) became the centre of a group of young Chinese intellectuals living in the British capital. It was Hsiung who first found fame as a "Chinese writer" in London, abandoning his dreams of writing modernist drama and instead, at the urging of British friends, producing a more "traditional Chinese" work, an adaptation of a Peking opera which became a hit under the title *Lady Precious Stream*. It ran for 900 performances in London from 1934-36, attracting a visit from Queen Mary - and one from First Lady Eleanor Roosevelt during its later run on Broadway. The Hsiungs featured prominently in the British media and Dymia later published a fictionalised version of their experiences in the UK, *Flowering Exile,* in 1952. It was Hsiung who gave Chiang Yee his first illustration work in London, in the programme for the play, and introduced him to his publisher at Methuen. It was also through Hsiung that Chiang met the famous Chinese artist and educator Liu Haisu, who subsequently included ten of Chiang's paintings in a prestigious exhibition at the New Burlington Galleries.

According to the book's co-editor Paul Bevan, such works contributed to something of a 'China craze' in Britain, which, while this initially focused on clichéd images of Chinese culture, it gradually evolved into a more genuine cultural engagement, particularly as

China and the UK found themselves allies in World War II, with British publishers releasing books by a range of Chinese writers, including Hsiao Ch'ien and Chun-chan Yeh (Ye Junjian 叶君健).

Yet this heyday was relatively short-lived. After the war, interest began to wane, as the Cold War became the prime concern, and some of the writers left Britain - including Chiang, who moved to the US in 1955. The BBC did make a televised version of *Lady Precious Stream* as late as 1950, yet by the 1980s, when I was studying Chinese at university in Britain, Hsiung and Chiang had been more or less forgotten; when I once chanced upon a copy of *The Silent Traveller in Edinburgh* in a local bookshop, I was frankly surprised to discover that a Chinese writer had even visited the city as far back as the 1940s, let alone published a book about it in English.

This volume therefore, plays an important role in helping to focus attention on the significant contribution of Chiang Yee and his 'circle', to enhancing both British cultural life and the status of Chinese culture and the Chinese community in Britain in the 1930s and 40s. Most of the book's eleven essays were originally presented at a symposium organised at the Ashmolean Museum in Oxford by co-editors Anne Witchard, whose volume *Lao She in London* for the RAS China series looked at an early interaction between the two cultures, and Paul Bevan, whose previous books *Intoxicating Shanghai* and *A Shanghai Miscellany* demonstrated the vibrancy of Chinese intellectual life from the 1920s-40s. The symposium coincided with the unveiling of a commemorative plaque at the house in Oxford where Chiang lived from 1940, after his London home was bombed; it's testament to his positive and endearing personality that he found these lodgings by knocking on doors at random, and was instantly taken in by the Keene family, with whom he subsequently lived for 15 years.

The book contains an impressive spectrum of research, from Bevan's essay locating Chiang and Hsiung amidst the British intellectuals and European exiles who were their neighbours in Hampstead (some of whom played a part in helping their work to reach British audiences), to Craig Clunas' analysis of Chiang's career as an artist and art writer, and Anne Witchard's fascinating and detailed account of his work with the Sadler's Wells ballet, where Chiang's 'delicate scenery' and 'amazing bird costumes and headdresses' helped *The Birds* play to packed houses and become 'one of the most popular and frequently performed ballets' of the war years.

Other authors delve into the pain of exile and the impact of the traumas of war on Chiang. Da Zheng, the third of the book's co-editors, notes that Chiang's hometown, Jiujiang, fell to the Japanese army in July 1938, and 'hundreds of local residents were slaughtered, houses burned, and villages and towns reduced to rubble'. Chiang's own family home was destroyed; two of his children fled to Chongqing with his sister-in-law, while his wife Zeng Yun took their other two children to the countryside, along with her own mother, sister, and uncle (the latter two of whom soon died). Zeng eventually found her way to Nanjing, but Chiang would not see her or two of his children for more than four decades; Da Zheng says Chiang 'cried the whole day' after going months without receiving letters from his family. His sense of pain was exacerbated by the death, also in 1938, of his brother, who had encouraged him to stay in Britain to avoid the war. Such sorrow is reflected in Chiang's memoir *A Chinese Childhood*, published during the war, which Zheng describes as a nostalgic elegy - or indeed eulogy - for 'the beautiful "old days "'now long gone.

Indeed, Paul French, in his chapter on Chiang's wartime activities and activism, argues that it was this personal experience of the horrors of war that inspired Chiang to begin writing *The Silent Traveller in War Time* so soon after the outbreak of hostilities in Europe. Even in Britain he could not escape the direct impact of war: French notes that his London home was hit by the first bomb to fall on Hampstead in September 1940; soon afterwards, Chiang was knocked unconscious when another bomb fell nearby. This prompted his move to Oxford (to where the Hsiungs soon followed him). And French points out that while Chiang did his best to remain 'publicly upbeat and optimistic' throughout the war, he acknowledged in the preface to the Chinese edition of *The Silent Traveller in War Time* that 'the pain I have suffered from the war is beyond description'.

At the same time, Sarah Cheang, in another essay, argues that it was the very 'horrors of the present' that may have encouraged Chiang to continue writing the Silent Traveller books about Britain throughout the war; she suggests that 'reassurance could always be found in the stability of ancient buildings, and traditions that Chiang Yee presented as appealing to both Chinese and British sensibilities'.

Yet she, and several other authors, note the prejudice and sometimes outright racism faced by Chiang and his friends in Britain - where, despite the welcoming attitude of some, the paranoid concept of the 'Yellow Peril' 'persisted as an influence in the collective British consciousness'. Cheang notes that Chiang Yee was confronted with children calling him 'Charlie Chan' (after the detective in the 'Yellowface' movies so popular at the time), while he wrote of avoiding Trinity College, Oxford, since this was 'now the only college which does not admit Orientals'. And though Cheang says Chiang Yee displayed 'great tact' and humour in dealing with such situations, she wonders whether it was the trauma caused by such experiences that encouraged what she calls the 'knowing silence' implicit in his penname.

And Diana Yeh, in her chapter on Chiang's relationship with the Hsiungs[A], emphasises that when there was interest in Chinese culture, it tended, at least until the late 1930s, to focus on stereotyped images. She cites Chiang's complaint that many western Sinologists were more interested in classical Chinese literature than in writing about the nation's contemporary development and problems - even though, as he put it drily, 'we try to read modern English rather than Chaucer'. Chiang also lamented that many western travel books on China 'laid stress on such strange sights as opium smokers, beggars, and coolies... pandering to an unhealthy curiosity in their readers'.

Diana Yeh says Chiang went out of his way to avoid such tendencies in his own writing, preferring to highlight 'similarities among all kinds of people, not their differences or their oddities'. However, she argues that Chiang Yee and other Chinese intellectuals in Britain had to contend with an 'economy of cultural representation', which offered just a 'few spaces to only those who offered specific representations of often highly exoticised Chineseness that appealed to British audiences'. This, she says, was the experience of Hsiung Shih-I, who 'had arrived in London, wearing a Western suit and clutching a realist play about the class divide in modern China', yet was encouraged to write a classical-inspired drama instead, and was later 'rarely seen dressed in anything but the traditional Chinese robe that was so essential to this visibility'. Indeed, Paul Bevan describes Hsiung's *Lady Precious Stream* as 'a distinctly Orientalist production', noting that fellow playwright Hong Shen saw it as an insult to 'both China and the Chinese'. Diana Yeh argues, however, that Hsiung 'sought to humanise the Chinese' through the play, 'by adapting a love story with universal appeal'. Yet his later attempts to write about modern China, in works such as *The*

A   See also Diana Yeh's RAS Monograph *The Happy Hsiungs*

Professor from Peking (1939) found 'only modest success'. And Yeh suggests that this 'economy of representation' forced Chinese writers in Britain to compete with each other for acknowledgement and status, 'fracturing their mutuality... and even throwing into doubt the strength of their political solidarity'. In evidence, she cites the fact that, despite their long years of friendship, Hsiung was sometimes patronising to Chiang Yee - and quotes Hsiung's grandson as saying that 'towards the end of their lives, they despised each other'.

Nevertheless, the book also makes it clear that the efforts of Chiang and his fellow Chinese intellectuals did contribute to gradual changes in this situation: Tessa Thorniley, in her chapter, describes how British publishers' and left-wing intellectuals' interest in Chinese authors grew as 'the brutality of the Japanese occupation of China began to be reported in the West' in the late 1930s. She cites the journalist Hsiao Ch'ien's remark that China really 'began to exist in the eyes of the British' after Pearl Harbor in December 1941, when 'he was immediately approached by publishers and film studios to work on cultural projects that might demystify China for British readers, listeners, and viewers', and suddenly found that he 'was no longer viewed as an "enemy alien" but instead as a "member of the grand alliance"'.

Thorniley highlights the close relationship between Chiang Yee and Noel Carrington, who first commissioned Chiang's writing for *Country Life* magazine, and later founded Puffin Books, which published Chiang's children's stories. Hsiao Ch'ien, meanwhile, published a collection of stories and essays, along with a book on Chinese culture and society, while the academic Tsui Chi's book *A Short History of Chinese Civilization* was published by Gollancz in 1942 with a preface by the poet Laurence Binyon. Chun-chan Yeh, who was invited by the British Ministry of Information to tour Britain and give public talks about China's war with Japan in 1944-5, forged close links with John Lehmann, editor of the journal *New Writing*, and the writers Stephen Spender and J.B. Priestley, and published several books, including the famous novel *The Mountain Village*, before he returned to China in 1949. Thorniley notes that British editors and critics 'found more than mere propaganda value' in these authors' writing, with Hsiao and Yeh's work being hailed as 'literature on a par with many great Russian, European, and British writers'. Thus, she concludes, these writers 'greatly improved the standing of modern Chinese literature in Britain

[and] offered anglophone readers alternative and contesting versions of China that pushed back against many of the negative stereotypes more widely associated with the country'.

A third Jiangxi intellectual who also won widespread recognition in Britain is the focus of another essay by Ke Ren: Shelley Wang (Wang Lixi) was a writer, poet and publisher of books by left-wing writers; he had been an early KMT activist before falling out with Chiang Kai-shek and taking part in an abortive uprising against his leadership. In 1934, he fled to London, where he and his wife later lodged with the Hsiungs and Chiang. Wang became a leading light in the International Peace Campaign, gave talks on China for the Left Book Club, and became a friend of writers including the Northern Irish poet John Hewitt. His book *Exile and Wars* was published in 1939, shortly before his tragic death from sepsis in China, where he had returned the previous year. His farewell party was attended by luminaries including the publisher Victor Gollancz and the future Indian prime minister Jawaharlal Nehru; at the event, Wang read a poem hailing the ties between the British and Chinese people, proclaiming that 'Neither distance nor language can divide our spirit'.

Frances Wood, meanwhile, highlights the role of other Chinese residents of London, including Sye Ko Ho, a former KMT diplomat who, after 1949, opened the upmarket Chinese restaurant The Asiatic, which attracted British politicians and the film star Ava Gardner; and the writer Ling Shu-hua, whose memoir *Ancient Melodies*, published in 1953, was championed by Virginia Woolf and Vita Sackville-West.

There are some minor discrepancies in tone and detail between different chapters. Craig Clunas' criticism of Chiang Yee's book on Chinese art as inaccurate and derivative of Liu Haisu's work contrasts with the generally celebratory tone taken by most of the writers in their assessment of Chiang, but such issues are perhaps inevitable in a multi-authored volume. And the plurality of topics does provide some intriguing tangents, such as Paul Bevan's tale of the British-Chinese circus impresario Lai Foun, whose troupe performed in some of the BBC's earliest television broadcasts and also appeared at the opening of the 1936 Berlin Olympics, where Lai was invited for a private chat with Adolf Hitler.

Overall the book makes an important contribution by lifting the veil on a largely forgotten but significant 'moment' in the often painful process of Sino-Western cultural engagement, and by highlighting the impact of Chiang Yee, the Hsiungs, Hsiao Ch'ien and other Chinese writers on Britain in the 1930s and 40s. In so doing, it provides a reminder of the benefits that can result when the two nations take an interest in each other's culture - and may also contribute to countering what Diana Yeh has described elsewhere as 'the lack of cultural visibility of the Chinese in Britain'. It will also help to ensure that the witty, humane - and perhaps surprisingly resonant - voice of the 'Silent Traveller' will continue to echo down the generations.

Duncan Hewitt's *biography appears elsewhere in this volume, below his article on JG Ballard*

SIR ROBERT HART (1835-1911): WHOSE HERO?

DOCUMENTARY FILM REVIEW BY EDITH TERRY

ABSTRACT

Born in Belfast, Sir Robert Hart arrived in China at the age of 19 in 1854. He would spend most of the rest of his life in China. By the time he retired at the age of 73 and returned to England, he was the most influential foreigner in China. The documentary For China and the World: Robert Hart *tells not only his story but also that of the Qing empire as it disintegrated under the pressures of western and Japanese imperialism. Controversial during his lifetime, Sir Robert Hart was gradually forgotten until an enterprising historian at Royal Holloway, University of London, Dr. Weipin Tsai, discovered his crumbling gravestone in a churchyard near London and decided to restore it as part of an archival project. I look at how the film resonates with the political context of foreigners in China in the last half-century, as China re-emerged on the world scene as a rising superpower.*

INTRODUCTION

At a time when globalisation is in retreat and China and the West have entered a new stage of confrontation, it is timely to look back at an earlier era of violence and change, and the individuals who were caught within it. This is the subject of a 31-minute documentary film commissioned by Professor Robert Bickers at the University of Bristol.

The film, which is available on internet video platform YouTube[1], starts in a quiet English churchyard, with birds chirping and the Waltham St. Lawrence Silver Band playing to an invisible funeral procession. Narrated by the late Tim Piggott-Smith, famous for his role in *The Jewel in the Crown*, the film begins with a reading from one of the 7,000 letters in the Sir Robert Hart archives at Queen's University Belfast, Hart's alma mater. Hart is voiced, in a strong Irish accent, by Conor Wilson:

> I have helped the Chinese toward a more intimate connection with the West, and of preservation thereby of peace and better understanding. I have aided them in

many troubles, internal and external, and have been of use to them in the settlement of many questions by the giving of much good advice. Thus, publicly and officially, I may lay claim to have done something for my fellows, and the world.

This combination of humility and pride would be familiar to foreigners in the China of the late 20th and early 21st century, 100 years after Hart had spent nearly five decades building the Imperial, later Republican, Maritime Customs Service and allied institutions including the Chinese postal service, Beijing University and the first translation institute. He did so much for China during his lifetime that it is easy to forget the context of brute imperialism as foreign powers, led by Britain and France, established the treaty port system, destroyed the Summer Palace in Beijing, and established extraterritorial powers and communities across China that were insulated, and when challenged, exercised their full punitive powers against the crumbling government of China's last dynasty, the Qing (1636-1912).

Directed by Jeremy Routledge of Bristol-based Calling the Shots Films, *For China and the World* recreates this history, using Hart's letters and photographs from the period. Its cast of interviewees includes Bickers, a historian whose *The Scramble for China: Foreign Devils in the Qing Empire 1832-1914*[2] is one of the authoritative texts on the period; Dr. Weipin Tsai, a historian and expert on the Chinese Maritime Customs Service at Royal Holloway, University of London; Professor Hans Van de Ven of Cambridge University; and Li Yan, currently a vice-chairman of the capacity-building committee of the inter-governmental World Customs Organisation. Li is interviewed in Shanghai at the China Customs Institute, part of the vast organisation that is the current incarnation of Hart's maritime customs service.

Given its short length, 31 minutes, and presumably academic budget, this is an extraordinary documentary, entrancing for both China hands who know the history as well as for non-specialists and the general public. It portrays an immensely appealing individual in the context of his times, including some of the less appealing parts—his cutting off of a relationship with a Chinese partner and their three children after nine years in order to marry a British woman for her social acceptability; his personal involvement in the Second Opium War and the sacking of Guangzhou (although he writes with empathy for victims on both sides); and his grand life in the insular Legation Quarters in Beijing, with his own brass band, the first western-style band in China that trained and used Chinese musicians. A plaque on a wall near the Peking Hotel marks the street where he lived.³

'We're not restoring Robert Hart to an iconic place in Chinese history', Professor Bickers says in the film. 'What we're doing is saying, let's pull away all these growths that have obscured him. Let's go back and look afresh at this man, warts and all, and let's just think about his role in the very complex relations between Britain and China.'

While the film takes a clear-eyed look at Hart in the context of its times, it is less sceptical when it looks at Hart's record in office. Others have dealt more harshly. In Jonathan Spence's profile of Hart and his erstwhile boss at the fledgling maritime customs service in Shanghai, Horatio Nelson Lay, his shortcomings are spelled out despite Spence's obvious admiration for the man.⁴ He was autocratic and secretive, enforcing strict discipline, including demanding the highest standards of Chinese from his foreign staff as it grew. On the first page of the chapter on Hart and Lay in his *To Change China: Western Advisers in China 1620-1960*,⁵ Spence quotes Hart as turning down an American who had come to him for employment:

> [There is] nothing whatever for you to do in the office at Shanghai, and, as you do not speak Chinese, I cannot put you in charge of a port...There's not the least use in your trying to learn the language; you must be now fifty years of age, and if a man begins after forty he can never acquire it...My advice to you is not to return to China; you will do best by resigning and asking for your year's allowance.

Spence notes that while the customs service was officially both Chinese and foreign, the Chinese 'invariably held low positions as clerks, accountants and copyists.'⁶ He also failed to train up 'an honest and efficient native administration,' Spence writes. 'The older he grew, the more his stake in China. The more his stake in China, the more he found it necessary to preserve the status quo in his own organisation', that is, with Europeans running the service.⁷ And he failed to groom a successor. Observes Professor Bickers: 'He was a happenstance actor on the Chinese stage, and it suited him well, and he it.'⁸

An issue addressed in the film, but not by Spence, is Hart's eight-

or nine-year dalliance with a young Chinese woman, Ayaou, whom he met in 1857. Like many other Europeans of his age and era, he had children by her without any intention of marriage. When he got ready to acquire a European wife in 1866, he gave Ayaou a settlement of $3000 and brought the three children with him to Ireland, handing them off to a foster family along with funds to cover expenses. He never saw them again.[9] During his brief visit home, he met a fellow Methodist, Hester Jane Bredon, and married her within three months. She stayed in China for 10 years, struggling with her introspective, workaholic husband, before returning to London. It was another 24 years before she returned to Beijing. The two rarely saw each other until Hart's retirement.

These failings have to be set against his monumental role in late Qing modernisation, which included not only the international civil service of maritime customs, but also his establishment of the *Tongwen Guan*, or interpreters' school and much more. He supported the first Chinese diplomatic mission to the West, preventing war between China and Britain in 1876 and arranging peace between China and France in 1885, and helped China float bonds in international markets after the disastrous Sino-Japanese war of 1894-1895.[10]

And redress is well deserved. Despite the honours showered on Hart during his lifetime, both by his Chinese employers and by Britain, his life and career came to be overshadowed in China by the demonisation of the European role in Chinese history; attitudes which, to some degree, were later shared in politically correct academic circles in the West. The post-1949 narrative on both sides was that no matter how good their intentions, the foreigners in China in the mid to late 19th century were largely playing to their own self-interest; denigrating Chinese capabilities when they were not outright destroying their cities and abusing their people.

The 19th century was as binary as our own age; China was seen as weak and declining, destined to be subservient to ascendant European, American and Japanese imperialists. Indeed, Hart was criticised by merchants and even consuls who claimed that he was using the customs service to help the Chinese, while senior officials on the Chinese side disliked and distrusted him. Spence writes: 'He was a man caught between two cultures, having to balance both at once, to keep them in proper perspective in his mind.'[11] Fast forward to 1949, when China became the People's Republic of China, and his achievements were ignored or lumped together with the evil machinations of British and European imperialism during China's '100 years of humiliation'. He was an early victim of cancel-culture as the 19th century and its heroes and villains receded into history.

WHOSE HERO?
For China and the World goes somewhat astray in describing Hart as 'forgotten' since he plays a large role in western historiography of the period, including that of Professor Bickers, and within the professional ranks of the Customs Administration of China there is a revival of interest in Hart, which the film captures. It's unclear from the film, though, whether Hart has actually been written back into school textbooks.

But 'forgotten' seems a little strong to apply to Hart in literal terms. Where it does resonate, especially with the present, is with the shift in geopolitics that redefined an entire period of history and the individuals who lived it to put them in the worst light. In the context of today's tensions between China and the West, the foreigners who 'engaged with China' over the course of the last four decades are now sometimes seen by China hawks in the West as deluded, while China's approach to foreigners, at the official level, can seem increasingly thin. A hero of one generation can become a devil for the next.

So, whose hero was Hart? And why does he make a compelling subject for a documentary? To answer this question requires a step outside the film to look at the broad historical record.

In the late 19th century, the faltering Qing dynasty and the rising empire of Japan were magnets for a particular breed of westerner. Both the Qing (1636-1912) and Japan's Meiji, led by its 'restored' emperor (1868-1912), saw the adoption of western technology as essential to 'self-strengthening'. Western experts were viewed as a temporary yet necessary evil. While Japan went on to build a powerful military and autocratic state along European lines and the Qing's Tongzhi restoration (1860-1874) ended in failure, the foreign experts of the time shared a singular faith in the superiority and inevitability of the transformation they heralded.

Hart was among the foreigners who crowded into China, looking for adventure, wealth, and trade. From a middle-class Methodist family in Belfast, he graduated at the top of his class at Queen's University Belfast, according to a 2017 biography, *Ireland's Imperial*

Mandarin: How Sir Robert Hart Became the Most Influential Foreigner in China[12] by Mark O'Neill. Arriving in Hong Kong at the age of 19 in 1854, and moving subsequently to Ningbo, he would spend most of the rest of his life in China, retiring at the age of 73 in 1908 to return, not to his native Ireland, but to an elegant, five-story house in Cadogan Place, Kensington, where he was greeted by London society as a hero of empire during the short reign of 'Bertie', King Edward VII. Not quite a rags-to-riches story, but still unusual at that time for an Ulsterman to be knighted, granted the hereditary rank of baronet, and bestowed China's highest accolades for a foreigner, the Ancestral Rank for Three Generations, as well as a red button and a peacock's feather.

Such outsize recognition was due to a successful example of nation building. By the time he retired in 1908, Hart had run the Imperial Chinese Customs Service for 45 years and turned it into an effective civil service that in many years generated up to a third of the revenue of the Chinese government. Sun Yat-sen, the 'father' of modern China and leader of the 1911 revolution that toppled the Qing dynasty, described him as an honorary citizen. Hart, he said, 'was the most trusted as he was the most efficient and influential of "Chinese"'.[13] The statue erected to Hart on the Shanghai Bund in 1914, three years after his death, described him as 'a true friend of the Chinese people'. Bickers writes in his personal blog: 'Aside from the Shanghai War Memorial, this was the monument that foreign observers seemed most invested in emotionally. In a couple of accounts published in wartime Britain, the statue is pointed to as representing all that was positive about the British presence in China, and what was presented as the selfless contribution of men like Hart to its development.'[14] By 1914, the quarrels of merchants and consuls, as well as sceptical Qing officials, were long gone. He was seen in subsequent decades as a hero of the British Empire—until the empire itself faded away in the decades after the second world war. His statue was taken down in 1943, at the insistence of Japanese war-time authorities.

Such is the narrative arc of *For China and the World: Robert Hart*. The film opens with the dramatic moment on 22 February 2013 when Bickers and Tsai assembled 60 guests, including the Waltham St Lawrence Silver Band, to rededicate Hart's tombstone, now polished, gleaming white marble. Wreaths were laid, including one from the China Stamp Society, Taiwan Chapter, because Hart also set up the Imperial Chinese Post Office in 1896.[15] The documentary was published a year later by the British Inter-University China Centre of the universities of Bristol, Manchester and Oxford, and had its premiere at the British Academy in London on 12 June 2014.[16]

The ceremony at the graveside was part of the first stage of an initiative to 'restore to public view' Hart's achievements as Inspector General of the Chinese Maritime Customs Service from 1863-1911, whose expansion and professionalisation were his life's work. The film also draws attention to the Hart archives at Queen's University in Belfast, where Hart matriculated, including 77 journals covering 57 years, from the first day he worked in China to a few days before he died. The Hart archive also has 7,000 letters and hundreds of photographs, many of which are used in the film. A brief reference is made to archives of 'Hart's era' held in the Shanghai-based China Customs Institute.

Among the points the film makes is that, while Hart has been forgotten in his homeland, in China he has been rediscovered. The film takes the viewer to contemporary Shanghai, and the Customs Institute under the General Administration of Customs of the People's Republic of China, where Li Yan, vice-president of the institute, and a former China Customs attache to the European Union, addresses remaining questions about Hart's legacy:

> The question of Hart's loyalty has often been queried by Chinese in general, and until recently, Hart was described as an agent of British imperialism in Chinese school textbooks. For Chinese people this time in history has some humiliating memories. That's why Hart received many unfavourable comments about his role at that time. As time has progressed and historical archives have gradually opened, people have started to revisit the history of the modern Chinese Maritime Customs Service, especially the academic field. From an historical perspective, Hart made important contributions to the development of modern Chinese society, particularly in laying the foundation for the modern Chinese Customs Service.

The audience for a talk at the institute by Professor Bickers is large; participants who are interviewed are ready to see a role for Hart in China's history. The occasion, on 29 November 2012, was a workshop on 'Lessons from Maritime Customs History for China's Customs Reform and Modernization'. The participants at the workshop, hosted by the China Customs Institute, the General Administration of Customs of the PRC and the European Commission's Directorate-General for Taxation and Customs Union included academics, customs officials and students. 'His long career in Imperial China left a valuable resource for scholars of modern Chinese history' says a fresh-faced young woman at the institute. 'I personally think he deserves more public attention' says a serious young man in suit and tie. 'This will depend on whether he receives greater acknowledgement from Western scholars'.

Hart's partial rehabilitation in China is in large part due to the enormous scale and confidence of China today, and the interest of maritime customs professionals in their own history. Today, the vast organisation that is his legacy is a ministerial-level entity under the State Council with 60,000 personnel and representative offices in the European Union, Russian Federation, the US and Hong Kong, overseeing the second-largest flow of trade in goods in the world, after the US.[17] Hart is no longer 'cancelled'. He may not figure as a popular hero, but there is an understanding that he played a part in strengthening China beyond the black and white perceptions of his ethnicity, nationality and the historical context of British and western imperialism.

Edith Terry *(edith.terry@gmail.com) is a writer and former correspondent for international media including BusinessWeek, the Toronto Globe and Mail Newspaper and the South China Morning Post. A student of Asian and Chinese history at Yale and Stanford, she began working on China issues in the 1970s with the National Council for US-China Trade, and was one of the first resident Americans in business in Beijing in 1980-81, before turning to journalism. Her books include* How Asia Got Rich: Japan, China and the Asian Miracle *(Routledge 2002). She has lived in Hong Kong since 2000.*

References

1. https://www.youtube.com/watch?v=zT-ImktiR3U
2. Robert A. Bickers, *The Scramble for China: Foreign Devils in the Qing Empire 1832-1914* (London, Allen Lane, 2011), p. 196
3. Xing Yi, 'A Briton's China Legacy' *China Daily*, 4 July 2017, http://www.chinadaily.com.cn/a/201704/07/WS5a2921d9a310fcb6fafd3d53.html, [accessed 14 October 2022]
4. Jonathan Spence, Chapter 4, 'Lay and Hart: Power, Patronage, Pay' in *To Change China: Western Advisers in China 1620-1960* (Boston, Little, Brown & Company, 1969), pp 93-128
5. Spence, *To Change China*, p. 93
6. Spence, *To Change China*, p. 116
7. Spence, *To Change China*, p. 116
8. Bickers, *The Scramble for China* p. 196
9. Mark O'Neill, *Ireland's Imperial Mandarin: How Sir Robert Hart Became the Most Influential Foreigner in Qing China*, (Hong Kong, Joint Publishing, 2017), p. 62
10. O'Neill, *Ireland's Imperial Mandarin*, p. 118
11. O'Neill, *Ireland's Imperial Mandarin*, p. 120
12. O'Neill, *Ireland's Imperial Mandarin*
13. The original quote comes from James Cantlie and C. Sheridan Jones in *Sun Yat-sen and the Awakening of China* (London, Jarrold & Sons, 1912) but is reproduced here from Mark O'Neill, *Ireland's Imperial Mandarin: How Sir Robert Hart Became the Most Influential Foreigner in China* (Hong Kong, Joint Publishing (HK), 2017) p. 381
14. Robert Bickers, 'Lost monuments and memorials of the Shanghai Bund 2: Statue of Sir Robert Hart', in Robert Bickers, History, empire, China and things found along the way, posted on 13 October 2014, https://robertbickers.net/2014/10/13/lost-monuments-and-memorials-of-the-shanghai-bund-2-statue-of-sir-robert-hart-1914/ [accessed 10 October 2022]
15. Robert Bickers, "Remembering Sir Robert Hart," in Robert Bickers: History, empire, China and things found on the way, posted on 4 March 2013, https://robertbickers.net/2013/03/04/remembering-sir-robert-hart/, [accessed 10 October 2022]
16. The film is available on Youtube at https://www.youtube.com/watch?v=zT-ImktiR3U, [accessed 13 October 2022]

17. General Administration of Customs, People's Republic of China, *2017 China Customs Annual Report*, http://english.customs.gov.cn/Uploads/Reports/2017 China Customs.pdf. [accessed 15 October 2022]

www.ingramcontent.com/pod-product-compliance
Lightning Source LLC
LaVergne TN
LVHW010315070526
838199LV00065B/5563